MW01484724

ONE RANGER RETURNS

THE RANGER'S PRAYER

O God, whose end is justice,
Whose strength is all our stay,
Be near and bless my mission
As I go forth today.
Let wisdom guide my actions,
Let courage fill my heart
And help me, Lord, in every hour
To do a Ranger's part.
Protect when danger threatens,
Sustain when trails are rough;
Help me to keep my standard high
And smile at each rebuff.
When night comes down upon me,
I pray thee, Lord, be nigh,
Whether on lonely scout, or camp,
Under the Texas sky.
Keep me, O God, in life
And when my days shall end,
Forgive my sins and take me in,
For Jesus' sake, Amen.

PIERRE BERNARD HILL
TEXAS RANGER CHAPLAIN

BRIDWELL TEXAS HISTORY SERIES

H. JOAQUIN JACKSON
WITH JAMES L. HALEY

One Ranger
RETURNS

UNIVERSITY OF TEXAS PRESS, AUSTIN

Copyright © 2008 by H. Joaquin Jackson
All rights reserved
Printed in the United States of America
First paperback printing, 2013

Requests for permission to reproduce material from this work should be sent to
Permissions, University of Texas Press, P.O. Box 7819, Austin, TX 78713-7819.
http://utpress.utexas.edu/index.php/rp-form

♾ The paper used in this book meets the minimum requirements of ANSI/NISO
Z39.48-1992 (R1997) (Permanence of Paper).

LIBRARY OF CONGRESS CATALOGING-IN-PUBLICATION DATA

Jackson, H. Joaquin. 1935–
One ranger returns / H. Joaquin Jackson with James L. Haley. — 1st ed.
p. cm. — (Bridwell Texas history series)
Includes index.
ISBN 978-0-292-71626-1 (cloth : alk. paper)
1. Jackson, H. Joaquin. 1935– 2. Texas Rangers—Biography.
I. Haley, James L.   II. Title.
HV7911.J23A3   2008
363.2092—dc22
[B]   2007038624
ISBN 978-0-292-74839-2 (pbk.)

doi:10.7560/716261

To all the Texas Rangers,
past and present

Contents

Acknowledgments

The Old Ranger is still pretty sharp, but even my memory does not have the photographic recall that it once had. I am indebted to several individuals for filling in some blanks.

I want to thank my old friends from the days of the Good Ole Boys at the FBI National Academy, Dave Gaylord and Ruben Archuleta, for sharing their memories to refresh my own.

The library at Sul Ross State University, in Alpine, provided access to newspaper articles covering the Frome murders, which were the most notorious of their day in Texas, but which have fallen from our common memory so completely that they had to be resurrected virtually from scratch.

To the University of Texas Press, in the persons of Dave Hamrick and Bill Bishel, and to my agent, Jim Hornfischer, for his advice and encouragement in maintaining a harmonious working relationship among all parties, my sincere thanks.

For my great friends Shelton and Sunny Smith, who provided a home away from home at their beautiful 4S Ranch on the Blanco River west of Wimberley, where James Haley and I could work in peace, no thanks can suffice.

Thanks are also owing to Bexar County deputy sheriff Bill Stanley, who helped gather information and photos for the Champ Carter chapter; to Russell Smith, author, friend, and fellow lawman, for his help on the hunt for Alfredo Hernandez; to Ben Ross, a friend originally from the Dryden area, in

Terrell County, for his help also on the hunt for Alfredo Hernandez; to Danny Rhea and Bill Gerth, former Rangers and Medal of Valor recipients, for their information about the Silver Badges of Courage; to Brian Kokernot, for the use of his ranch near Alpine as a place to work on this book away from the telephone; to Kim Keith, our great friend, who makes our trips possible by taking care of our home place, and Will, when needed. And to all the readers of *One Ranger* who wanted to read more.

Finally, and this is going to be hard to word in a proper way, there would be no interesting crime stories to read if there were no crimes, and there would be no crimes without victims, some of whom survive from the incidents I relate, who could be reminded of painful episodes in their lives. Where appropriate, I have changed the names and some circumstances to protect their privacy and peace of mind.

Prologue

As I sit down to think about how to introduce a second volume of my Texas Ranger memoirs, Ann Richards, the former governor of Texas, has just passed on to help the Big Boss guard the pearly gates. She was a great lady and a great leader, but many readers don't know, and indeed Ann probably didn't know, that she played a major role in the success of my first book, *One Ranger: A Memoir*.

As the manuscript was being prepared for production, Shelton Smith, who had been Ann's lead counsel while she was governor, and who I met because he was chairman of the Former Texas Ranger Foundation—and who has become a very close friend—told me that I needed a strong woman to give me a blurb for my book. Having never been involved in the literary world, I did not know what the hell a "blurb" meant, except it was similar to "blurt," and in my world that was some kind of spontaneous response. And I said, "Well, who do you suggest to do this?"

Shelton replied, "Ann Richards."

My former cowriter David Marion Wilkinson was also present, and I looked them both right in the eyes and said, "Hell, she's one of the reasons I left the Ranger service."

They still thought we should give it a shot, and after Shelton sent the manuscript to Richards, several days passed before she called him at his office in Wimberley. She didn't say hello or "This is Ann" or anything else.

But Shelton knew her voice instantly as she said, "You tell that old bastard that I'll give him a blurb for his book, but I know he rode his horse from Amarillo, Texas, to Austin, Texas, to turn in his Ranger badge when I was governor, and I damn sure don't appreciate it."

Shelton said, "No, Ann, that's not right."

Richards insisted, "I know it's right. I know what he did."

He said, "No, Ann, that's not right." Pause. "He rode his horse from *Alpine*, Texas, to Austin, Texas, and turned in his Ranger badge."

In point of fact, it was my retirement papers that I turned in, not my badge, and I rode from Alpine to Austin in my state-owned Jeep Cherokee, which had about six lame horses under the hood and was the sorriest vehicle I ever drove for the state.

When I first entered law enforcement, the thought that I might live a life worth writing a memoir about was the furthest thing from my mind. But when I was approached about doing a book, a fine and seasoned writer named Robert Draper prepared a proposal. When the New York publishers read it, they thought the big story would have to be about my alleged objections to women serving in the Texas Rangers, and their reaction wasn't just no but hell no. A couple of them sniffed that the book had possibilities, but it was probably right for a regional press, which in New York is rather a put-down.

After David Wilkinson came aboard as my cowriter, the book was indeed placed with a regional publisher, but a very distinguished house with national reach, the University of Texas Press. Imagine my surprise when *One Ranger* became the fastest seller in the Press's history. We are now waiting on the ninth printing, having sold over 30,000 copies. Reviews of the book appeared in places we might have expected, such as *Persimmon Hill*, the quarterly magazine of the Cowboy Hall of Fame, but others were in the unlikeliest of places, including an enormously flattering piece in *Southern Living*.

I began getting invited to give talks about the book to a variety of civic and literary groups, which quickly became a cottage industry for Shirley and me. Hundreds of fans—and we were so taken by this that we saved their letters—wrote to me of the ways they responded to the story: perhaps I used an expression they hadn't heard since they were children, and it awakened some early memory, or a landscape in the book evoked a nostalgic childhood. Many told me that their only complaint with *One Ranger* was that it wasn't long enough. I guess that planted the seed for this new book, although UT Press, being smart and adaptable, liked having a commercial success and suggested preparing a second book even before I could mention it to them. And then one day Robert Utley, the extremely distinguished historian, buttonholed me after he read *One Ranger*. After telling me it was a great read, he asked why I didn't have a chapter on the United Farm Workers strike in the Rio Grande Valley in 1966–1967, which became a defining moment in American labor history. As it happens, I am the only surviving Ranger of that Company D, which some people find so infamous, and indeed some of my vivid memories of those weeks bear sharing, not least because they differ materially from what has become the accepted history of that incident.

As I began considering such a new effort seriously, it became clear that David Marion Wilkinson, who contributed so mightily to the success of the first book, would not be available for a second one. My agent, Jim Horn-fischer, suggested I meet with James L. Haley, an experienced writer who has been pretty versatile, in that he does both history and fiction. He drove out to Alpine and we got acquainted. I think he was concerned that I might have told all my good stories in the first book and that there might not be enough additional raw material to draw on. We spent an afternoon in my garage, poring through my crime files, and at one point I looked up just as he was taking a picture. He later e-mailed it to me with the title "One Ranger, Many Boxes."

We went through the folders. He winced over crime-scene photos of a young mother in Uvalde who had been murdered; it had taken five years to pin it on two of the most notorious serial killers in American history. He met some truly remarkable characters who did not make it into the first book, among them Tom Bybee, a man of strange contradictions. He supported himself by bootlegging, but he himself never touched the stuff, nor did he ever sell to drunks or minors, nor did he begrudge me my duty in trying to foil him. He was quite modest and likeable in every other way, but after he was insulted by the town bully in a poker game, he excused himself, returned, and took the man's head off with one swing of his cedar-chopping axe. Or there was the murder case I worked on that had been open since I was three years old. Jim Haley became more and more engrossed and decided this was a project he wanted to take on.

But aside from just relating further adventures, *One Ranger Returns* really has a different job to do than *One Ranger* did. Because so many people took such a kind interest in the first book, I thought it appropriate to introduce readers more intimately to my family. My wife, Shirley, whom no one ever accused of being shy, speaks in her own voice in this volume, as do both my sons. I wanted to bring back real folks who were in *One Ranger*, like Jake, my buddy, and a great story he relates about Hank the Cowdog (and that's an earlier Hank, not John Erickson's famous Hank the Cowdog literary character). And I needed to say more about Captain Allee, of course, and Bill Cooksey, and other friends and good lawmen who were not given their due in the earlier volume.

I also felt it was important to introduce readers to more of my Ranger family, brave men whose services have perhaps not been as widely acknowledged as they should have been. Having been humbled by serving with them, I dedicate this book to them with all the respect in the world. All Rangers know that we have been part of an organization with a long tradition of service and courage, but what many readers don't know is that the storied Ranger heroes of days gone by, Leander MacNelly and John B. Jones and Bill McDonald and Frank Hamer, still have their equals today. To paraphrase Gloria Swanson in *Sunset Boulevard*, it is the times that have gotten small.

ONE RANGER RETURNS

CHAPTER I

La Huelga

THE UNITED FARM WORKERS STRIKE OF 1966–1967

In all my years of active Ranger service, the incident that caused the most controversy, and damaged the reputation of the Rangers more than any other, was *la Huelga* ("the Strike"), the United Farm Workers strike of 1966–1967 in the lower Rio Grande Valley. Since I am the only Ranger involved in the affair who is still alive, that makes me what they call a primary source, and I have some issues to take up with the way this episode has been related by historians.

In today's popular perception, the actual events have become shrink-wrapped into a passion play of social stereotypes, of potbellied, bullying Rangers swinging nightsticks and pistol-whipping hapless, terrified Hispanic farmworkers, who were only seeking to better their destitute and exploited lives. As reinforced by many politically correct writers, this view was quickly extended back into Ranger history. As one writer summarized it in the *Southern Patriot* at the time of *la Huelga*, the Rangers "were formed in the old days of the Texas Republic to keep Mexicans in line. They merged with the Confederate Army . . . to fight to preserve slavery, and in the Twentieth Century they have been used repeatedly as strikebreakers." Even without the breathtaking historical errors packed into those few lines of text, I would still have to say, sorry, but as a former member of Company D, which some people find so notorious, I'm not buying this.

It is important to understand the Farm Workers strike in a context that extends back not just to the previous trouble in the Rio Grande Valley, during World War I, but back through the Mexican War to the Texas Revolution itself, with fault and virtue on both sides. Originally, the Rangers were formed as patrolling companies for defense against hostile Indians, since the Mexican government did not provide this service to the Anglo colonies. During the Texas Revolution, bad blood existed between the colonists and the Mexican Army because of massacres at the Alamo and at Goliad, which together cost the lives of nearly six hundred Texans—including some Tejanos. The deaths at the Alamo you might defend as the natural outcome of a fierce battle, but at Goliad about four hundred prisoners of war were lined up and shot in cold blood. The Texas victory at San Jacinto was, equally, a slaughter of vengeance that is hard to defend on any moral grounds, and it assured continued ethnic animosity.

Texas Rangers who saw service during the Mexican War came close to running amok in Mexico, so much so that not even the American generals could contain them. That was when Mexicans began referring to them as *los diablos Tejanos*; in the Texans' minds, they were still getting some vengeance for the Alamo and Goliad. Contrary to the assertion in the *Southern Patriot*, it is absolutely not true that Texas Rangers fought in the Civil War. One regiment, the Eighth Texas Cavalry, was known as Terry's Texas Rangers, but that designation was purely a nickname. In fact, the lack of Texas Rangers during the war led to a near collapse of frontier defenses against hostile Indians, and settlements were defended by ragtag home-guard units of young boys and old men. However, many Hispanics did fight in the Civil War, mostly as pro-Union guerillas along the Rio Grande and in the Nueces Strip. So the *Southern Patriot* got it not just wrong, but backward.

I would concede that many of the Rangers' actions in the Rio Grande Valley during World War I spread terror among the Hispanic population. It is also likely that some Rangers, as well as local sheriffs and deputies, gave in to racist feelings and overreacted to the threat that they perceived. But that threat, the "Plan of San Diego," seemed real at the time. It was a plot calling for Mexican Americans and African Americans to rise up and reconquer Texas and the Southwest for Mexico, killing all Anglo males over the age of sixteen. This only fueled any existing mistrust and hostilities. A couple of recent books have made it clearer that the Plan of San Diego was really the work of Mexican president Venustiano Carranza, who wanted to blame it on his enemies and enlist the American government to help keep him in power. Most of the murder, arson, sabotage, and pillaging that took place in Texas during this time was carried out not by Texas Hispanics, but by Carrancista soldiers who crossed the border out of uniform. That was little comfort to the hundreds of Texas Hispanics who were killed both by Rangers and by federal troops in the actions that followed, and their hatred of the Texas Rangers simmered from that time on. So when a labor dispute erupted in 1966, the events surrounding it were colored by a long and sad history.

Late in the spring of that year, a California labor organizer named Eugene Nelson arrived in the lower Rio Grande Valley. He was an affiliate of the Chicano labor leader Cesar Chávez and a veteran of the grape strike in California. His mission now was to organize Texas farm laborers and affiliate them with his own union, the National Farm Workers Association, which later became better known under the name United Farm Workers. He centered his operation in Rio Grande City, the seat of Starr County, which is the third county upstream from the Gulf of Mexico and for many years was the poorest, or one of the poorest, in Texas.

The conditions under which he found the Texas farmworkers laboring could only be called horrible: they cultivated vegetables with short-handled hoes and picked melons ("stoop labor") for up to sixteen hours a day, without any sanitary facilities in the fields. Nelson quickly signed up a large number of laborers into his new organization, which he called the Independent Workers Association, for a membership fee of one dollar each, and they decided to strike. His main target was La Casita Farms, a truck farm of 1,600 irrigated acres near Rio Grande City, where a wide variety of melons, fruits, and vegetables were grown. Cantaloupes are especially perishable, and their upcoming harvest was highly vulnerable to any kind of work stoppage. The workers' principal demand, beyond recognition of their right to bargain, was for a wage increase to the federal minimum of $1.25 an hour, which was, on average, about double what they were being paid.

Local law-enforcement authorities, including elected county officials who were beholden to the large farm operations, reacted vigorously with injunctions and arrests, sometimes of doubtful legality, until the harvest was over and further striking would have lost its effectiveness. Undeterred, the organizers determined upon a march to Austin, a walk of nearly four hundred miles, to demand attention to their grievances. You might remember that this was also the time of the high-water mark of the civil rights movement for African Americans, and the whole country was sensitized to marches. Nelson, several clergymen, and hundreds of workers set off on July 4, 1966, for a long hot walk—and a slow one—intending to finish in a rally at the state capitol, in Austin, on Labor Day.

In August, Governor John Connally, along with other high state officials, met them in New Braunfels. At first the marchers were prepared to greet Connally as a hero, but as his lack of sympathy became more apparent, they raised the cry of *¡Viva la Huelga!* (Long live the strike!). The day was a public relations disaster for Connally, and the march continued on to Austin. For the last few blocks, Ralph Yarborough, who was Texas's liberal U.S. senator and Connally's deep political enemy, walked with the strikers to the capitol to show his solidarity. The *huelgistas* got lots of sympathetic attention in Austin, but as usually happens with politicians, no meaningful action. So they went back to South Texas and resumed beating their heads against the wall, striking, being arrested and roughed up, and getting nowhere.

The Texas Rangers were called down to the Valley late in 1966 to investigate conditions. We scouted the area and found the strikers doing nothing illegal or threatening, but still we asked some of the workers if anyone had tried to interfere with their jobs, and they said no. Texas was, and still is, a "right to work" state, and under the law it was illegal to try to force a worker to join a union. That sounds innocent enough to write about, but this is the first of many places in this story where the perception gets disconnected from reality. The truth was that we merely looked the situation over and found nothing wrong, but because of the long history I've outlined of hard feelings between Hispanics in the Valley and Rangers, and because of the way the subsequent history has been written, our presence itself has been treated as an attempt to intimidate the union. Well, if they were thinking of illegally interfering with the laborers' right to work, I should hope we were intimidating them, but that not being the case, we left and resumed duties back in our home stations soon after.

Things heated up particularly as the next melon harvest approached, in May 1967. A couple of unionists were pretty badly beaten, and the word came down that the Rangers were to gather in Rio Grande City to assess the situation again. South Texas was served by Company D of the Rangers, each of us in our different stations. I went down from Uvalde, Glenn Krueger went down from Beeville, Jerome Priess was nearby in Harlingen, and Tol Dawson went from Carrizo Springs, along with our sergeant, Selman Denson, and

Joaquin's junior days as a Ranger, with Captain Allee, 1966–1971.

Jack Van Cleve from Cotulla. Frank Horger came from McAllen, which was close by; Captain Allee's son, "Little Alfred," also came in for as much as a week at a time; he was in E Company, stationed in Ozona, but his captain would allow the Old Man to claim him on request.

We stayed two to four in a room in the old Ringgold Hotel on East Main Street, which was built in the 1870s. It was quite a historic old place, with a big wide gallery porch lined with rocking chairs facing the street, which was a great place to lounge around for an hour or so after a long day. I arrived in Rio Grande City, then a town of fifteen hundred to two thousand folks, on May 12. It sits a few miles north of the Rio Grande, and the harsh land is full of heavy brush, cactus, and some of Texas's biggest rattlesnakes. Most folks were hardworking, honest people; of course there were also a few crooks and deadbeats. On the 14th, I was assigned with most of the others to ride the daily produce train sixty or seventy miles east to the terminus in Harlingen, which was the destination of most of the produce trains. Several days before we arrived there had been an attempted arson on one of the three major railroad bridges between Rio Grande City and Harlingen, and threats had been made to disrupt the train service.

Debris heavy enough to derail a train had been removed from the tracks in several places by Missouri Pacific Railroad employees. Sabotage of public transportation is a serious matter. In performing our duty, however, we Rangers lent ourselves to another unfortunate disconnect between reality and perception. It was the trains, bridges, and right-of-way that we were protecting, but a photograph taken of this would make it seem as though we were protecting shipments of nonunion melons and taking sides in the conflict, which we most emphatically were not doing.

This job of riding the train to Harlingen and back became our principal job for several days. Typically two of us would ride on the train, one on the engine and one in the caboose (trains still had cabooses in those days), and then two more Rangers would follow in one of our state cars. There was an unpaved road that paralleled the tracks the whole distance, and it was surfaced with either gravel or shell, but whatever it was, it tore the living hell out of the tires on our state vehicles, and we had to replace them after every five to six trips.

On one of these trips I was riding in the caboose, and I had my state issue riot gun with me, a Remington Model 11 with an eighteen-inch barrel that kicked like a Georgia mule. Glenn Krueger had been following in the car, and about the time we started pulling into the station, he called me on the walkie-talkie and said I could get off and join them in the car and we'd go back to the hotel. I went to step off while the train was still moving—I don't remember that I had ever been on a train before—and when you do that, you get off with your feet moving so you're going about the same speed as the train. I did this, but, unfortunately, I got off in the direction opposite that which the train was still going, and the only thing that kept me from cartwheeling boots over Stetson was that I jammed my shotgun into the dirt to keep my balance. When I got into the car, Krueger was weak from laughing at me; he said he'd never seen such long legs flying so high in the air before. I made some lame remark like "Okay, asshole, next time you can ride in the caboose." I was the least experienced of the Rangers down there, and hated doing anything that made me look like it and receive the razzing from my fellow Rangers in arms.

Guarding the trains became something of a routine, but one that afforded an opportunity for Krueger to demonstrate an unusual skill he had acquired somewhere along the way. On the southeast side of Rio Grande City there was a shopping center, which was sort of a novelty, and there was a little restaurant in it, which did not have the best food in town but did have the best coffee. Glenn Krueger, Jerome Priess, Tol Dawson, and I met there one afternoon about three for coffee before escorting the train to Harlingen. We were sitting at a round table, and Krueger had his back to the door. I noticed that there were several flies buzzing around; Krueger was very quick with his hands, and he snatched one of these flies out of the air, put it down into his ice water, and started stirring it around. Krueger, always the prankster, asked, "You guys ever see someone drown a fly and bring it back to life?"

We had to admit that we hadn't, and wondered what the hell he had up his sleeve this time. Krueger stirred the fly in the ice water for a good minute or two, until we figured if it didn't drown, it would certainly freeze to death. Krueger fished him out with his spoon, and then poured out about half a shaker of salt onto a napkin, making this little hill of salt, and he put the fly in the salt and started stirring him around in it. Just about that time Captain Allee walked in and came up behind Krueger. We weren't expecting the captain for another day or so. Kruger's head was down, and with his usual exaggeration, he was concentrating on stirring this fly in the salt. When he looked up at me, he saw me looking behind him, and he turned around. Krueger had these big brown calf eyes that, when he was surprised, popped open to about twice their normal size, which is just what happened as he blurted out, "Oh, hello, Captain! How you doing, Captain?"

Allee had gone home for a couple of days to rest and do his laundry and get a prescription refilled. "I'm just fine, Glenn," he said. "But, what in the *hell* are you doing?"

"Well," Glenn explained, "I caught this here fly, and I drowned him in the ice water, and now I'm going to bring him back to life in this salt."

Captain nodded. "So you're going to bring him back to life?"

"Yes, sir."

"Well, you damn sure better!" He stood there, foursquare, with a look on his face that suggested that if Krueger failed, Captain was going to drown him and stir him around in some salt.

Krueger went back to work, with a little more riding on the outcome now (we were all rooting for the fly—to save Krueger's ass), until finally that fly appeared on top of the mound of salt. He wiggled around, then righted himself, stretched his wings for a bit, and, sure enough, flew off. Krueger wiped his forehead and breathed an audible, "Whew!" He was sure Captain would have given him some time off if he hadn't managed to resurrect that poor critter.

And Captain Allee watched all this with a look on his face that said here he was in Rio Grande City with a man's job to do, what with bridges burning and people getting beat up, and he turned his back for a couple of days and ended up having to babysit this bunch of pranksters. He didn't have to say anything; he just walked away.

*　　*　　*

Protecting the trains was not the only issue we had to concern ourselves with. In Texas, it was legal to picket on roadsides and so forth, but it was not legal to block the ingress or egress (entrance or exit) to places of business. "Secondary picketing," the practice of picketing a business other than the one that was being struck, was also illegal, as was interference with those who were working. Faced with a strike and the loss of their melon crop, La Casita and the other struck farms used green-carders, Mexican nationals with papers for day labor in the United States, to keep picking. The details of the laws were quite restrictive, and I don't give an opinion whether any of those laws were right or wrong, but they were the laws we were sworn to enforce. When picketing in lawful ways brought little attention to the union or its cause, its members began picketing illegally, and many of them were arrested. That's what the press was waiting for: action.

Much has been made of the alleged brutality of these arrests, and I cannot vouch for the conduct of local and county authorities, who were also on the scene, but all of the Ranger arrests that I saw were by the book. That does not mean we politely asked folks to follow us to jail, either. When you're in a situation of public unrest, arrests have to be made swiftly, efficiently, and without discussion. You never negotiate an arrest in front of a crowd; to do so invites a disaster.

Certainly the most celebrated arrest was on May 26 at a railroad bridge near Mission, and involved the Reverend Ed Krueger of the Texas Council of Churches, who was heavily involved in the labor action. (This was a great opportunity to tease Glenn Krueger with repeated questions whether the two weren't kinfolk, to which his standard reply was "Go to hell.") Much was made in the media and in the history books of the arrest of the Reverend Krueger. The part I'll bet you never read about—but I was there, and these big old ears heard it—was the Reverend Krueger making a total nuisance of himself to Captain Allee: "Arrest me! I want you to arrest me! You've got to arrest me! I *demand* that you arrest me!" acting like a small child having a tantrum.

Captain finally had enough and said, "If that's the way you feel about it, I'll sure as hell accommodate you," and he took Krueger by the seat of his pants and hustled him to the unit. That was when Mrs. Krueger produced a camera and began taking the publicity pictures they had been hoping for, of her poor husband being victimized by Rangers, whom they wanted to depict as state thugs: bingo! The Captain moved to seize her camera, but she hid it behind her back until he took it from her and exposed the film. Of course, if we'd had modern technology available then, we would have videotaped the whole altercation to show that we were acting completely within the law.

I can say further that the Captain had not particularly been of a mind to arrest anyone at that time, and probably would not have if Krueger had not pestered him like a six-year-old to be taken into custody and get the arrest ball rolling. They certainly got a ton of publicity for their trouble. It was a setup deal from the start.

The Rangers were not the only law enforcement on the scene that summer. The local police and county sheriffs were also actively engaged, but I'm not going to try and account for the impartiality of their actions as I can for the Rangers. In fact, I knew that the Rangers would get blamed for some arm twisting and head busting done by the local authorities, whose allegiance was more to the local politicians than to enforcing state law. I do know that after we had been down there awhile, the strikers were a lot more afraid of the local officers than they were of us Rangers.

Since the first incidents of railroad destruction, the Missouri Pacific had brought in its own detectives to protect the rail line and keep it under surveillance, and we worked with them. They were good at their job, but were in a different environment than they were used to. We got to know them pretty well because they were stationed out in the brush to keep their eye on the bridges and railroads, and we would go by and visit with them just about every day. There were two in particular who had come down from Missouri and were pretty clueless about the country and the animals, and a few of us used the opportunity to play a really scary trick on them. The first major bridge on the line was six or seven miles east of Rio Grande City, and these two particular railroad detectives would sit out in the brush and keep it in view. It gets hotter than hell down there in the summer, so they made themselves a shade on the northeast side of the tracks, a sort of lean-to out of sotol (a Texas cactus bush that grows six to seven feet tall) stalks and roofed with grass and brush, with some cardboard furnished by the railroad thrown

Glenn Krueger and Joaquin with a railroad detective in their camp, 1968.

in. It was a flimsy little thing that would have fallen over if you looked at it hard enough, but it kept them out of the sun.

One day Rangers Krueger and Priess went by and visited with them right before dark, and Krueger told them (in a voice like Alfred Hitchcock's) to be on their lookout because huge man-eating black jaguars came up from the Mexican jungle and hunted along the Rio Grande. And that was even true; there were a few jaguars in that country that had migrated in from Mexico. But he went on to elaborate about this one huge black jaguar that had been seen in the area, a man-eater that had killed several people along that stretch of the river. This was a big windy story, but these detectives from Missouri had never been to the Valley before. Krueger went on to tell them that jaguars are totally fearless, that everything they see is just something to eat, and he went on and on. His final message to them was STAY ON YOUR GUARD!

These wide-eyed gumshoes took all this in, and after Krueger and Priess left, those two Missourians built a fire you could have seen all the way from Harlingen, which was about fifty miles from there. Krueger and Priess knew this because they snuck back up near the bridge after dark. To make the story real in the detectives' minds, Priess—being, like many Rangers, pretty inventive—made some kind of contraption consisting of a one-pound coffee can, open at one end, and a piece of rawhide stretched tight over the other end. There was a hole punched in the center of the rawhide, and a string that he could pull through the hole. When he did so, the metal can became an amplifier, and it made the most godawful moaning roar you ever heard. At least to someone who had never heard a jaguar, it sounded just like a huge, hungry man-eater. Priess was a real artist with his invention, and could generate the maximum horror with its sounds. They crawled down the arroyo to within sixty or seventy yards of these two detectives huddled by their bonfire, and Priess pulled the rawhide through the coffee can.

They heard those detectives startle up, and one said, "What the hell was that?"

"Maybe it's that jaguar."

They started down the railroad bridge with their pistols in their hands, shining their flashlights, one off the left side and the other off the right. Krueger and Priess were looking at the detectives' searching flashlights when one of the beams landed on something black and shiny, and Priess, who was hiding behind a big rock, realized one of his black boots was exposed.

"Look there!" hissed one detective. "I think that's him!" And Jerome thought, oh shit, now I'm going to get shot in the foot, but he froze, thinking that moving his foot might start a barrage of pistol fire.

Finally the other one said, "No, that's nothing," and they went back to the lean-to. Very, very shortly after that they abandoned their big bonfire, which had gone down considerably, and left their duty station.

Krueger and Priess got back to the hotel about six or seven the next morning and flopped into bed. Captain Allee and Frank Horger were staying in the room next to theirs, and the Captain arrived in the middle of the afternoon, totally exhausted, and flopped on his bed. No sooner had he dozed off than Priess playfully pulled on his bullhorn one more time. Horger said that when the Captain heard that screaming noise through the wall he went straight into the air, and then landed on his feet. "What in the hell was that?"

Horger tried to throw him off the scent. "Cap, I think it's just the water pipes."

The Captain said, "That ain't no damned water pipe," and stormed next door. Of course he found Krueger, and Priess with his coffee can with the rawhide strip, and the whole story came out what they had done. Captain Allee might have thought this was as hilarious as the rest of us did, but he would never have shown it. He yanked up Priess's bullhorn and said, "You scared off those railroad detectives with this damned thing after you told them your stories. If this shit happens again, you are going to work your shift, and when you're done, you're going to work their shift as well. So if you want to work a twenty-four-hour shift, pull this caper again." And twenty-four hours a day was damned near what we were doing anyway.

Because Captain Allee projected such a fearless image for the public, people imagined that the strain of this duty had no effect on him, but that wasn't the case. In fact, he did not even want to be in the Valley, but the Rangers' colonel, Homer Garrison, had ordered him down there, and we all knew for sure that the instructions had come from Governor Connally himself. And I soon discovered why the Captain was so suspicious of everybody. He told me early in the morning one day, on the hotel's porch, that his acid indigestion had gotten bad, and he gave me a five-dollar bill along with instructions to go to a drugstore down the street and buy the biggest bottle of Pepto-Bismol they had. So I took off to the nearest drugstore, probably the only one in Rio Grande City, which was within walking distance of the hotel. On my way back to the hotel, a reporter leaning against a telephone pole pointed to the paper sack I was carrying. "What's going on, Ranger?" he asked.

I should have told him to mind his own damned business, but not really thinking this was a secret mission, I casually told him that the Captain had a little stomachache. It turned out he was a wire-service reporter who was down there covering the strike, and the next time he saw Captain Allee, he asked him if his stomach was feeling any better.

Captain Allee pulled me aside later, as he sometimes did, especially since I was a rookie Ranger still learning the ropes, and said, "The next time I ask you to get me something, I don't want to hear about it later from the damned Associated Press."

I said, "Yes, sir," and assured him it would not happen again. All in all, the

Captain took a pretty lenient approach to me. At thirty-one and with only a year in the Rangers, I was the greenest member of Company D. I did have three months' seniority on Glenn Krueger, but he was older and had been in the Texas Highway Patrol longer than I had before joining the Rangers and had more experience. I, on the other hand, was still learning that when A. Y. Allee told you to do something, he meant every damned word of it.

I found this out soon after, when the Captain called us all together and informed us that a death threat had been received. This was something that he took very seriously: to keep the strikers in line and intimidate green-carders from crossing the border to work the harvest, the *Huelgistas* had engaged the services of an enforcer, a cross-border thug and convicted murderer named Magdaleno Dimas. We were sure that there were others involved who were also about that tough, and in the world of machismo, it would be a big feather in someone's cap to be able to say that he had killed a Texas Ranger. Captain told us that from then on we were not to go anywhere alone.

Soon after this I was having a conversation with Homero, who owned the local gas station—I seem to remember it was a Humble station—where we got our state cars serviced. Homero was tall for a Hispanic, six feet or a little more, about 180 pounds and athletically built. He was very friendly and had a high regard for the Rangers; I think that some members of his family had been in law enforcement, and he understood that we were there to protect lives and property, not to take sides in the dispute. That was back in the days of full-service stations, when someone would check your oil and windshield-wiper fluid and the pressure in your tires; Homero had two or three young guys working for him. And we gave him a lot of business during our weeks in the Valley because it was important to know that we weren't buying gasoline from someone who might put water in our tanks. And that road along the tracks that one of our units had to drive on every day to follow the train just ripped our tires to shreds.

Homero came by the Ringgold Hotel around nine one night and invited me to go with him for a Coke. The other Rangers and Captain Allee had gone across the street for coffee, but I declined with thanks, saying that Captain Allee had told us not to go anywhere alone. Homero said, "You won't be alone, you'll be with me." That sounded sensible, and I thought it was important to keep good relations with him, so I accompanied him to a local drive-in place a few blocks away and had a Coke with him.

When I got back, the curb in front of the Ringgold Hotel was bare; all of the Ranger cars, every one of them, were gone, and I thought, oh hell, I'm in trouble now, they've gone out on some call to trouble and I wasn't present. With a lump in my gut, I sat down in a rocking chair on the gallery porch and awaited my fate. I was thinking about making a radio call to see where they had gone when the cars started showing up again, driving fast and stopping hard. I could tell by the way they were driving that everyone was pissed, and all the Rangers went up the steps and into the hotel without saying hello, where you been, or kiss my ass. No one even looked my direction, they were so pissed off at having been out looking for me, until at last Captain Allee came up the steps and sat down in a chair next to me.

He said, "Joaquin, did you hear what orders I gave about not going off by yourself?"

I said, "Yes, sir, I did."

He said, "Where the hell did you go?"

"I went down the street there with Homero to have a Coke with him. He said we wouldn't be gone five minutes, but when we got back, you were all gone."

Captain said, "Well, you know what my orders were, you know what I told you, and by God, you'd better not let it happen again or you'll be working for Homero."

"Yes, sir."

"Get your ass upstairs and go to bed."

"Yes, sir." So up the stairs I went and started getting ready for bed. Krueger and Priess and Dawson were sitting up there playing dominoes when I walked in, started taking my clothes off, and went in to take a shower.

Krueger had this high fast nervous little voice, and he said, "Joaquin! Joaquin! What did the Captain say to you? What did the Captain say to you?"

Not wanting to talk about it, I said, "Not a damned thing," and I went on to bed.

It got to be a running joke between us for many years. He would ask me, "Joaquin! What did the Captain say to you when he came up them steps after we was out looking for you?" I'd tell him, "Glenn, that's between me and the Captain. Go ask him if you just got to know." And bless his heart, he went to his grave without ever learning how Captain Allee had dressed me down. We still had a lot of laughs about it, though. I sure miss him.

But that's how watchful the Captain was over us even while he was taking the heat for what was becoming a very bitter political issue. And there were also times when he put his own life on the line. Of all the misrepresentations in historians' reporting of the farmworkers' strike, nothing has gotten under my skin more than the depiction of poor Magdaleno Dimas, struck down and brutally arrested with his hands in the air as he tried to surrender to Captain Allee. This is horseshit.

In the later days of May, Dimas and a sidekick of his named Benito Rodríguez were seen strutting around the picketing areas, stoking the strikers. Dimas had been seen brandishing a rifle, and on June 1 he had a confrontation with Jim Rochester, La Casita Farms' foreman, and threatened his life. Rochester fired his own gun into the ground to get them to move off, and Dimas and Rodríguez sped away in a car. Rochester called the Rangers, and Captain Allee went to the union headquarters to learn where they were. A union clerk named Chandler told Allee that he had no idea, which the Captain figured for a lie, and he and Tol Dawson staked out the headquarters for a while. Sure enough, Chandler and another man rushed off soon after, and they led the Captain and Dawson to a house, where they saw Dimas carrying his rifle.

The Captain immediately shined a spotlight on him and ordered him to surrender, and as Dimas threw down the gun and ran back into the house, Chandler got in the way, hollering, "Don't shoot, don't shoot, he isn't armed!"

The Captain of course had no idea what kind of arsenal Dimas had concealed in the house. Going by the book, Allee obtained a warrant to enter the house and arrest him. Armed with an issue riot gun and with Dawson right behind him, he kicked down the kitchen door and found Dimas and Rodríguez sitting at the kitchen table, their hands concealed beneath it. This was a situation in which pussyfooting around could have been deadly. Even while ordering them to get their hands in the air, Allee upended the table as Tol Dawson butt-stroked Dimas in the head with his shotgun, and they got the cuffs on them.

Dimas later claimed that his hands had been in the air when the Rangers came through the door, and several years after the events, when the U.S. Supreme Court handed down its decision in the union's lawsuit against Captain Allee, part of the recitation of facts was that Dimas was dealt a concussion that put him in the hospital for four days. I know for a fact that was not true, because I returned to the sheriff's office from my train duty somewhere between ten thirty and eleven that night. The lights were on, and I saw Dimas inside with his head bandaged, and learned that he had been treated at the emergency room and released. I suppose it is possible that Dimas later went to a hospital looking for a friendly diagnosis to help him claim brutality, but he did not appear to need more treatment at the time I saw him. Some Tejano political leaders believe to this day that Allee eventually had Dimas eliminated, which simply isn't true; we later received information that he had been killed in a bar fight in Mexico. But how people choose to feel about Magdaleno Dimas just mirrors their feelings about the political situation generally, for at some point this simple labor dispute became transformed into a much larger affair that the Rangers were caught in the middle of, having to enforce the law in conditions that the public was coming more and more to see as unjust. So many different groups found a stake in it: for students and liberals it became a civil rights cause; many Hispanics in the Valley hoped it might be the beginning of the end of the traditional power structure; Texas liberals saw it as a weapon to use on Connally and his establishment. And Captain Allee was the one who had to face the Hispanic politicians who, drawing on that long, bad history in the Valley, were determined to make the Rangers out to be the bad guys. The Rangers found themselves caught in a time warp of history; as the historian Ben Procter wrote, it was simply an impossible situation. God knows, that's the truth.

One politician who wanted to make sure his name got associated with the strike was Joe Bernal, a state senator representing Bexar County in the legislature. He called a press conference to take place at the courthouse in Rio Grande City. His opinion was already very well known, since he was famous for calling the Rangers "the Mexican Americans' Ku Klux Klan. All they need is a white hood with 'Rinches' written across it." (*Rinches* is border Spanish for "Rangers.") Captain Allee did not want to go to this press conference. He knew it was a setup for Bernal to grandstand and use the Rangers as his whipping boys, and the Captain meant to have none of it, but Colonel Garrison ordered him to go.

We walked into the rotunda of the Starr County Courthouse, where the press was set up. Bernal was there in a high-dollar suit. Cap got delayed and showed up ten or fifteen minutes late in his tan gabardine suit. Bernal and Allee were standing ten or fifteen feet from Tol Dawson and me, so we couldn't hear everything, but things had hardly gotten started when it broke up. Rangers are trained to notice eye movements and body language, and Allee suddenly poked Bernal on the lapel of his suit and said loudly, "When you talk to me, by God, look at me. Otherwise, I don't have anything to say to you." And he stormed out. He was just as capable of knocking him across the room as he was of poking him on the lapel, but Senator Bernal never got his opportunity to ham it up for the cameras that day.

This depiction of Allee as an anti-Hispanic racist ignores his own history. In the early fifties, long before these events, Governor Shivers had sent Captain Allee to South Texas to protect Hispanics from abuses being practiced by the Parr regime in Duval County. On that mission the Captain actually got into a physical altercation with George Parr, son of the Duke of Duval County, the infamous Archer Parr, for which Parr got the Captain indicted for attempted murder, but had to drop the charges.

A further fact is that many of the *patrónes* and *patrónas* of the large haciendas had a world of respect for Captain Allee, but that introduces another aspect of the Valley labor troubles that people have proved reluctant to write about. It was more a class struggle than a racial struggle. Workers on those large Tejano-owned spreads, some of which had been in the same families since the days of Spanish land grants, did not enjoy conditions any better than those of workers on the large Anglo-owned truck farms. However, it does not serve anyone's political interest to elaborate on that today.

Much of what was written about the Rangers' supposed brutality has gone unchallenged, and the Supreme Court's summary of what happened was called uncontested. That was because by the time the testimony was taken and the stories were written, Captain Allee and the other Ranger principals had become so disgusted by the circus-like quality of the proceedings that they refused to acknowledge a no-win situation, since no one was going to believe them anyway. They were not without defenders, however. One of the most important was Congressman Henry Gonzalez, one of the twentieth century's most dedicated champions of the little guy. He read a report by the Texas Advisory Committee of the U.S. Commission on Civil Rights and called it mediocre and unfair. He also criticized the rush of recommendations to disband the Texas Rangers in the wake of *la Huelga* as wrong-headed.

I do remember that, when questioned, Captain Allee would answer with no more than the minimum number of syllables and with an exact meaning. In fact, during one of the legislative hearings later, some lawyer asked him if it was true that he had attempted to arrest Magdaleno Dimas, and the Captain said, "Nope."

This lawyer started getting excited, thinking he had caught the great A. Y. Allee in a lie, and said, "Do you mean to tell me that you did not attempt to arrest Magdaleno Dimas?"

The Captain said, "Nope. I have never *attempted* to arrest anyone in my life. I either arrested him, or I didn't."

After the La Casita strike blew over, which was within a couple of weeks of Dimas's arrest, and long after I was pulled from the lower Valley, the United Farm Workers sued Captain Allee and the Texas Rangers for alleged violations of their civil rights. The case eventually reached the U.S. Supreme Court, which agreed with the union, not because the Rangers had acted outside the law, but because several of the statutes under which we acted, and had to act, were declared unconstitutional.

I do not want to end this chapter and have anyone believe that we Rangers were unsympathetic to those poor people. I'm glad that conditions improved for the farmworkers, but my conscience is clear that we did our jobs. I think it was Shakespeare who wrote that all the world is a stage, that all of us in it are players who come out and deliver our lines, and that was what the Rangers did: we performed the role that fate placed us in. For all the things that have been written about the strike that are critical of the Texas Rangers, that we were tools of oppression, that we were echoing those repressive days of a half century before, I take comfort in believing that we did our job, which was to enforce the law as it was written at that time. The Rangers do not have the luxury of deciding which laws are fair and which are not. God knows, those farmworkers deserved a living wage and access to sanitary facilities and other things that would give them a dignified life. And they had the right to protest and demonstrate, but they did not have the right to block a railroad right-of-way or engage in secondary picketing, and that is why they got arrested. Moreover, they blocked the tracks exactly in order to get arrested—that is just Gandhi Tactics 101: you protest in such a way that you cannot be ignored. If they had demonstrated on the sidewalk, no one would have paid much attention. In fact, when they did demonstrate without blocking roads or rights-of-way or access to property, nobody paid attention and nobody got arrested. As it happened, when they broke the law, the whole country paid attention, and their situation eventually improved. There were certainly aspects of the farmworkers movement that history has proved willing to soft-pedal, such as its leaders' use of brutal enforcers like Dimas to keep people in line, but the same thing is probably true of every revolution, good or bad. Greater justice resulted from the whole drama, and that has been, and should be, the story of human progress.

CHAPTER 2

By the Light of the Rustlers' Moon

Rustling may be the plot of many a Western movie, but it remains a modern plague and a major source of concern for ranchers. It will usually come to the attention of both rural law enforcement and the Texas and Southwestern Cattle Raisers Association (TSCRA). To law enforcement and livestock owners, a rustler is someone who steals stock by rustling, or gathering, it up and using it for his own gain, depriving the owners of the value of their livestock—in other words, a rustler is a damned thief!

This is a highly professional and modernized organization, and important enough in Texas history to have acquired its own little legend. The story is that it was started under the boughs of an oak tree on February 15, 1877, in the town of Graham. Actually, the meeting took place in the less romantic setting of the courthouse, but it was indeed attended, as tradition says, by such legendary ranchers as Jim Loving and C. C. Slaughter. Their purpose was to regularize the "spring work" and to try to put a stop to the rustling that was hurting them all. Rustlers did not surrender the range easily, and well into the twentieth century a number of early association officials were killed in either ambushes or gunfights. One of the most famous incidents occurred on Easter Sunday 1923. Two TSCRA inspectors, W. E. "Dave" Allison and H. L. Roberson, were in the lobby of the Gaines Hotel in Seminole, Texas, the seat of Gaines County, north of Odessa near the New Mexico line. Both had been Texas Rangers in earlier years and were experienced theft investigators.

They were in town to testify against two cattle thieves, one a rancher named Tom Ross, from nearby Seagraves, and the other a no-good named Milt Good, who was already under indictment for other cattle thefts. These two strode into the lobby of the hotel with six-shooters and shotguns ready, spied the inspectors in the lobby, and gunned them down in a hail of bullets.

Roberson's wife was in her room when she heard the gunfire. She ran to the lobby and saw her husband lying mortally wounded. Well, this tough little lady went for her husband's holster, but found that the handle had been shot off the pistol. Knowing that her husband kept a hideout gun, she reached inside his belt and with this weapon opened fire on the two assailants as they backed out of the door. She hit one in the belt buckle, the bullet grazing his stomach; the other she hit in the arm, and the bullet went into his side. Both thieves fled, but being wounded, they turned themselves in the next day to the local sheriff. Both men went to the pen but later escaped. Ross was later located in Montana, where he committed suicide after killing another man. Good was recaptured, served more time, got out on parole, and was later killed in Cotulla, Texas. There's just no changing or reforming some men.

From its rustic beginnings, the TSCRA has grown into a protective army of twenty-nine field inspectors and eighty market inspectors who cover all 119 livestock markets in the state. By 2007 there were more than 14,500 association members, who owned an aggregate 5.4 million cattle. In 2005, the inspectors, often working with Rangers or local law enforcement, accounted for or recovered nearly 5,200 head of cattle, 40 horses, and hundreds of items of ranch property, all worth well over $6 million. Although many cases were deferred or dropped by the victims, the thieves were meted out actual or suspended sentences totaling 133 years.

In other words, this is a formidable organization, and it is no wonder that rustlers have changed their method from the brazen thefts of the old days to stalking, often by night. Like many aspects of the vast Texas landscape, the nights are timeless, and not many images from the Old West stay with you longer than a big full moon hanging over the desert or prairie. Away from city lights, the nights are as dark as ink, and when the moon comes up in the flat country, it seems as large and brilliant as an old silver peso. The amount of light it throws over the ground is just astonishing. Indians considered it big medicine. Comanches believed that the most favorable time for an attack was at dawn after the night of a full moon, and in fact the full moon after the grass got high enough to graze the ponies of a war party was known on the frontier as a "Comanche moon," a time to keep your guard posted and your guns ready.

A "rustlers' moon," in contrast with the brilliant Comanche moon, is something else again; the light of a full moon is so revealing that thieves are more likely to be discovered than concealed. Modern rustlers often prefer to work after dark. But when they are active at night, they prefer the light of a half-moon, or a moon that is a little more or less than half full. This gives them just enough light to see what they're doing, but it is dim enough to make them difficult to see from a distance if someone should come through the country. And there is a second reason for using moonlight: cattle, and more especially sheep and goats, will avoid dark shadows at night. They've learned that nocturnal predators use those shadows for cover while stalking, so the stock will bed down on high ground if there is any, or else out in the open. Thus, they become easier pickings for thieves using the light of the rustlers' moon.

Some rustling occurs during the day, but when that happens, it is usually done by someone on the inside—either the foreman of the ranch or the straw boss or one of the cowboys. I would guess that 80 percent of all stock thefts are committed by someone connected with the ranch. It may be the guy who tends the windmills or the fence builder, but it'll be someone who knows the outfit's routine: which pastures the stock will be grazing in or bedding down in, where the owner will be at any given time, where the entrances and exits to the ranch are, where the loading pens are, and, therefore, where he has the greatest chance of success.

If the loading pens are handy and available, they can be used by someone rustling after dark, but often the night rustler moves about with his own portable panels and an eighteen- or twenty-foot cattle trailer, and they'll just set the chutes up and funnel them in. Now, when they do this, they'll use a dog—a cow dog, sheepdog, or goat dog, depending on what they're looting—and they never have to get on a horse. Day rustlers will generally work from horseback with a couple of accomplices, including a good dog or two, and if you have an experienced dog to herd the animals, you don't need a horse at all, especially to get cattle to go into pens or a funneled cattle trailer.

Once the rustler has his cattle, he has several options for disposing of them. A lot of times he'll take unmarked or unbranded livestock to an auction ring and sell them there, but to do that it helps to be someone who is known for having his own operation, perhaps just a lease with a few head of stock. However, every stockyard has a market inspector from the TSCRA, who is not a peace officer but who notes the source of every animal that moves through there and records the brand, which is logged in a computer data bank at the association headquarters, in Fort Worth. When checking records, you can go to the local livestock auction, or you can get hold of the association's local inspector, or you can check with headquarters itself.

Naturally, the rustler prefers to find unbranded cows and calves. Breeding is timed so that the cows will have their young in December or January. The calves will be up to 350 or 400 pounds by spring, when it's time to work them—brand them, mark them, vaccinate them, castrate the young bulls to make steers (which, as we like to say, diverts their attention from ass to grass), and dehorn them. Sometimes there is another roundup in the fall, but the whole system depends on ranchers paying attention to their herds. The weekend ranchers who let their calves go unbranded and don't keep a tally book and don't know where their animals are at any given time are the ones most susceptible to becoming a victim of rustlers.

In fact, the best ways for a rancher to protect his stock are similar to the commonsense precautions that city people should take to keep their homes safe: keep gates locked and fences mended, and be cautious who you give keys or combinations to; keep stock marked or branded; mark saddles and tack with indelible identification; ideally, keep a videotaped record of animals and equipment; don't build loading pens by the side of the road; count cattle regularly; and vary ranch routines such as feeding times. Displaying Cattle Raisers Association signs prominently along the fences lets potential rustlers know that the stock is identifiable and will be difficult to dispose of.

Just like city thieves, rustlers look for easy victims, and there are enough lazy stock raisers to keep them in business. There is a long Texas history of lazy cattlemen. The term "maverick," referring to cattle that are unbranded and unmarked and therefore easy to steal, comes from an early mayor of San Antonio, Sam Maverick. He had originally intended to become a stockman, purchased a herd on the Matagorda Peninsula, and left slaves to look after them. His other interests quickly took over his attention—he joined the revolution, and was one of the last couriers to take messages out of the Alamo before it fell. Then he went into business and politics, and it was some years before he turned his thoughts to his cattle again. By then his inattention had caused the loss of a large number of livestock, and he was the butt of jokes about "maverick" cattle, free for the claiming. (A "dogie," by contrast, is simply a motherless calf, although the term is sometimes used incorrectly when "maverick" is meant.)

One way that a cattle rustler might deceive lawmen and the Cattle Raisers Association is for him to have his own place. He will have a branded or marked cow that he has stolen, and he will just keep her. He'll have his own bull or a stolen one, and just use up the stolen cow by making her produce calves for him, of which she might have several before she dies, and no one will ever know where she wound up. Another way to evade the authorities is to take stolen stock out of state, although that is not as easy as it used to be. Oklahoma is also covered by the TSCRA, New Mexico has its own system of brand inspection, and Louisiana also has a livestock board that investigates thefts.

* * *

During a livestock-theft investigation, the first thing I did when I arrived at the scene of a possible stock theft was to ask to see the rancher's or manager's tally book (a written diary of which animals were on what part of the spread). A good tally book would have the brand and markings of each animal and note when and where it had been acquired. It would also show whether it had been branded before the current owner's brand was applied. The tally book is a quaint piece of the past, for few if any ranchers use them today. On the huge corporate operations, cows are accounted for by embedded identification chips, and still more ranches are just weekend showplaces for rich city people. Both are aspects of the decline of family ranching culture, which is not the subject of this chapter but is never far from the mind of any real cattleman.

The ranchers who were diligent about maintaining their tally books, and usually that meant the old-timers, the ones who inspected their herd every day and knew the animals probably well enough to name them, seldom had problems with theft, but when they did, they would know within twenty-four hours more or less how many head were gone and from where.

Once it was ascertained that stock was in fact missing, the first step was to make sure they did not merely go astray. When that happens, a friendly neighbor will often pen them up and let the owner know to come get them. One of the college kids in Uvalde once reported his five-thousand-dollar quarter horse missing, and I tracked him out five or six miles east of town, down the highway, and then up a dirt road, and when I got up there, a rancher had seen he was a stray and penned him up. A little neighborliness goes a long way in these parts, or anywhere else, as far as that goes.

One way stock gets out of its pasture is through water gaps, where a fence will cross a dry wash or seasonal creek, which, when it floods, will take the fence down. One of the first things I would do is borrow a horse and ride the fence line, looking either for places where the fence had been cut or was down, or for water gaps where the stock could wander through. Water gaps have to be repaired several times during the rainy seasons, and many ranchers secure them just enough to keep the stock in, but they will break away and swing aside when a flood comes roaring down the wash. I don't think I ever met a stockman who cared much for mending fences at any time, and they just hate securing water gaps, but it's all part of the job, especially knowing that sometimes cattle will push up against that part of the fence and ease on through. In later years, for high-dollar thefts on large ranches, the Department of Public Safety (DPS) would make a helicopter available to me to check the fence line, and I could do in thirty minutes or an hour a job that would take all day on horseback. If there were any loading pens, I would check around for signs that they had been used recently, or for trailer paint markings on the loading chute.

Another potential fate of lost livestock, and this is most true of Angora goats, is that they become entangled in catclaws. These vicious little shrubs spread their seed by means of sharp, hooked pods that will catch onto a passing animal. Out here we call them wait-a-minute bushes because once you get caught up in one, it takes a minute or two to free yourself. Unlike the short-haired Spanish goats, Angoras are raised to be sheared for their mohair, just as sheep are sheared for wool, and when they get caught in thick brush, the catclaws just dig in deeper as the animal struggles to free itself. If the rancher doesn't comb through the thickets on his place regularly, Angora goats can stay hung up until they die of thirst or exhaustion. Getting caught in a catclaw also leaves them easy prey for predators such as coyotes, which love sheep and goats, so that is another possibility for the fate of missing stock. In fact, we have a saying out here that Angora goats are born looking for a place to die. Coyotes aren't big enough to pull down grown cattle, but they may attack a newborn calf if they can get around the mother cow.

Another problem with Angora goats, although it happened with other kinds of livestock as well, was that it seemed as if I'd get calls every November and December from several ranchers saying they were missing a hundred or two hundred head, and they would want an investigation done and written up before income-tax time so they could take a write-off on the missing animals. Ranchers did have a lot of deaths with Angoras, and maybe the coyotes ate them. I know that most of the coyotes in goat country were usually good and fat around Thanksgiving, but then again, not that many coyotes could know when the tax deadline was.

★　★　★

Many of the calls I had to answer were from absentee ranchers, men who owned the land and hired people to run the ranch but didn't visit it very often. In Texas, this practice is as old as the influx of foreign capital in the 1870s; even the great Charles Goodnight ran the famous JA Ranch on behalf of a British moneybags named John Adair (hence, JA Ranch). I remember one of the few nights I got to sit home with Shirley: we were watching television when I got a call from a rancher who lived in South Texas and had pastured some steers on land between Alpine and Marfa. He had gotten into a dispute with the "so-called cowboy" he had hired, who was now holding four of the cows in lieu of pay, which is illegal in Texas. The caller had to come up to West Texas to collect his stock because his lease was up, and since his helper had threatened to "whip his ass," he thought it would be wise to have some law present when they met.

When the time came, I called Bobby Upchurch, the TSCRA inspector in Alpine, to go with me. Well trained and a fine lawman, he had been chief deputy in Pecos County for years before becoming an inspector. Bobby called the helper, told him he was violating the law by holding the cattle, and directed him to bring them with him. The owner, who was actually a mild-mannered little man of about five-eight and might have weighed 160 pounds soaking wet, hired new help to get his stock off the expiring lease. We all rendezvoused out at the lease, waiting on the miscreant helper to show. When he rolled up in his pickup truck with the trailer behind, he proved to be about six-six and would have dressed out at about 280 pounds of solid muscle. As he approached, I noticed the handle of a six-shooter protruding from his legging pocket, so I stopped him.

I asked him if that was a revolver in his pocket and he replied yes.

I said, "You turn around and go back to your truck and put that gun in it, as there is not going to be anyone packing a gun here except me." He did as he was told, but when he came back, he and the owner began their verbal tiff.

At one point the helper dropped his shoulder as though he were about to throw a punch, but the little landowner looked him straight in the eye and said very calmly, "Damn you, don't you hit me," and glared him down until the helper returned to his truck and left, without his cows. Bobby told me later that they settled their differences without any violence, but it always warms my heart to see a little guy who is not afraid. It reminds me of one of the great Ranger proverbs: No man in the wrong can stand up to a man in the right who keeps on coming.

It was also refreshing to witness this little reenactment of a scene from the Old West. Back when there was a frontier and ranchers had to look after themselves, enforcing the law with regard to cattle rustling was simpler than it is today. Justice, however, was often summary, as they say, and sometimes carried out at the end of a rope beneath a convenient tree. When more people arrived out West, such "necktie parties" came to be frowned upon, but to say the country became thickly settled would be an exaggeration. The counties out in West Texas are large, predominantly rural, and very sparsely populated, by modern standards. Terrell County, where Sanderson is the county seat, covers 2,357 square miles and has only a thousand people in it. Brewster County, the largest in Texas, sprawls across 6,193 square miles and contains fewer than nine thousand people, and nearly two-thirds of them live in Alpine. That's why I like to tell folks that when you drive on the highways out here, people in the car or truck coming the other way wave at you. They're lonesome.

*   *   *

After the frontier closed and automobiles arrived, Texas Rangers were often called in to help solve stock thefts, since elected local sheriffs in these vast rural areas often had little or no training in investigative techniques. I remember Dalton Hogg, who was the Terrell County sheriff at Sanderson. He had been chief deputy under Bill Cooksey, whose shooting I've written about elsewhere in this book, and he succeeded Bill when the latter left to teach law enforcement at Odessa College. Dalton called me to help investigate some missing goats reported from a ranch north of Dryden, which is on Highway 90 about twenty miles east of Sanderson. Bobby Upchurch went with me, and we picked up Dalton and drove over to Dryden; that was a real throbbing metropolis, with a population of about a dozen. When we got to the ranch, the first thing that Dalton noticed was that the barn doors were open, and sitting inside was a 1954 Chevrolet, up on blocks. Dalton liked to rebuild old cars—that was sort of his hobby—and it was apparent from the start that he was more interested in that old car than he was in a bunch of silly goats. He eyed that thing the way most men in that day would have ogled a beauty like Marilyn Monroe: you could almost see the spittle coming down from the corners of his mouth.

We went into the house, the family gave us coffee, and I started asking the usual questions: could I see the tally book, when was the last time they saw the goats, who all had access—the who, what, where, when, and how that opens any investigation. Dalton, for his part, learned that the '54 Chevy had been bought new by the owners' parents, driven home from the dealer, and parked in the barn. It was still dealer fresh and in mint condition, and you could just sense his heart begin to ache for it. I think he probably made them an offer for it later, but never acquired it. But gradually he started paying attention to how I did my job, and I could tell when he was thinking because he twiddled his thumbs while he thought. I'd always heard about people twiddling their thumbs—knitting the fingers of both hands together and twirling the thumbs around each other—but I'd never seen anybody actually do it. When we got back to the car, I started to drive off, and Bobby was in the backseat and Dalton beside me, and then I saw Dalton looking at me, twiddling his thumbs. I'm sure he'd heard a lot of things that day he'd never heard before, and finally he said, "Ranger, you're just a regular damn Dick Tracy, ain't you?" I took that as a compliment from one officer to another. He was a good man and I liked him, and he tried to do a good job, but he'd never had any real training—in Texas, you don't have to be a certified peace officer to get elected, although starting in the 1970s, officers had to get certified once they got elected. Before that, deputies never got formal training either, which is why Rangers were so important in rural areas. I think a lot of them never even read the damn penal code. Now, however, new officers have access to law-enforcement-officer training, so it's getting better. The police departments in large cities have their own academies now, but when I was working in Uvalde, the city officers there, apart from their junior-college program, didn't even get basic training.

The Rangers, therefore, were called on to cover a good many aspects of individual situations—not just finding stock and culprits, but sometimes playing negotiator and peacemaker. Some of these ranchers are hard-bitten old cusses who get along with their neighbors about as well as Charles Bickford and Burl Ives did in *The Big Country*, which is to say, they live just a short comment or two away from starting a big row. I got a call once from Clyde Watkins, who was a rancher and the father of a close friend of mine, Beau Watkins, the sheriff in Uvalde for two or three terms. Clyde asked me to meet him at six o'clock one morning at the Kinkaid Hotel, an old landmark in Uvalde, where all the area stockmen used to hang out. I was expecting maybe this was about a stock theft, but when I met him, he said he was pissed off at Red Nunley. Nunley, another good friend of mine, was a big rancher who shared cattle interests with Dolph Briscoe. Clyde said he wanted to show me something, so we headed out of Uvalde on Pearsall Road and drove about fifteen miles to the Kinkaid Ranch, where he had leased some land next to Nunley's lease. As he directed me, I pulled up to a cattle gate, and he pointed to a brand-new lock on it. "The SOB has locked me out of my own lease," he said, and he asked me to get my bolt cutters and remove the lock.

I figured this was a hired-hand mistake of some kind, and I told Clyde that I didn't have any bolt cutters. He gave me a squinty look and said, "Who in the hell ever heard of a Texas Ranger without bolt cutters?"

I told him they just hadn't issued any, which was true, but I got a set a few years later. "Well, Clyde," I said, "I do have a damn good bolt cutter under my front seat," by which I meant a Winchester .30-30, but I knew there was a better solution than that.

I told Clyde to wait and that I'd take care of it in a couple of hours, maybe sooner. I telephoned Nunley, and he was very surprised and completely unaware of the situation. He told me that he had sent one of his cowboys over to put a lock on his gate, but he must have put the lock on the wrong gate, since they were on neighboring leases. From the time I talked to Red, the lock was off the gate within an hour. These two men were old, tough, grizzled big-time ranchers, and the incident could have sparked into a fight—or a killing—had I not stood in as a mediator between them, which is all in a Ranger's job: keeping the peace.

*   *   *

This lack of expertise on the part of a lot of rural law-enforcement officers certainly helped some rustlers skate by in years gone by, because some of those perpetrators never exactly obtained advanced degrees in their craft either. I remember being called out to La Pryor, in Zavala County just across the line from Uvalde County, on a hog theft. These guys had pulled up, knocked a couple of hogs in the head with a hammer, loaded their carcasses into the back of their pickup, and driven away. We could tell from the tracks that their tires had a very distinctive tread, so we made plaster-of-Paris casts of them, and when we found the likely truck, discovered blood and hog hair in the back of it. Once we questioned them, they gave it up pretty quick, since we had good evidence on them; you'd think they would have at least hosed out the bed of their truck.

Or there were the college boys (and one fun-loving girl) who drove some trailers south of Uvalde and stole about twenty-five or thirty young steers in broad daylight, never really thinking about what kind of trail they were leaving behind them. One of the kids took several of the calves and sold them in the auction barn under his own name, which raised some red flags right there because they were all branded and marked, and the rest of them he penned at the Uvalde County Fairgrounds. Of course, he didn't have any permission to do this, and the suspicious groundskeeper called the police, who in turn notified me to round them up. That wasn't a hard job, but not all investigations are this easy. They paid a fine and got probation, which was fair enough because all the stock was recovered undamaged and lots of young folks just need a second chance.

About 1970 I got a call that led me to a dead 450- or 500-pound calf under the bridge over the Nueces River west of Uvalde. It had been shot, and the hindquarters and backstrap (tenderloin) taken. It took only a little inquiring to learn that there were a bunch of college kids who were planning to have a big barbecue on a ranch just two or three miles west of there. I drove to the ranch in my state unit that night and met Sheriff Kelly and game warden Raymond Custer there. There was a big party in progress, involving college students and maybe some high school students, and as at many college barbecues, quite a bit of beer was being consumed. Once the kids saw us drive up, they started scattering in different directions like a bunch of quail. The owner met us at the gate, and I told him what the situation was and that I knew the names of the ones I believed responsible. When the owner told us that one of those named was his son, Sheriff Kelly told him we needed to come in and take a look. He told Kelly that he didn't have the authority to enter, then he looked at me and said, "But that Ranger does," and he let us in. Now, really the sheriff had just as much authority to search the place as

I did, but it's sort of comforting that the Texas Ranger badge will still get gates opened for you. We found some of the meat cooking on the grill and the rest in the freezer. It didn't take the ringleaders long to fess up to what they had done, and I believe they paid a fine or got probation, which again was okay with me. Any time there is free beef and beer, people will show up, including college kids. They don't always think about the consequences before they act, and I always tried to help them keep from getting a rap sheet.

There were times when tracking and locating animals—and the thief—could simply be fun. I got a call early one morning that a rancher near Uvalde was missing a palomino horse, along with its saddle, bridle, blanket, and a pair of chaps. It was apparent from the trail that the thief had gone off west down Highway 90, sometimes on one side of the road and sometimes on the other, sometimes in a lope and sometimes in a trot, but he never got the horse into a full run. I trailed him forty miles, to Brackettville. He was just feeding the horse in a wooden trough and hadn't been there more than thirty minutes when I drove up. He saw me and looked as if he were going to pass out. I arrested him, but if I remember correctly, he received probation also.

Or there was another rancher, who owned a buffalo that got through a fence and into a neighbor's pasture. A lot of people don't understand what powerful animals buffalo are, even a female, let alone a big old tough bull. You can fence them, but buffalo go where they damn well please. This neighbor shot the trespassing buffalo, then took the body to a local processor for butchering. He gave his real name and phone number so he could be contacted when the job was done. He wasn't particularly hard to find either, since slaughterhouses don't generally process buffalo.

Most of these cases, like many, many other instances of stock theft, ended when the victim declined to press charges. The thief typically offered to make restitution for the animal, or otherwise got the owner to feel sorry for him and not bring the full weight of the law to bear. Of all the hundreds of cases that I worked, maybe only half a dozen thieves whom I caught actually went to the pen; the rest got probation. Some of those even got adjudicated probation, which means that as soon as your term is up, if you have behaved yourself and your probation wasn't revoked, the whole conviction gets stricken from your record and you come out as clean as a choirboy. Sometimes it made me wonder what the hell I was doing out there, but in another way it was understandable, because a lot of the perpetrators were people with whom the ranchers had a previous or an ongoing relationship and had kind feelings toward. There was even a case in which a rancher lost about a hundred head of Angora goats, and when the identity of the rustler was discovered, it was the rancher who went down to the jail and made his bond.

Farmers and ranchers are the bread and butter of this country, and they grow up knowing that being merciful at times is all part of it. It has a different quality than the easy leniency handed down by a busy judge, a more human touch to it. And besides, it kept me out of courtrooms and in the field, chasing criminals who needed to be locked up worse than this bunch did.

CHAPTER 3

My Own Good Ole Boys

THE FBI NATIONAL ACADEMY

In 1978 that great Texas novelist, Elmer Kelton of San Angelo, published one of his very finest books, *The Good Old Boys*. For some reason, it wasn't until 1994 that it was made into a superb television movie with Tommy Lee Jones, who was the creative force that made it happen, Frances McDormand, Sissy Spacek, Sam Shepard, and other actors of equal caliber—including a grouchy old retired Texas Ranger, who, thankfully, wasn't given more lines than he could remember as he played the Upton County sheriff. The whole thing turned out a hell of a lot better than Elmer thought it would, especially me.

Oddly enough, it was also in 1978, when I had no knowledge of Elmer Kelton, that I left Texas to attend the FBI National Academy, and I and some of my classmates, sort of like Elmer's heedless and free-spirited character Hewey Calloway, founded our own pistol-packing group that we called the Good Ole Boys. Even more oddly, it was not with any thought of making myself more promotable as a Ranger that I went up there. I was perfectly happy being a private, but I was already forty-three, and I knew that going through the program would add to my resumé in case I decided to seek further employment after I retired. When I retired, I started a private-investigation company, so the FBI Academy expertise came in mighty handy.

Chasing cattle rustlers with my well-intentioned sheriff friend Dalton ("You're just a regular damn Dick Tracy, ain't you?") Hogg seemed light years away from the FBI training program. The campus was on 385 acres of the

United States Marine Corps base at Quantico, Virginia, forty miles down the Potomac from Washington, D.C. At the time, only the FBI and the National Academy were trained there, but it is now used by the Drug Enforcement Administration and other agencies also. There were dormitories and a dining hall, a classroom building and a separate forensics-training building, a large auditorium, a gymnasium and an outdoor track, eight outdoor firing ranges, and a 200-yard rifle range. Our Texas Department of Public Safety Training Academy would sit inside it—probably a good example of the power of federal money versus that of the state. Just outside the gymnasium begins what they call Hoover Road, the obstacle course that you see Jodie Foster running at the beginning of the film *The Silence of the Lambs*, and at the start of Hoover Road was a sign: HURT, PAIN, AGONY: LOVE IT. There is even a chapel, and anyone who thinks officers don't pray has never been shot at. One of the first impressions that struck us all was that all the buildings are connected by covered walkways; in fact, we began calling the whole complex the "gerbil cage" because it was quite possible to cover the whole complex and, except for physical training, never be exposed to the outdoors.

The idea for this school began with a government report in 1930, during the height of Prohibition, when gangsters would go careening around corners with tommy guns blazing. This study concluded that law enforcement needed to be regularized around the country by giving officers better and standardized training. The academy opened in 1935 with a class of only twenty-three students. Eventually they settled on a three-month course of study, and classes now can number up to 250.

The National Academy is an advanced course of study intended to raise the standards of law enforcement, promote cooperation among the many justice agencies around the world, and, most importantly, reach these goals by producing highly trained professional leaders in the justice field. Which made me wonder what the hell I was doing there. And, of course, for us old country boys, a few politically correct courses were thrown in for good measure. Lord knows how many would be required today. Candidates are drawn from state and local police forces, sheriffs' departments, military police, federal law-enforcement agencies—any organization concerned with protecting life and property and providing justice. What it boils down to is that the FBI building itself houses one hell of a reserve service at all times, if one is ever needed.

*   *   *

Joaquin and Shirley at the FBI National Academy, 1978.

The entrance requirements are pretty strict. You have to be at least twenty-five years old, have five years of continuous law-enforcement experience, and have earned a high school diploma or its equivalent. You have to be in excellent physical condition, which they define as being capable of sustained strenuous exertion, and if they require a physical, the candidate or his agency has to pay for it. Most stringent of all, you have to be nominated by some high law-enforcement official in your state who can swear to your character and reputation for having professional integrity, the potential for leadership, and the respect of your fellow officers. Also high on the list of what they look for in candidates is a sense of compassion; at this high level of training, borderline badge packers are not welcome. My nomination came from the director of the Department of Public Safety, Wilson Speer, through the recommendation of my captain at the time, Jack Dean.

The state paid for my travel up there without my having to take any vacation time, so Shirley and I used the occasion to make a road trip out of it. She had a good friend, Peggy Nichols, whom she had kept in touch with since her days of doing classified cryptography under that mountain around Shepherdstown, West Virginia, and Peggy still lived there. Don Joaquin was fifteen and Lance was nine, so we turned it into a vacation. We stayed a couple of nights with Peggy before we drove down to Quantico to drop me off. I don't know if Shirley ever told Peggy about our skinny-dipping in her swimming pool one night around one o'clock while everyone else was sleeping. Man, those were great days. The last time I had been in Quantico was for Marine Corps Officer Candidate School (the Platoon Leaders Class program for college students) in 1956, and at that time our housing was in Quonset huts. Some of the experiences from that time are still as sharp and clear as yesterday: a memory of the gunny sergeant making us stand in the rain all night so they could get our barracks ready (screw with our minds and test our physical stamina would be a better description) flashed in my head. Harsh, we thought at the time, but something that now brings a smile to my face. That location was only about half a mile from the National Academy site, so we drove by there and I discovered that those primitive huts had been replaced by modern dormitories. The ever-evolving times make me remember the Quonset huts with fondness. Sometimes traditions are a good thing.

The academy has an impressive appearance, an imposing glass building with a circular drive in front and lots of parking. The receptionist checked my ID and assigned me to Room 707 on the seventh floor, which seemed lucky enough, and Shirley and the boys got a tour of the place before they went back to Peggy's house for a couple of days, and then started the long drive back to Uvalde. They weren't gone an hour before I started missing them.

The study courses included long classroom hours over a period of three months in the areas of law, forensic science, behavioral science, health and fitness, communication skills, modern investigative techniques, and so on. They also offered courses on supervisory skills, but I didn't take them. I was a Ranger private (although for payroll purposes, the legislature later made all us privates sergeants) and was very happy to remain so. The reason I became a Ranger was to be active out in the field, not to sit in a company headquarters office, look over damned reports, and get calluses on my rear.

*   *   *

One of the things that made the course work so interesting was that my classmates were all seasoned officers to begin with, and in the classes they shared their own experiences in the field to help make the course work more useful and applicable. One very practical benefit of going through this training was the high regard you earned from the FBI, which followed you throughout your career. Before I attended this program, every time I asked for cooperation from the FBI, they never showed me their own folders on the cases, but after I graduated, they never failed to do so.

There are four three-month sessions every year. Mine occupied July, August, and September 1978, and about the first thing we had to do was to meet our "class counselor," Chuck Stephenson. He was a commissioned FBI agent who had been detached from his regular duties to serve as our class monitor, with a little bit of nursemaid thrown in. We were the 114th session of the National Academy; I was in a section of fifty men housed on the seventh floor, and there were four other sections of fifty men, each housed one section to a floor in the high-rise dormitory. Chuck's principal job was to keep us in line and focused, which is to say, to keep us from reverting into a bunch of drunken Good Ole Boys. He started by giving us a very stern speech about what a special group of men we were, and because we represented the essence of our nation's strength and character, a high code of behavior would be expected from us. This inspired some, but went right in one ear and out the other for others of us, who began living, or reliving, the college dorm days we always wished we'd had but probably never did.

The dormitory where we stayed was huge, an eight- or ten-story building housing not only the 250 National Academy students, but also the regular FBI trainees. We were housed two men in a room, and a pair of rooms separated by a bathroom formed a suite. Each room had a desk and a bed for each guy. The roommate I drew to share Room 707 with was Dave Gaylord, formerly of the police department of Holley, New York, and more recently assistant director of the police department at the State University of New York at Brockport. He was several years younger than I was, pretty moderately sized at about five-eight or five-nine and 160 pounds, fair complexioned but with dark hair and a moustache, and smart as hell, which turned out to be a benefit for a country Ranger.

We were a various bunch, to put it mildly. There was Carl, who came to the academy after working undercover narcotics for several years in Victoria, Texas. He arrived with a Buck knife and shoulder-length hair (the Buck knife stayed, the hair went), and his inevitable reaction to any news, good or bad, or to any situation, was some slight vocal variation of "Well, that's a hell of a deal." He had a wicked sense of humor, and in fact it was at Carl's suggestion that we called ourselves the Good Ole Boys and had T-shirts printed to seal the deal. Eventually we learned to figure out whether Carl was enchanted

Dave Gaylord at the FBI National Academy, 1978.

or disgusted or amazed by his tone of voice, because that's about all he ever said: "Well, that's a hell of a deal." And boy, did he have a hollow leg when it came to drinking; his buddy Jim Billesbach, from the police department in Everett, Washington, once tried to keep up with him, but surrendered after half of a quart of rum, which Carl then finished before chasing it with a quart of tequila.

Carl drank almost as much as Ray, who came to the academy from the Chicago Police Department, who turned the desk in his room into a full-service bar, and who would literally pull guys in from the hall to have a drink with him. Floating above all this was Chuck, our counselor, although it was apparent from the beginning that alcohol counseling had not been part of his training. One night shortly before the end of the course, when several of us were up, well, being boys, a private security guard for the Justice Department showed up at our room and ordered, "Get up to your counselor's room right away." We thought we were probably in deep shit, but when we got up there, we found Chuck and a couple of other agents, wanting to visit and have a drink. I guess he wanted to show us he could be one of the Good Ole Boys, too.

One of my favorites in the class was Ruben Archuleta, who is still one of my close friends. He had been a sergeant with the police department in Pueblo, Colorado, and after the academy he worked his way up through the

Ruben Archuleta—a Good Ole Boy—at the FBI National Academy, 1978.

ranks until he retired as chief of police a few years ago. Also standing out in my mind is Steve Smith, who was with the Suffolk County Sheriff's Department on Long Island. I got a real lesson in life when he invited some of us to go up to New York for a weekend. I'd never been to New York and was eager to see it; also going with us was Ray Cesaritti, who was an NYPD sergeant and worked the Harlem area. We left on a Friday afternoon after class and drove up; I think we might have dropped Ray off before going on to Steve's apartment on Long Island. Saturday night we went over to Harlem, and from Ray's tour we learned that normally on a Saturday night every street corner has its complement of pimps, prostitutes, and drug dealers, but on this night they made a liar out of him. There was not any illegal-looking element to be found, and Ray just shook his head and said, "Well, I guess they heard the Rangers were coming," and we all had a good laugh.

But I saw right away that this was no place for an old country boy. One officer pulled up in his Suburban to chat with Ray; he was a "special response team" (SRT) officer, sort of like a member of a SWAT team, which meant that he responded to officer-down or shooting-in-progress calls, or to other situations that might require his special arsenal of tear gas, automatic weapons, bulletproof vests, and other tactical equipment. I was introduced to him, and he said, "Ranger, I've got to check out this old hotel. Would you like to come along and see some of what goes on here?"

I said, "Sure, why not?" Why would he think I would be concerned about a hotel?

He looked at me and asked, "Are you armed?"

I answered, "Yes, I'm always armed." I was carrying my .45 Colt Lightweight Commander. I had a jacket on, and it was tucked down in my belt, off my right hip. It was fully loaded and "cocked and locked," as we like to say, the thumb safety engaged. After many years of carrying that weapon, I could have the thumb safety off and a live round in the chamber by the time it was leveled. It was about as close as a modern Ranger could come to a Western-style quick draw.

We went into this old hotel, just the SRT officer and me. He had his hand on his gun. Looking over to my right, I saw what appeared to be a bulletproof glass cage with a black fellow inside it, who apparently was the hotel clerk. As soon as I saw the bulletproof glass, I thought to myself, this is a badass part of town, something you definitely would not see in my part of the country, and certainly not a place I would ever want to work in, even if I could handle it.

The officer said, "Come on, let's go upstairs and check a room or two." There was no elevator in the hotel, so we went to the staircase. It was a "winder" that had two landings and changed direction at each one. The officer unsnapped his gun and had his hand on the butt of it, and at each landing he would stop and look around the corner to see if anyone was on the stairs. It was like inching our way through a jungle, and each turn might have revealed some bastard high on dope ready to shoot my tall, lanky butt off.

We got to the second floor and reached the door of one of the rooms; he motioned me to stand on one side of the door, and he stood on the other. He pulled out his revolver and tapped on the door with the barrel of it. The Old Ranger was definitely on the alert. I placed a hand on my Colt and a thumb on the safety. The door had a peephole so the people inside could look out and see who was there. A voice inside said, "Who is it?"

He said, "Police. Open the door."

The door opened, and to my surprise, this being Harlem, it was a white man, and I mean he was as white as a sun-baked cow chip. You could tell by his looks that he was a dope addict. I've seen dead people who looked better than he did.

As soon as the door opened, the SRT officer stuck his revolver right under the guy's nose and marched him back into the room; I followed in behind them. It was a small room, and sitting on a couch inside was a black man.

The officer poked around the room and asked some questions. These New York police officers don't take crap from anybody. Their efficiency is just as you see it on TV and in the movies: cold, calculating, and "right on target" with their mission. Impressed the hell out of this Texas cowboy. I guess he was satisfied with the answers because we left without bothering them further.

Back down on the street, we ran into this big uniformed African American NYPD officer, almost as tall as I am and built like he was a tight end for a professional football team; believe me, he could have gone bear hunting with a switch. He had heard of the Texas Rangers but had never met one, so he was quite interested in me and asked several questions. Finally I said, "Look, officer, I want to tell you something, mi amigo. I got all the admiration in the world for the job you are doing up here. An area like this, I couldn't work it unless I was totally retrained." An officer, a Ranger or anybody, is only effective when he gets to know his territory, gets to know the people in the territory, and develops his sources of information and such things, and from what I'd seen so far, doing that in Manhattan could take a spell. Of course, I heard that there are other parts of New York that are just as rough as Harlem, but seeing this made me count the blessings of my own job, of moving in free, wide-open spaces. There was a reason we were called Rangers: we ranged over a wide swath of country, keeping the settlers safe. As I said, New York City was just not a place for an old country boy to be.

But those New York cops were as tough as any I've seen. They told about one officer who was late to a briefing and missed the word that a movie was being filmed in his district. The scene that was being shot, as he came upon it, involved two actors, one chasing the other and shooting at him. Thinking that he had come upon a shooting in progress, he stood behind a building corner and waited. He allowed the actor being pursued to pass, but then as the "shooter" approached, running at full speed, he clotheslined him in the throat with his nightstick and put him in the hospital. I figure he didn't miss any more briefings.

*   *   *

Life back at Quantico, in the gerbil cage, seemed pretty tame after that. Dorm life resumed, and I guess it would be only fair to acknowledge, men being cooped up together and all, that on the weekends they would go to mainside Quantico (the area of town opposite the mainside marine barracks) or to

D.C. for a little R&R. One of the places we would go in Washington was the Officers Service Club on 14th Street. If not for the small brass plaque by the door, you would never have guessed it was a bar; in fact, the first floor was a restaurant, and the bar was upstairs. They were always partial to National Academy boys; on our arrival, the maitre d' would clue the single officers in on the male-female ratio, and once we got upstairs, there was a bartender who was a wizard—he could associate a face with his favorite drink after just one or two visits and not forget him.

It is important to understand that these recreations were not an everyday occurrence. In fact, if the combination of course work and physical training had not been so rigorous, there would have been little enough reason to escape from it. A course that stands out in my mind particularly was called Biorhythms. I first thought, "Is this about music—a lead guitar accompanied by a rhythm guitar, or something like that?" But biorhythms were a major focus of attention in the seventies, and we were required to plot major crimes, such as serial killings, by the full moon or high tides, which are known to affect animal and human behavior. We had an exam at the end of each one-week unit, and failure was so unthinkable I don't even know what would have happened if someone had failed one. And considering that we were each representing a home agency, the pressure was considerable. Playing havoc with our mental capacities, the instructors also challenged us with courses in criminology, forensic sciences, and other highly technical subjects that lifted this training far above the demands of local law enforcement. After going through all this, we deserved a beer. A little Jack Daniel's and water couldn't be totally excluded either.

When manly bonding was more in order, we would frequent the Globe and Laurel Bar and Restaurant, whose proprietor was a retired Marine Corps major, and a guy from the National Academy who made his first visit there had to deposit a patch from his home department. The major had lined the ceiling of the bar with hundreds of them. There was a small joint there at the academy called the Boardroom, although we called it the Slopshoot, which was what we called bars when I was in the Marines. The Boardroom could serve only beer and wine, which was okay as far as it went, and it was a friendly place to relax before turning in on school nights. There was also a theater that showed a movie every evening.

Dave was more enamored of the campus than I was, and on most weekends I would tag along with one of the Good Ole Boys who had brought his own transportation, and we would head into D.C. or someplace for some recreation, leaving Dave to hold down the fort. Not only did Dave never complain, but if I had reports that had to be typed up, he'd say, "Don't worry about it, roomie, I'll take care of it for you," and he would; on a couple of occasions, he even threw my laundry in with his. Man, what a great roomie!

★   ★   ★

Even with all this camaraderie, after a few weeks in Quantico I got so homesick I couldn't stand it; I had been away from Shirley and the boys before, when I was chasing fugitives in Mexico or when other duties carried me far from home, but this was drastically different. The gerbil cage had all the amenities of home except family, and they were fifteen hundred miles away. In fact, there was one night I went up to my room and started packing my stuff. About then, Chuck the resident counselor came by. My door was open to the hall, and he saw me inside. He said, "Ranger, what are you doing?"

I answered, "I'm packing my stuff. I'm going home."

He said, "You can't do that."

I said, "You just hide and watch. I'm hauling my lanky ass back to Texas. I'm homesick as hell, I've had all of this I want, and I'm going home."

Chuck got thoughtful and said, "Well, I'll tell you what, let's go up to the Slopshoot and I'll buy you a beer." We went upstairs, and after about three pitchers of beer and a couple of bags of popcorn (I remember my blood pressure later shot up and I was called to the nurse's office. It was because of so much salt in the popcorn, along with the beer.) I mellowed out enough to think I could stick it out for maybe another week or two. And that week went by, and after another week I began to see an end to it all, so I lasted. I tell you, it's no accident that compassionate psychology is part of what they teach, and if Chuck hadn't offered me a little downtime, I would have walked out that night. I would have had to pay my own way back home, catch a train into D.C., and then fly, but I would have done it.

★   ★   ★

There were aspects to life there that were more like boot camp than Animal House: we had to make our beds every morning, and the physical training was rigorous. At forty-three, I was one of the elder statesmen of this class, but I am proud to say I held my own in this department. One of the things I have always hated to see is an officer who lets his physical conditioning go.

A slob of a cop is a danger to himself, his partner, the force, and the citizens who are depending on his protection, and right up until I retired, I was in pretty damn good shape for one of the Over the Hill Gang. After calisthenics, we had to run a mile every morning, and I came in second every time, which at forty-three was pretty good. But I got annoyed at the guy who was always, always in front of me. He was military—probably Special Forces—and every morning this little bastard would take off like he had a lion on his tail, which I guess in a way, he did (me). I also finished second in marksmanship, although I was a master shooter; Jim Billesbach, the lightweight drinker from Washington state, was the only one of us to ever score a "possible" (a perfect score) on the pistol range.

The food at the academy dining hall was catered by the local Marriott, and was uniformly excellent—Wednesday was steak night—and some evenings after dinner our spirits would run kind of high. Our floor once staged a jousting tournament, which was more like rousting (knocking the hell out of your opponent), fought with mop handles, the object being to unhorse your opponent from his mount, which was a big laundry cart. The halls in this dormitory must have been a hundred and fifty or two hundred feet long, and the guys pushing the knights in the laundry carts could get up a pretty good head of steam. Since there were no fair damsels to win, the prize for victory was a bottle of whiskey. The jousting was finally deemed a little out of bounds, though, and Chuck put a stop to it—reining in the Good Ole Boys.

★ ★ ★

Some of the students were foreigners, of course, and one of the nicest and most studious was Hsin-Chung Yang of Taipei, Republic of China—or just Taiwan, as we're supposed to call it now so as not to get the mainland Chinese worked up. When not actually in class, he was forever in the library studying or in his room studying. He was very polite to everyone, but he was a perennial no-show at the hall parties.

One night one of our students, Billy Ray Wooten, of the Alabama State Police, produced a bottle of moonshine that had supposedly been "seized" from an illegal still somewhere. He was even able to swear that it was "certified . . . won't even make you go blind or nothin'." Well, that was reason enough for a hall party, and on this occasion Dave Gaylord went down the hall and rapped on Yang's door. He was studying, naturally. Dave explained that for him to not ever have a drink with his fellow officers was considered a serious insult. "Losing face" was a concept that Yang understood immediately, and he produced his polite and smiling self in a heartbeat. We drank several toasts, each of us taking single shots while we double-shot poor Yang, and he got drunker than a waltzing pissant.

He came out of his room the next morning, as Dave tried to describe it, holding both halves of his head together, and probably the first twenty-five words we heard out of him that morning exhausted his vocabulary of English cussing. Yang, if you ever read this: We're sorry. We apologize.

★   ★   ★

At our graduation, diplomas were handed out by FBI director William Webster, who later became director of the Central Intelligence Agency. I have recently taken some pleasure in the fact that Webster in 2005 received the William Penn Award, a prestigious honor that is bestowed by the Penn Club of Philadelphia for outstanding merit in various fields—arts, humanities, science, public service, etc. Previous winners have included President Ulysses S. Grant, the poet Walt Whitman, and the British war hero Lord Mountbatten. I received the same award in 2006 for public service, so despite the partying that went on amongst the Good Ole Boys, if the Old Ranger could rise to the same level of recognition as the director of the bureau, I must have done something right, or wrong.

Law-enforcement training has advanced a great deal since I graduated from Quantico, thirty years ago. The curriculum has kept abreast of criminal activity by adding courses in such areas as computer forensics and counter-terrorist measures. To date, nearly forty thousand officers have completed studies there, of whom more than 6,300 went on to occupy the top positions in their agencies, which speaks volumes about the place. More than 1,300 women have graduated, as have more than 2,500 foreign students from 152 countries, everywhere from Albania to Zimbabwe.

Ruben Archuleta went on to achieve significant things in the arts—he has written two or three books, and he is an accomplished sculptor, working out of his home studio in Pueblo, Colorado. My only regret is that we didn't know his artistic interests at the time. We could have given him hell about being the "pistol-packing painter." Dave Gaylord went back to work for the State University of New York at Brockport police force for thirty-two years,

Joaquin getting his diploma from William Webster
at the FBI National Academy, September 1978.

and eventually became its chief in 1992. He has published extensively in various police periodicals; received advanced training in areas such as crisis intervention, bomb disposal and weapons of mass destruction; and taught seventeen sessions of SUNY's police academy in Albany before being named its deputy director. He finally retired a couple of years ago, and has more time now for golf and his collection of vintage military rifles. He remains a fast friend, and still signs his letters "Yer Roomie," a fresh reminder of our youth—well, his youth and my earlier middle age—of serious training and high jinks.

After I retired and became involved in the filming of *The Good Old Boys*, I never made the connection to my old dorm buddies until I visited with Dave and Ruben and they pointed it out to me. Looks like the Good Ole Boys came full circle.

CHAPTER 4

Sadistic Deaths in the Desert

THE FROME MURDERS

The FBI training I received stood me well in all my subsequent years of Ranger service, but there are times when all the training in the world will not be able to overcome bad clues, the calendar, or circumstances that just favor the criminal. Once a crime is solved, you can look back down the trail of an investigation and see a kind of inevitability about it. But when you are still at the outset, not knowing where the trails will lead, there is no sense of certainty whatever. Freshness of evidence, of course, is always desirable. Whenever I was called in to investigate a crime, especially one as dire as a homicide, I, like any officer, would prefer working with a crime scene that was as pristine as possible. But during those days when so many rural sheriffs were lacking in training, a lot of times a Ranger would not be called in until the local authorities had given it their best shot and given up, or maybe until some of the local citizens had begun to suggest that the sheriff wasn't doing his job. I went down to Uvalde in 1966, and I think the coldest case I was called in on was a murder that had been committed in 1938.

Culberson County, in West Texas, is just a touch smaller than the state of Connecticut, its beige desert stretching south from the New Mexico line for nearly a hundred miles, almost to the Rio Grande, divided north to south by the Delaware and Apache mountains. During frontier days, this area was the scene of the last Apache Indian fighting in Texas, which was brought about by a band of raiders under the famous chief Victorio. After decades of mayhem and bloodshed, the army's ace cavalry raider, Benjamin Grierson, finally stopped chasing the Apaches and began seizing the water holes in their path, turning their own desert against them. It took twenty years to figure out how to best the wily Victorio, but far longer than that to make any progress in the Frome murders.

In 1938 the population of Culberson County was about sixteen hundred people, a lonely enough place even to live in. Van Horn is the seat of government, and five out of six Culberson County residents live in that town. But for Mrs. Weston G. Frome and her daughter Nancy the hot silent desert near Van Horn was an even lonelier place to die in. Mrs. Weston G. (Hazel) Frome was forty-six, a prominent socialite in Berkeley, California. Her husband was assistant sales manager of the Atlas Powder Company, a DuPont subsidiary that made a variety of industrial and consumer filters out of charcoal that had been reduced from lignite coal. Her daughter Nancy, twenty-three, was a doe-eyed brunette, very pretty and winsome, a member of Delta Delta Delta sorority and a graduate of the University of California. Mr. Frome had just given his daughter an expensive new automobile, a silver-gray Packard, in which she and her mother set off on a cross-country trip to visit another daughter in Parris Island, South Carolina. Originally, Nancy had intended to travel by train, alone, for an extended visit, but her mother was worried about her traveling alone, and at the last minute they opted to break in the new car with a road trip.

With their luggage in the rear, and with a jar of fruit and a gallon of olives to snack on, they journeyed from Berkeley to El Paso, where they developed engine trouble and stopped to have the car fixed, as Mrs. Frome wrote her husband. That was on March 25, and over the next five days mother and daughter played tourist, staying at the Hotel Cortez, where they became friendly with other California travelers, and taking shopping trips to Juárez. The automobile was repaired, and they resumed the trip on Wednesday, March 30.

One hundred thirty miles east of El Paso they entered vast, lonely Culberson County. The highway from El Paso that passes from west to east is the only one, and the next town of any consequence after El Paso is Van Horn. Somewhere on that stretch of highway, Hazel and Nancy Frome vanished.

About halfway between Van Horn and Pecos the highway splits, the northern route bound for Dallas, the southern route for San Antonio. On March 31, near Balmorhea, Texas, seventy miles east of Van Horn on the highway to San Antonio, Deputy Sheriff Sam Davis found the Frome car abandoned on the Old Spanish Trail. The engine worked perfectly, and there was five gallons of gasoline in the tank, but there was no sign of luggage or tools. One of the tires was flat, and the inner tube was missing, a sign that perhaps a passerby had given them a ride to get it patched; the tire-repair kit had not been removed from its factory packaging. There was no blood or other sign of foul play, but also no fingerprints, and, oddly, a comparison of the odometer with the notation from the repair shop in El Paso showed that the car had been driven about forty miles more than the distance between the two locations.

Scores of officers and even Civilian Conservation Corps workers fanned out to search a ten-square-mile area near where the car was located, and discovered a number of rattlesnakes, but no sign of the women. A Coast Guard airplane searching overhead had no luck either. Local Justice of the Peace R. F. Ross told the press that he could not explain their disappearance, but had no reason to believe that they had come to any harm. Back in Berkeley, California, Weston Frome, paunchy and gray haired, feared mightily otherwise, and boarded an airplane for El Paso to join in the search. He knew that his wife and daughter intended to go through Dallas, and their car should not have been on the road where it was found. He was able to tell officers that the women had left home with about $125 in spending money, and the last he had spoken to his wife, she still had $90, tucked into the safe hiding place of her brassiere. His daughter was wearing a French watch, which hung from a neck chain, and two gold bracelets, one with an elephant hanging from it. His wife wore her wedding ring and a diamond solitaire; also in the car had been an Indian blanket—all items that could be identified if found in the possession of someone else.

The first real break in the case came when Jim Milam, a truck driver who lived in El Paso, came forward to say that the Frome car and a coupe had passed him on the highway east of Van Horn. A man and two women were in the Frome Packard, and a third woman was driving the coupe. It had two sets of license plates, one from Texas and one from either New Mexico or California; and he noted there was printing on the door of the coupe, but did not notice what it was. The two cars appeared to be traveling in tandem, because they passed him, then stopped and turned around. At this location, the tracks showed that the Frome car veered crazily for over 250 yards before regaining the highway, indicating that a struggle had possibly taken place within. The Frome car passed Milam again, going in the opposite direction, and then suddenly turned off into the desert. With Milam guiding them, the authorities, including federal agents who had been called in because a kidnapping was suspected, found the spot where tire tracks turned off the road. It was six miles east of Van Horn, by an abandoned caliche pit, where road crews had once mined crushed limestone to use as roadbed when the highway was paved. The trail headed south toward the Wylie Mountains. Following the tracks for some four-tenths of a mile, they came to an isolated clearing of bare dirt and a spread-out blanket concealing some objects underneath.

Beneath the blanket were the corpses of two seminude women, carefully laid facedown, each bearing signs of savage beating, torture, and gunshot wounds to the head. One was a matronly, middle-aged woman who had stood about five-three and weighed about 140 pounds. The other woman was much younger, in her early twenties, a willowy brunette about five-six and 115 pounds. There was no sign of a struggle, but the younger woman had dirt under her fingernails, a sign that she was not dead at the time she was covered, and had tried to move. She might also have tried to resist her attackers, for blood and skin were also found under her nails. One hand tightly gripped a man's monogrammed handkerchief. She had a French watch chain around her neck, but the watch was missing.

Most of their clothing had been stripped away, but their undergarments remained in place, leading investigators to doubt whether they had been sexually assaulted. The older woman's shoes, stockings, girdle, and brassiere were in place, and her eyeglasses had been fitted on as well; the younger one was clad only in shoes, socks and panties. Both women had been repeatedly burned with cigarettes—no fewer than eight times on the back of one of the young girl's hands, searing it to the bone—and finally each had been shot in the left temple. It didn't take long from this gruesome scene to identify them as Hazel and Nancy Frome. Autopsies showed that neither woman had been sexually molested, but Nancy's diaphragm, which is located directly above the stomach, had ruptured from the force of being stomped. The fatal weapon used on Hazel Frome was a .32-caliber revolver of foreign make, probably Spanish. At first it was thought that Nancy had been killed with a .38, fueling the belief that more than one killer was involved, but closer study revealed both bullets to have been .32s and probably fired from the same gun.

According to the medical examiner, Dr. W. W. Waite, the suffering that the women endured while being beaten and burned was beyond belief. It ap-

Hazel and Nancy Frome, 1938.

peared that a chunk of flesh had been bitten from Mrs. Frome's forearm. When
told that his daughter had apparently made a struggle of it, a grief-stricken
Weston Frome commented, "She would. She was the gamest little thing in
the world." The bodies were quickly released; Frome visited the mortuary
where they were taken, but could not bring himself to view them. After they
were prepared for burial, he had the caskets sealed, and they remained so
after he took them back to California for interment.

From the tire tracks, it was deduced that the car that dumped the bodies
had turned around and returned to the highway from an acceleration spin,
turning a large doughnut before regaining the road two-tenths of a mile west
of where it had left it. When word of the grisly discovery spread, curious

onlookers flocked to the scene, destroying any other evidence that might have remained.

One man who went virtually into hiding was Milam, who was terrified that the killers would find him and silence him. Ten days after the murders, he was the subject of a front-page feature of the El Paso newspaper, in which he claimed that he had been shot at on the same stretch of road where the Fromes were taken. Rangers investigated and determined that a wind charger on top of his truck had snapped off, making a sharp bang that made him believe a bullet had struck his vehicle. Milam sounded less than convinced. "I want the murderers caught," he said, "but I don't want them to get me. I have a wife and ten children, too."

Also in seclusion was an El Paso fortune-teller, her name withheld, who said that Mrs. Frome had called on her the Monday before she left town. The seer dealt her Tarot cards: "I saw enemies around her in the reading—I saw the death card. Not wishing to frighten her, I did not reveal this until she asked, 'Do I have an enemy who would do me bodily harm?'" The authorities thought she might be a publicity seeker, but she accurately described Hazel's outfit, a black serge suit, black felt hat, and brown oxfords, and she described the jewelry, saying that Mrs. Frome kept nervously turning the

Joaquin at the Frome crime scene, thirty-two years later, 1970.

diamond solitaire on her finger. She did not fear for Nancy, only herself. "I want to help police as much as I can," said the card reader, "but I fear giving my name because I feel the killers are in or near El Paso yet."

Further motorists, including a mother and grown son who contacted authorities from their home in Massachusetts, substantiated Jim Milam's description of a coupe following the Frome car, and officers acquired a description of the two others as a blond woman and a "burly" man. Some days later, a Berkeley, California, newspaper dated March 23, the day of their departure, was found about forty miles east of the scene, indicating a possible direction of flight. A large portion of the Ranger force was assigned to the case, and they cast a wide net: hundreds of people were interviewed and put on the spot to account for their whereabouts. When El Paso sheriff Chris Fox turned up what he called "definite evidence in the murders," the Texas Rangers requested authorities in Denver, Colorado, to arrest a thirty-eight-year-old itinerant railroad brakeman. Because of his railroad-circuit rounds, he traveled over and over again to areas under investigation. Ranger A. L. Barr went up to take custody of him, and then hauled him all the way to Winslow, Arizona, to check his alibi, which was substantiated. He was released.

The few clues were baffling. At first it was thought that robbery might have been the motive, for Mrs. Frome's diamond solitaire and the stash of money from her brassiere were missing, and it was believed that the women had carried two thousand dollars in traveler's checks. However, her wedding ring and a diamond wristwatch remained in place, as did another diamond ring worn by Nancy. Further tire tracks matching those from the two cars, and blood-soaked tissues that were of the same brand as those found in the Frome car, led authorities to search an abandoned mine six miles west of Van Horn for the missing luggage, but to no avail.

At least the time of their deaths was narrowed, since two army privates from Fort Bliss were certain they had seen the Frome car near Toyahvale, sixty miles east of Van Horn, at five thirty in the evening on March 30, the date of their disappearance. They said no other car was following them at that time.

Theories of the crime abounded. One, developed and espoused by Captain S. D. Shea, head of the Criminal Division of the El Paso County Sheriff's Office, was that it was a case of mistaken identity in a drug deal gone sour. Their car was similar to one that local authorities had pegged as belonging to narcotics runners, and the torture, which otherwise would have been attributable to hate, could have been inflicted to learn the hiding place of a drug stash. In another theory, the El Paso district attorney, the Van Horn sheriff, and some others believed the women's killer might be a man who had befriended them in El Paso, while their car was being repaired. They were known to have been escorted by someone on at least one of their trips across the border to Ciudad Juárez, Mexico. There was some thought by investigators that espionage might be involved, since German spies were in Mexico at this time, just before World War II. Investigators mentioned that the Frome family was originally from Germany.

The gruesome slayings aroused such fear locally that state police announced in June that they were opening a substation in Van Horn and would begin patrolling that stretch of highway more closely. Federal agents were pulled off the case once it was shown not to be a kidnapping, but they stood by to cooperate when asked. Various rewards, including one for a thousand dollars announced by Governor Jimmy Allred, were posted until they totaled some ten thousand dollars, enough to bring private gumshoes into the search. One of them, an El Paso private eye named Bennett, was certain he had solved the case with a laundry ticket and a scrap of black satin, but he, too, came up empty.

The first several days of April 1938 were a bad time for anyone in the Southwest to behave erratically or be caught out of an established routine. The Rangers pounced on any person who could remotely be tied to the case, and in the depth of the Great Depression, a ten-thousand-dollar reward brought a flood of hopeful tips. Fourteen months after the slayings, they detained twenty-two-year-old Robert Burgunder, Jr., a student at Arizona State Teachers College. He was being extradited to Phoenix to face charges of killing two automobile salesmen when it was learned that he had been a student at the University of California while Nancy Frome was there. As did many, many people who drove through Van Horn, he had stopped and asked directions to the murder scene, and that was his downfall.

He was not the only man wanted elsewhere who was caught in the Frome dragnet. An anonymous tip to the Dallas Police Department, that the couple wanted for the Frome murders could be found in a West Dallas tourist camp, led authorities to an ex-con named John Mahan and a red-headed female companion. They were wanted in Duncan, Oklahoma, for robbing a grocery store, and in Kilgore, Texas, for robbing a baseball ticket office. No link to the Fromes could be established.

Similarly discovered in Dallas, only ten days after the killings, were two three-time ex-cons: Jack Flippen, age thirty, and Jack Barnes, thirty-four, who were traveling together. The pair had been sought in El Paso, where their mug shots had been published in the *El Paso Times*, since the beginning of the investigation. They had been seen heading north toward Roswell, New Mexico, not east toward Van Horn, but after being given the third degree late into the night, they admitted to robberies in Tulsa, Oklahoma; Fort Smith, Arkansas; and Fort Worth, Texas, but adamantly denied involvement in the Frome murders. The next day a Dallas newspaper reported that no murder case could be made against them. However, they eventually admitted to, or were identified by eyewitnesses as, being involved in as many as thirteen heists in Texas, Oklahoma, and Arkansas.

Authorities tracked down guests who had been registered at the Hotel Cortez in El Paso, where the Frome women had stayed, causing them to develop an interest for a time in a "Doctor" Romano Nicholas Trotsky, who was wanted for having abandoned a wife and toddler in Las Cruces, New Mexico. He had a long criminal record and multiple assumed names, and had been convicted more than once for performing abortions, including one on a woman who died as a result. Despite his ties to the town of Richmond, California, next to Berkeley, including having been married there, and despite his admission that he stayed overnight in the Hotel Cortez at the same time Mrs. Frome and her daughter were there, he couldn't be tied to their killings. The local press still made some sensational mention of his claim to be a nephew of the Bolshevik Leon Trotsky, then living in exile in Mexico.

During a barroom conversation in San Antonio, a young married couple was overheard talking about a party in Berkeley at which they met Nancy Frome. This led to a tip being phoned in to police, and the couple was tracked to a motor court in Laredo and arrested. In McCamey, Texas, a man attempting to sell a bag containing expensive women's clothing was taken into custody; the clothing subsequently proved to be his wife's. A blond woman who happened to be hitchhiking near Temple, Texas, was picked up and questioned even more closely when it was learned that she had been in Van Horn a couple of weeks before the killings, but she was also released. A lunatic in Bisbee, Arizona, mumbling that he had left them face down and had to go bury them, was arrested. A bullet was removed from a suicide victim found on the banks of the Rio Grande with three cents in his pocket—he had shot himself with a .32-caliber revolver—and compared to the one that killed Hazel Frome. A lead that a romance of Nancy's had resulted in an annulment in New York was checked out. All were investigated exhaustively, but none of them panned out.

Suspicious luggage, such as a Gladstone traveling bag thrown from an eastbound train near Sanderson and recovered by a motorist, was examined thoroughly. It fit the description of one of the missing Frome bags; an inventory of all five pieces was circulated as a hundred state and local officers combed the brush between Van Horn and Balmorhea. Eventually, a cache of probable Frome luggage articles was found by a team of twenty-two Civilian Conservation Corps workers. The workers found the articles nineteen miles west of Balmorhea; the materials included California newspapers, green eye shadow, and a receipt for expensive perfume.

On April 7, a week after the murders, the funerals were held in California. Weston Frome had maintained since learning of their disappearance that robbery was the only possible motive. Even so, El Paso County sheriff Chris Fox altered his theory to one of personal vengeance. "I am strongly of the opinion that the murders were premeditated," he said. "They appeared to be the work of someone inspired by intense hatred."

Once, just once, they came tantalizingly close. Nine days after the killings, a dark coach with writing on the side, bearing California and New Mexico license plates, pulled into a mechanic's shop in Del Rio, Texas, for repair. In it were an extremely nervous, small blond woman and a male companion. There were a number of expensive pieces of luggage in the rear; the mechanic noticed a pistol on the floor, which the woman placed in her handbag. A black coach of that exact description soon turned up at another mechanic's shop in Sonora, Texas, ninety miles almost due north of Del Rio, where a similarly described blond woman said she didn't have time to wait for the car to be fixed, and the garage workers took her luggage to the bus station, where station employees stated that she nervously told several people that she was going to Florida. She boarded a bus to San Antonio. It was believed that the blond and her male companion rendezvoused in San Antonio, for the next day, April 10, they and their distinctive car were seen in Carrizo Springs at a roadside café, and thence headed to Laredo. Local Texas Rangers A. Y. Allee (my captain some twenty-eight years later) and Pete Crawford took up the chase as soon as they learned of it, and roadblocks were thrown up around the city, but the car was gone, doubtless driven into Mexico and oblivion.

Two weeks after the murders, Sheriff Fox went back to square one, retracing the women's route in his own car, hoping to glean some insight that had escaped him up to then. The next day he turned his attention to Juarez, where Hazel and Nancy Frome's photographs were recognized by a nightclub waitress, who said the women danced with two men who had identified themselves as fellow Californians.

But the Laredo lead was as close as they got; subsequent clues all led to disappointment, and the case got colder and colder as leads faded into increasingly improbable rumors. The last really good candidate was lost the following August, killed by police while resisting arrest in Hot Springs, Arkansas. His name was Earl Young, twenty-six, wanted for the murders of women in Kansas and South Dakota, attacks that were as savage as the Frome killings. He was also wanted for questioning about murders in New Mexico that had peculiar similarities to those in the Frome case, and he was known to have been in El Paso at the same time the Fromes were there. But Hot Springs police ended that line of inquiry.

Authorities again thought they might have caught a break in the case in March 1940 during the murder trial in Odessa of a New Jersey jail escapee named Isabelle Messmer, who claimed self-defense in the shooting of a semiprofessional baseball pitcher. She was the strongest possibility to date. She fit the description of the woman seen following the Fromes' car on the day of the murder. She told officers that she had obtained the gun she used to shoot the baseball player from "two Mexicans who had murdered two California women," and the Frome murder weapon was believed to be a Spanish revolver. Most tantalizing of all, she had in her possession photos taken near the Frome murder scene at the time she was taken into custody. Like many once-promising clues, however, this turned into a flash in the pan, as Ranger Barr, who was a ballistics expert, was apparently unable to tie the bullet taken from the ballplayer to the bullets that killed the Frome women.

It happened again in January 1942, with the arrest of Charles Hatfield, a thirty-eight-year-old truck driver from Bakersfield, California; his thirty-one-year-old wife, Bonnie; and Mrs. Wood Butler of Mexia, Texas. With the involvement of the FBI, the Hatfields were taken into custody in Los Angeles and secretly removed to El Paso for questioning. Ranger Captain Royal G. Phillips, who later became chief of the intelligence section, and another Ranger worked for weeks, snooping from El Paso all the way back to Los Angeles, trying to break their stories, but they were unable to do so. Van Horn sheriff Albert Anderson was at one time under the impression that Mrs. Hatfield had given a voluntary statement, but after being held for ten days in El Paso, the suspects were released and the case, as the newspaper lamented, "reached another dead end."

By the time another story was written about it, the Frome case had become "Texas' costliest, most intensive and most complex crime detection project" up to that time, and that was in February 1953. In 1937, Homer Garrison had become colonel of the Texas Department of Public Safety, and therefore colonel over the Texas Rangers, so the Frome murder had been with him almost his entire tenure. "I still believe one of these days we will break it," he said. "As long as two people were involved, there is always a chance. One of them may talk." Thousands of index cards had been dutifully filled out with tip information, and the aggregate paperwork filled three large filing drawers. Garrison did say that at one time they had gotten a red-hot lead from a prison stool pigeon, who identified the Fromes' killer and recited details of the crime. After more investigation, the case appeared airtight, and the Rangers prepared to celebrate bringing this long-cold case to a close. And they did indeed apprehend the alleged killer, but then quickly learned that he had a fail-safe alibi: he had been incarcerated when the murders were committed. Colonel Garrison actually had a brief laugh over this. "There was one man," he said, "who was actually happy he had been in prison."

*   *   *

On September 13, 1970, Captain Allee called me to the Ranger headquarters in Carrizo Springs and briefed me on the Frome murders. He wanted me to go to Dallas and interview two brothers, G. W. and Leroy Garner. Three days later I drove to the DPS office in Austin and familiarized myself with the Frome file. The following day I drove to Dallas and telephoned G. W. Garner, asking for an interview. We met at the DPS office, which was the headquarters of the Rangers' B Company. In that interview, G. W. and Leroy told me that their father, Howley Garner, had been told by his brother-in-law Leslie Daniels that he killed two women by torture out in the desert and that their bodies were found three or four days later near Van Horn. The Garner brothers went on to say that in early 1940 their father was found shot to death in Plainview, Texas, along with his housekeeper, Mildred Franks. They believed that the brother-in-law Daniels had done it, his motive being to keep Howley Garner silent about the murders. Leslie Daniels was living in Los Angeles at the time.

With this information I returned to Austin and reviewed the Frome murder file again, and then went back to Carrizo Springs to report to Captain Allee. The captain asked me if I would go to Dilley, Texas, which is in Frio County on the road between Carrizo Springs and San Antonio, and interview M. R. Gill and a Mr. Coyne and question them about Roy "Monk" Thurmond, who had been a suspect in the Frome murders. I met these contacts, and they told me that Thurmond and his wife, who was a small blonde, had been in Dilley a couple of days after the Frome murders in a black Chevrolet or Plymouth, and that Mrs. Thurmond had attempted to sell Mr. Coyne some jewelry. She had three rings and wanted five dollars each for them, but he turned her down. Thurmond told Coyne that he had followed the Frome women from California to El Paso, but he had had car trouble and had not seen them anymore. There was a suspicion that the rings that Mrs. Thurmond tried to sell had belonged to the murdered women, but that evidence was never developed. Gill went on to say that the Thurmonds had camped in the Dilley area for a couple of days before moving on, so apparently they were living out of their automobile.

On September 22, 1970, Captain Allee got my travel orders approved in Austin to journey to Los Angeles and follow up the investigation. Leaving Uvalde, I stopped in Sierra Blanca, which is in Hudspeth County, a little over thirty miles west of Van Horn. There I talked to Jim Nance, who had been the Ranger for that area for many years and was about to retire, but he recalled nothing about the Frome case that I didn't already know. I drove on to El Paso that afternoon, visited the *Herald* newspaper, and combed through its "morgue" of past articles to see what else I could learn about the Fromes. I was there until midnight making copies of articles. I left feeling pretty well informed. The next day, September 23, I drove on to Phoenix, Arizona, to spend the night. While there I telephoned ahead to the Los Angeles Police Department and spoke to a Detective Broda and his partner, Detective Cornell, who advised me that he had an address for Leslie Daniels, and possibly an address for Thurmond. After that long drive I was really relieved to hear that. Especially since so much time had passed from the time of the murders.

Living in West Texas, you begin to think that the Chihuahuan Desert is about as hot and dry as it gets, but driving through the Sonoran Desert west of Phoenix changes that notion in a hurry. The yuccas and chollas and oco-

Joaquin with LAPD detectives Broda and Cornell in downtown Los Angeles, 1970.

*Interviewing Leslie Daniels, a suspect, before
administering a polygraph, Los Angeles, 1970.*

tillos of Texas are replaced by the huge saguaro cactus, standing in the desert like giant criminals, surrendering, with their arms in the air. I arrived in Los Angeles on September 24 and met with Broda and Cornell at their central headquarters downtown. For a Texas Ranger who was used to tracking cattle rustlers from horseback and living in Uvalde, Texas, Los Angeles was quite a change of culture.

A reporter from *Life* magazine, David Snell, who lived in Houston, heard about the resurgence of interest in the Frome case and approached me with a request to accompany me to Los Angeles. I had met him in Uvalde when he was working on a story about the Newton boys. With the captain's permission, I let him keep me company. On the way west we stopped in Tombstone, Arizona, and I visited with the local city marshal, who gave me a personal tour of the OK Corral, before we went on to Los Angeles, which was by far the biggest city I had ever seen.

The two LAPD detectives and I talked about the suspects Daniels and Thurmond, and I also learned that they were looking at two more possible suspects, named Jack Barnes and Jack Marvin Flippen, and another one named James O'Brien. That rang a loud bell, because Barnes and Flippen had been arrested together in Dallas a couple of weeks after the Fromes' bodies were found. They had been questioned, and were known to have been in El Paso shortly before the time of the killings, but they were released for lack of evidence. The next day, Detectives Broda and Cornell and I went to interview Leslie Daniels at his apartment in Los Angeles, and he denied having anything to do with the Frome murders. He further volunteered to take a polygraph test; in fact, he was given four different examinations by a Lieutenant Burdick, who was very skilled at his work. Burdick pronounced all the tests inconclusive. Daniels was in his seventies and in poor health, at least in part from a lifetime spent drinking heavily and abusing drugs, and was now on various medications for a bad heart. I was not all that hopeful of getting a good polygraph result from him—just too much water had flowed under his bridge. Burdick said that as far as he was concerned, Daniels had cleared the polygraph, but only because it was impossible to tell if he was being truthful or not.

On September 26 we began trying to locate an address for Monk Thurmond, but with no success, and then we tried to find Flippen. He, at one time, had worked for the Diamond Cab Company in LA, and we had an old address for him. We found records showing that O'Brien had been arrested in 1954, so we got an old address for him as well, but all three had fallen from sight, and despite two days of work, we never located them. I just wanted to have a friendly chat with them. Just a little bit of their time. I spent all day on September 29 in the Hall of Records, but was not able to find death reports for Flippen or Thurmond, but at least I learned that O'Brien had died two years previous, in 1968. Because of my type A personality and propensity to value success in all areas, I disliked not getting results from this case. I was not a particularly happy camper. The next day I drove angrily straight through from Los Angeles to Alpine, Texas. I arrived in Alpine after dark and left early the next morning for Carrizo Springs to report to Captain Allee. It's ironic to think back that this stopover, Alpine, Texas, would be the place where I would spend my last six years as a Ranger and then make it my retirement home.

The captain had turned sixty-five on September 14 and prepared to retire, which he did on September 30. He was hopeful that these new leads would solve this vexing old murder and finally bring some closure to the Frome family—and it also would have been a sparkling way to end his career, to finally apprehend the murderers who had so narrowly escaped his grasp thirty-two years before. There was a retirement party for the captain the week before he first called me to Carrizo Springs to brief me on the Frome murders, and at this party he told a reporter from the *Dallas Morning News* that he believed they had a lead in the case. This was highly unusual because the Captain was always suspicious of and even a little hostile to the press—usually for good reason. I guess he figured that after retiring he would be out of any more contention and so didn't have to guard his words so carefully now. "There were two of them," he told the reporter of the Fromes' assailants, "and I think one of them is still alive."

The Frome murders, however, are an open investigation to this day; therefore, the DPS file on it is not made available to the public. It is frustrating to give your best professional effort to a case and still come away empty handed. The truth is, though, it doesn't take a perfect crime to foil the lawmen who investigate it. It only takes time—time for suspects to vanish and witnesses to die and the trail of evidence to grow cold. But the British have a saying, "Truth is the daughter of Time," meaning that all secrets will eventually be revealed. Certainly, if that proves true of the killers of Hazel and Nancy Frome, the Rangers will take it up again with their Unsolved Crimes Investigation Team, with all their modern technology, under the command of Lieutenant

Hank Whitman, a crackerjack Ranger. Unfortunately, as I write this book, it's my opinion that all the witnesses and suspects in this case are deceased.

Captain Allee lived just over sixteen years in retirement and remained a treasured friend until he passed away of cancer in San Antonio in January 1987. During his career of thirty-nine years he killed one man, and certainly he knocked some heads together from time to time to keep order, but no man cared more for the law or was more protective of the men who served under him. I'm sure that is one reason why he had three heart attacks before he finally retired. He is still vilified by Hispanic activists who continue to make trade on the farmworkers strike of 1967, but in the latest work by the great Ranger scholar Robert Utley, Captain Allee's professionalism is vindicated. At his retirement party, the reporter from the *Dallas Morning News* asked him yet again about putting Magdaleno Dimas in the hospital for four days with a fractured skull, and the captain replied, "I sent him to a doctor in Roma and there was no fracture to it." And as I noted earlier, I saw Dimas in the police station that night. But for a lot of people, history becomes what they want to hear.

CHAPTER 5

A Man Not to Mess With

The country around the little town of Leakey, Texas, is the heart of the Hill Country, known now mostly for its deer hunting, dude ranches, and a sprawling church youth camp owned by the Butt family, owners of the HEB grocery store chain. It is a lot more peaceful now than it used to be. During my years in Uvalde, it was known as a tougher area, populated by hard-bitten sorts of independents, people who were not vicious, particularly, but who were used to doing for themselves without outside help, and therefore did not like outside interference. If Texas has a sort of self-identified insular area like the Ozarks, it is the country around Leakey. In the words of a good Texas expression, many of these are people who just do not like to be messed with.

I heard of Tom Bybee by reputation when I was first stationed in Uvalde; he was something of a local legend for an incident that had happened back in 1959. Although Bybee lived in Leakey, he would come down as far as North Uvalde to take part in a poker game. This was an unincorporated area, not within the Uvalde city limits, so the county sheriff's department had jurisdiction, not the city police, and it was a decidedly separate community from Uvalde proper. In fact, it was one of those places where you could come literally from the wrong side of the tracks, since it was divided from Uvalde by the railroad line. It had long had a reputation as a tough place; those Depression-era train robbers, the Newton boys, had a house there. (I was in that house once, with Sheriff Kelly, who had some civil papers to serve on one of the brothers. Kelly actually was on good terms with them, and while they didn't exactly give me a Cook's tour, I remember that the house faced south, and the living room had four windows covering the east, south, and west, and leaning against the frame of each window was a Winchester lever-action rifle.) People who lived in North Uvalde didn't want much to do with the people in the rest of the city; the southern and western portions of the town were predominantly Hispanic, and North Uvalde was predominantly Anglo, with a few Hispanics mixed in.

Another of the participants in the poker game was the acknowledged town bully, a big old meaty guy by the name of Burleson who enjoyed throwing that weight around. At one point he started screaming at Bybee, claiming that he was going to whip his ass if he didn't get out and that he was no longer welcome at that game. Calmly, Bybee went out to his truck, fetched his short-handled double-bit axe, the kind cedar choppers use, with an edge on both sides—a razor could only wish to be so sharp—came back inside, and took the bully's head off with one swing. Amazingly, the grand jury no-billed him, for the victim's reputation was such that, in their view and in frontier parlance, he needed killing. But clearly, Tom Bybee was a man not to mess with.

Bybee was on the small side of average, five-seven, skinny, wiry, and with skin like rawhide. He was a cedar chopper. Originally, the Hill Country had featured grassy prairies on the hilltops and hardwood forests along the streams, but going back as far as the Spanish ranches, the land had become overgrazed and the cedar moved in. Actually the tree is mountain juniper, but everyone calls it cedar. Tough and invasive, it has no real business being there, and millions of acres are now covered with it. The land can be brought back into grazing, but it has to be cleared of cedar first, either with draglines, chainsaws, or axes, and the cedar is useful for fence posts, foundation pilings, mulch, and other things. Men like Bybee make this their business. He had always been a hard worker, all of his life—born in 1915, he was fifty-five and had solid gray hair when I first got acquainted with him. In October 1969 he was arrested for driving while intoxicated and for transporting beer in Uvalde County. When he didn't make his court date, bench warrants were issued, and I had to drive up to Leakey to arrest him. I left about ten and arrived at his home forty-five minutes later, but he wasn't there. The main service station was an Enco operation at the intersection of Ranch Road 337 and U.S. Highway 83. I stopped to ask the attendant if he had seen Bybee, and just as he started to answer, the man himself pulled up to the intersection in his green Chevy pickup and turned north on Highway 83.

I don't know that having a foghorn of a voice was ever a requirement for getting into the Rangers, but I can make myself heard over a pretty good distance, and I bellowed at him to pull over. He obeyed right away, parking near the Frio Canyon Lodge and getting out of the truck. I told him I had two warrants for his arrest, and as we were talking, I noticed a large sheet of plywood lying in the bed of his pickup, and between the edge of this panel and the tailgate I saw a case of Lone Star beer. I raised the plywood and found not one case, but thirty; I advised him of his rights and told him he was going to be charged in Real County with transporting the thirty cases, which was a new and separate issue from the matter already pending in Uvalde. Just no keeping a good man down, I guess.

Bybee immediately protested that he drank twelve cans a day and that all this beer was for his own use, but that was a matter for the court to decide, not me. It says something about Real County that I tried to contact, in turn, the justice of the peace, then the county judge, and finally the sheriff, but all three were not at home and couldn't be found. Bybee was not at all un-cooperative about the situation; I asked him if he wanted to drive his truck down to Uvalde, and he agreed. Once we got him into the Uvalde County jail on those two warrants, I finally got the Real County sheriff on the phone. He advised me that he had no safe place to store thirty cases of Lone Star, either in Leakey, which was the county seat, or in Camp Wood, which was the other principal town, although neither of them had more than a couple of hundred residents, and he asked us to keep it in Uvalde. We took the thirty cases and stored them in the jail alongside the fifty cases of Falstaff that were the evidence in the Uvalde charges. I was mildly curious about why he had changed brands, but never thought to ask him about it. A couple of days later the grand jury in Leakey indicted him for hauling the Lone Star, but since they had no county criminal court there, he was scheduled for trial in the state district court.

As far as I know, Bybee didn't hold any animosity against me for enforcing the liquor laws on him, although, in hindsight, the laws of the time seem pretty stupid. He took the attitude that I was just doing my job, and he was just doing his job, and occasionally we would run foul of each other. This certainly wasn't the only time we talked over beer, as it were. He would come down to Uvalde now and then to pick up a carload, and I would stop him.

Busted stock from Marshall Williams's .22 rifle
on Tom Bybee's carport, Leakey, Texas, 1971.

You can tell by looking at how low in the rear a car is sitting whether the trunk is loaded with something heavy, and that plus his record as a bootlegger added up to probable cause to pull him over. And we'd go through the court rigmarole again.

Still, I'm certain that he made it to his house with most of his merchandise, and I would get information that he was selling out of his house, but short of an exhaustive stakeout, it would have been hard to prove. I don't think a stranger could have driven up and bought beer from him—he was too smart for that—because that stranger might be a state liquor control agent. And he did answer to a pretty strict moral code—he really wasn't much of a drinker himself, despite his claim that all those suds were for his own use. He would never sell to a drunk, and he wouldn't sell to minors. He really wasn't a bad guy: he served his own small clientele, he kept to himself, and he minded his own damned business. But by God, he was not a man to mess with.

Two years after Bybee got caught with the thirty cases of Lone Star, he had to teach this lesson to still another guy, a local laborer named Marshall Williams, who was ten years younger than Bybee. I got the call at 1:10 a.m. from a local telephone operator, who advised that Bybee had called her and said a man had come to his house with a gun and there was likely to be a shooting. As usual, she was unable to find Sheriff Wright at his home in Camp Wood, so she called the local Ranger. By the time I contacted Real County's deputy sheriff, Maxey Carter, he was already at the Bybee house, off Ranch Road 337, and had come upon a scene of mayhem. He found Williams in the carport, savagely beaten and unconscious, lying in a pool of blood, and he was bringing him down to the hospital in Uvalde. I told him I would meet him there and asked him to bring any witnesses with him. I met them at Uvalde Memorial about two fifteen and saw what was left of Williams in the backseat of the car. The emergency physician noted three separate blunt-force-trauma wounds to his head, two to the forehead, and one to the right rear, each one of which had broken the skull and exposed the brain. I don't know why he was still alive, but he was taken by helicopter to Santa Rosa Hospital in San Antonio for surgery.

Deputy Carter had brought Bybee down with him, along with two Hispanic women, whom I interviewed. Typically for Bybee, he was cooperative and straightforward. Marshall had been at his house all day, drinking beer, and Bybee had called the two women to come over and do some domestic chores—do the laundry, clean house, and cook some supper. They were Betty Garza, twenty-seven, and her sister, Feliz Garza Becker, thirty-nine. After they did the work, they wanted to watch some television. Marshall got it in mind to go home and get his record player so they could dance, and when he returned, he had his wife with him. The others were watching a movie on television, and since no one would dance with him, he danced alone. When the movie was over, Marshall asked Feliz to dance, but she told him to dance with his wife, which he did. Later she relented and danced with him, but became offended when he kept trying to kiss her hand and neck, saying repeatedly, "You love me, don't you?" Feliz kept pushing him away.

Marshall's wife never objected to any of this. Probably she knew that he was also a man not to mess with, especially when drunk, but Bybee told him he had gone too far and he should leave. Feliz helped carry the record player to the car, and Marshall and his wife left, but with a threat from Marshall that he would be back the next day and "get him." About twenty minutes later,

Bybee heard Marshall calling him from the carport, and when Bybee got out of his chair, Marshall told him to sit back down, but Bybee continued to the door. When he opened it, he saw Marshall with both hands at his right side, concealing something. As Bybee approached him, Marshall produced a .22 rifle and started to level it, but Bybee, being a wiry little guy with cat-quick reflexes, seized the gun. As they struggled over it, the .22 went off, piercing the tin roof of the carport. When Bybee wrestled the rifle away from Marshall, he held it by the barrel and swung it at Marshall's head with such force that the stock broke off. Bybee didn't remember how many times he hit him, but said that Marshall was still fighting after the first whack—which I doubt, since it broke his skull open.

Statements I took from the Garza sisters backed Bybee up in all the particulars. I drove up to his residence to investigate the scene. It was just a small frame house on an acreage on the south side of Leakey, but he owned it himself. The yard was tidy and mown, with no weeds, and the house was clean and well kept, I guess by the Garza sisters, if they were his housekeepers. It was apparent that Bybee lived modestly, but not like white trash at all; everything about his life seemed orderly, except this penchant for killing people who messed with him.

The evidence at the scene supported Bybee's story. I found a Springfield Model 87A semiautomatic with the stock broken off; the safety was off, there was a live round in the chamber and eight more in the magazine. Considering the force with which Bybee hit Marshall, he was lucky the gun didn't go off and shoot himself. There was a bullet hole in the carport roof, and a pool of blood about the size of a football on the carport floor, on the side opposite the house. I interviewed Mrs. Marshall, who said they left the Bybee residence about midnight, but after dropping her off at their home, he got back in the car and said he would be back in a little while. She did not see him take the rifle, but noticed later that it was gone.

Even when I wrote up my case report, I wrote in the blank labeled "Status of Case to Date" that he had been released on a five-thousand-dollar bond pending grand jury action, but that he would probably be no-billed on the grounds of self-defense. That was on August 31, and on November 1 the Real County grand jury met, returned a no-bill, and the case was closed.

Tom Bybee eventually died of natural causes, one of the last of the breed of Hill Country cedar choppers, and by God a man not to mess with.

CHAPTER 6

To All the Dogs I've Loved Before

This land out here—Alpine, the Big Bend—is timeless. Just look at the photographs: pictures taken of Fort Davis a hundred years ago are no different from the same view today. So it's not that hard to see myself as a Texas Ranger back in those earlier times. And if I had gone about my duties back in the 1860s or '70s or '80s, I would have had a good mare, a good saddle mule, and a good dog, because they would all three bond—the dog and the mule would form a strong attachment, and the mare and the mule would bond, whereas a horse and mule would likely get into some sexual-dominance kind of thing and not get along, although there are exceptions to prove the rule. (In Spanish, "horse" automatically means a male of the species, and the term for mare, *yegua*, is a sharper distinction than it is in English. Modern city dwellers might refer to a mare as a horse, but it happened less often in frontier days. In fact, just over a century ago, one of the most famous pursuits of a fugitive in Texas history occurred when some ignorant deputy translated *yegua* as "horse," causing Gregorio Cortez to be accused of a horse theft he did not commit.)

In those places where the country is open or rolling, and the footing isn't that difficult, you'd ride the horse and pack and lead the mule. Then when you enter the mountains, where there are precipitous canyons, and even the slopes where you have to ride are steep and dangerous, you change their roles, riding the mule and leading the horse. A mule won't commit suicide, whereas you can sometimes make a horse go where he really doesn't want to go. In movies and cartoons this is played up as a mule's stubbornness, but those who know mules learn to respect their common sense.

Traveling through this wide dry country back in those days was a slow and dangerous enterprise. Given the prevalence of Mexican bandits, American outlaws, and Apache or Comanche raiders, and given a Ranger's job in previous days of tracking down all of them, a violent death might be only a sniff or a twig snap away. Whether riding by day or camping at night, he felt protected by this group of bonded and befriended animals, whose senses are so much keener than our own that we can hardly explain it. It was a comfort to lay out your bedroll and sleep soundly, knowing that you were watched over, and if riders or animals or anything got close to you, the mare and mule and dog would all alert you to it.

I call up this imaginary memory to explain to people why I have always over the years loved and felt close to animals. I have never found any use in the world for anyone who would mistreat or be cruel to an animal. If a person will abuse an animal, he will abuse a human being, and that's a fact. Mistreating a person is bad enough, but an animal can't normally defend itself, and a man who would take advantage of that and abuse an animal is just no kind of a man in my book. A dog will even remain loyal in spite of it, because he looks at the man as the head of his pack and will accept the treatment that is given. I suppose that loyalty is the main reason why I have always liked to have a good dog. A dog's a great companion. He'll never argue with you, he'll never talk back to you, he's always your friend—important qualities when so much of your work involves catching people in lies—and if you take care of him, he will take care of you. Your dog, unlike most of your friends and sometimes family, will never tell on you about anything, but just for a while I'm going to tell some things on some of the dogs I have loved over the years.

*   PENNY   *

The first dog I remember ever having, when I was six or seven years old, was a crossbreed bulldog. His name was Penny because of his copper-colored spots on white. He had a dark spot over one eye and probably weighed twenty-five or thirty pounds, built stocky as bulldogs are, so he might have weighed a bit more. That was before I was old enough to be allowed to have a .22 rifle, which didn't happen until my teens, so whenever I went out with my BB gun, hunting meadowlarks or quail or maybe rabbits, Penny went with me, as well as everywhere else I went. Our farm was up on the Llano Estacado, and I remember once Penny and I went prowling out on the plains. We came across what was originally a badger hole, in all likelihood, but at this time a big mamma skunk had taken up habitat in there and was raising five or six little ones. Penny got the scent of them and went down into the hole to get them. There was nothing I could do to stop him; he was a bulldog, and once their blood is up, you'd best not get in their way. He dragged the mamma skunk out of the hole and killed her, then went back down and dragged all the kits out one by one and savaged them. In the process, of course, he got thoroughly sprayed, and stank to high heaven. Mamma and Daddy made sure I kept Penny a far distance from the house until it wore off.

Penny also taught me my first lesson in a dog's loyalty. I got lots of whippings in those days, which I probably deserved, and my dad was pretty quick to resort to it, but he had to take me into a room and close the door, or into the garage or the barn or somewhere that Penny couldn't get to him to help me. If Penny had gotten to him while he was on me with a belt or a strap or whatever, he would have chewed him up pretty good. I must admit that even to this day Penny's protective behavior still gives me a little satisfaction. I guess I was pretty much a rascal and deserved a fair number of the whippings, although discipline is usually handled differently today. (I'm not sure if I would have responded any better to a "time out," as they call it today, any more than Penny would have once he got after something.)

I remember one time we had a couple of milk cows, and after my dad would finish milking the one that was my favorite, I'd get up on her back and ride her around the cow lot. One time my sister Dorothy Gail, who was nearly two years younger than I was, started hollering that she wanted to get up on the cow and ride too, and he let her get up there behind me. I didn't think she had any business being up on my cow, and I was really ticked. While dad was milking the other cow, I started scooting back and scooting back until I finally scooted Dorothy Gail off the end of the cow, and she landed in a big fresh pile of manure and started screaming and hollering her head off. My dad jumped up from the cow he was milking and ran over and grabbed a lariat rope from the barn wall, and I never figured out whether it was intentional or accidental, but he dragged the end of the rope through the water trough. And I can tell you, if you've never been taken down with a wet lariat rope, you've never had a really good whipping. But even then, I remember, he had to lock Penny in the corn shed before he could start on me. Good boy, Penny.

★ COUPLE OF UVALDE GERMAN SHEPHERDS ★

Now if Dad had ever gotten so serious that he would have taken out my dog if he'd defended me, I can't say whether Penny would have waited around. Dogs are loyal but not, generally speaking, stupid. I saw something similar when I was stationed in Uvalde. Morris Barrow and I were on a stakeout in south Uvalde. Morris was the chief of police and formerly chief deputy sheriff for Uvalde County—Morris replaced Vance Chisum, a close friend of mine, as chief of police when Vance went to Big Spring as police chief. They had gotten information from Arturo Rodriguez, who was a fine Ranger, and I will write more about him later, that a notorious San Antonio drug dealer named Fred Carrasco had had some of his people store six pounds of high-grade black tar heroin in a house on South Getty in Uvalde. We made a raid on that house and seized the six pounds of heroin, but there was no one home at the time. So Morris and I undertook some surveillance just on the chance that someone would show up to collect the drugs. We were in an unmarked police vehicle, monitoring the police radio.

During the wee hours of the morning, we heard a dispatch call to respond to a domestic disturbance at a house in North Uvalde. There were about twelve thousand residents in the town at that time, and there were two officers on duty that shift, each in one vehicle. Both of them responded to this call that some guy was roughing his wife up. Back at our stakeout, we listened in amazement to this conversation between the two officers (they sounded like Howard Cosell, the sports announcer, delivering blow-by-blow accounts of this man beating his wife.) The officers arrived at the place, shined their headlights on the house, and saw the man whipping his wife on the front porch. But they seemed to have a problem. They said they couldn't get up there, because there were these two big German police dogs in front of them that looked really vicious, and they were afraid they would attack if they got out of their cars. Morris and I couldn't believe what we were hearing: two armed officers felt trapped in their car by a couple of dogs while some guy was whaling on his wife. Morris looked at me, and I looked at him and said, "Let's go."

Not believing our ears, we took off to see for ourselves. The Uvalde Police

Department always kept a Remington Model 870 pump shotgun in their cars, so we had that in place. I said, "Morris, when we get there, I'll take care of the dogs. You get the guy who's whipping his wife." We got there, and sure enough, there were the two officers, each in his own car, with their lights shining on the front porch where this man was still pounding his wife. I stepped out of our unit before Morris had even come to a full stop, and headed up the sidewalk to the house. I don't know whether it was due to my being six-five, or the look in my eye, or the riot gun in my hands, but those two German police dogs just ducked and ran with a whimper. Now I turned my attention to this poor excuse for a man on the porch.

Once he saw us, he stopped pounding on his wife and came down the side-walk toward me, swinging a big heavy iron pipe about two inches in diameter, the kind used for tamping fence posts, from side to side. I told him to drop the rod and had the gun raised, ready to blow his legs out from under him if I had to, but I was wondering where the hell Morris was, not knowing that he had had some trouble getting the car into park. I told him again to drop the rod and was just about ready to squeeze off on him when Morris came crashing into him from the side and took him down. Morris was carrying a snub-nosed .38 special tucked into the front of his waistband, and as they hit the ground, this guy got hold of it and pulled it out. I was able to seize his hand and wrist and twist the .38 away from him. He was still struggling, and Morris said to give him the gun, which I did, and he whacked the guy in the forehead with it. That cut the skin and broke a blood vessel, and a jet of blood came shooting out of his forehead every time his heart beat, just like when you dehorn a steer. It was the damnedest thing you ever saw. Then out of nowhere a squatty little dachshund appeared, avidly licking at the blood as it squirted out of this guy's head. I swear you couldn't make this stuff up.

We finally got the handcuffs on him, and with the German shepherds out of the picture, those two brave city officers emerged from their units. Needless to say, they got a couple of withering looks from us. Morris had them take the guy to the hospital to get patched up—I don't recall that he was hurt badly enough to even need stitches—but if anybody needed to be pistol-whipped, it was those two bozos sitting there in their units, scared of two German police dogs, watching this woman get the hell beat out of her. Morris was more lenient with them than I surely would have been; if I had been running the Uvalde police force, those two lumps would have been gone in a hurry.

And the behavior of the woman in this case, following and pawing after us, hollering "Don't hurt him, don't hurt him," was so tragically typical of what I observed of domestic violence incidents. I served back in the days before psychiatrists used terms like "codependent" or "enabler," which is usually how they are described today. I have always been pretty old-fashioned when it comes to what they call gender roles, but no woman should become so dependent on a man that she accepts abuse from him. I love my wife and would never raise a hand against her, but Shirley has always been highly independent—her own job, her own money. She loves me because she chooses to, not because she has to, and that is a mighty gift that I have always been grateful for.

Fred Carrasco, incidentally, whose drug stash had begun the whole evening for me, came to a bad end in the prison in Huntsville two or three years later. He tried to stage a breakout, took some hostages, and killed one or two of them. The authorities wound up killing him and one of his henchmen.

* FRITZ *

Shirley and I had been married eight or ten years, the boys were small, and we lived in a three-bedroom, two-bath house that was maybe 1,550 square feet, so we had plenty of closeness. We had a dachshund—some people call them wiener dogs—whose name was Fritz, which was appropriate, since they are of German descent. Actually they were bred to hunt badgers (*dachs* is German for "badger"), so they have the long body and stumpy legs to go down in burrows after them. That's also why they were bred to have loose skin, so they could turn and bite while being bitten. But you'd never guess that Fritz shared such a violent heritage, he was so sunny and friendly and lovable with everybody, and he just thought that's the way the world was.

Uvalde didn't have any detectives then, and part of my duty at that Ranger station was to respond to the police or the sheriff when they needed something investigated. One day the chief of police, Vance Chisum, and I were investigating a string of burglaries south of town when I got a call from radio dispatch saying to come home immediately because there was a problem. I knew Shirley wouldn't call me home unless it was something pretty dire, so I hightailed it to the house and discovered that Fritz had gotten himself into some trouble. We had a neighbor directly across the street from us, a nice, friendly woman whose daughter was visiting from Corpus Christi, and she had brought with her these two huge German shepherd police dogs. They were a fierce couple of watchdogs, but Fritz didn't know that, and so went trotting across the street. The neighbor's yard was enclosed by a chain-link fence, but dachshunds are bred diggers, and he went right under it to meet his new playmates.

Shirley heard this awful commotion of snarling and snapping and Fritz squealing, so she ran and got the only handgun in the house, which was a big Colt .45 single-action revolver that I had purchased from the widow of John Sitter, a Ranger from the early 1900s, and it was a pretty powerful old gun. I'd had the barrel cut down from five and a half to four inches to carry in my high-ride holster; since it was an old single-action, the hammer had to be pulled back and cocked before it could be fired, but once it was ready, it had a hair trigger. Shirley got across the street, and the neighbor's daughter was in the yard beating on her dogs with a broom handle, trying to get them off Fritz. Shirley got the hammer cocked and was threatening to shoot the SOBs if she didn't get them off, and to this day I don't know how that revolver kept from going off: she either had her finger off the trigger, or else she had a lighter touch than she ever used with me (although I don't think one could fairly say that I have a hair trigger). Of course, the dogs' owner ran into the house and called the police, saying there was a crazy woman in her yard waving a gun and threatening to kill her and her dogs.

By the time Vance and I got to the house, the daughter had gotten her dogs back inside. Because there was so much damage and bleeding, we had to wrap Fritz in a sheet to take him to the vet. His hide had been ripped open to the raw flesh, and he needed about twenty stitches in his back. I could see why Shirley had been so upset. Fritz recovered from that ordeal and became a wonderful pet. I never saw such a well-mannered dog. Unfortunately, he had a habit of getting behind my vehicle in the driveway. It was a sad, sad day when I backed out of our carport in a hurry and ran over him. That time he didn't survive. Man, that was a bad scene.

⋆ HONEY ⋆

During my Ranger duty in Uvalde, about the only time I had with my family was on Saturday nights and Sundays, and that was usually the time when locals got together for their cockfights. Many a late Saturday night or early Sunday morning I'd get a call from the police or the sheriff that a rooster

Lance with Honey at our house in Uvalde, around 1980.

fight was going to be held, and I got to where I really resented those damned chicken fighters for spoiling my Sundays—I already worked on Saturdays. Before long, I learned who the local ringleaders were, and when I'd get notified of a pending cockfight, I'd call them up and tell them that I knew they were going to fight chickens at such a place and that they needed to knock it off because it wasn't going to happen. That usually did the job. I'm sure that a lot of times these guys would just change the location to one I didn't know about, and I'm sure that animal activists and PETA would prefer that I had gotten more worked up about chicken fights, but at the time, it just wasn't worth ruining a Sunday with my family.

But there's a big step up from fighting chickens to fighting dogs, which is just a cruel and sadistic thing to do. I know that these breeders and guys who run dogfights will tell you that the dogs are bred to fight, that the pain is something that they endure or even love—and that is just a cartload of bullshit. Anytime I got a call alerting me to a dogfight, day or night, I got right there and had no moral dilemma about putting everyone involved in jail.

Still, I was never taken with pit bull terriers as a breed, but in the years after Fritz, we acquired one. Shirley had a sixth-grade student who she thought needed some special attention, and he insisted that she take one of his dog's puppies. Her coat was just the color of honey, and that became her name. I now understand their reputation among people who are partial to them, since Honey was intensely loyal and affectionate. She became especially drawn to my younger son, Lance, and slept on his bed at night, and was a full and trusted part of all the family outings.

Lance was the pitcher on his Little League baseball team, and he had a sinking curve ball that would almost wrap around the batter and come at him from behind. It was just amazing to see. One day when I was on some distant assignment, I think I might have been in Mexico, Shirley put on our catcher's mitt and, using the house as a backstop, decided to catch him while he was practicing. He loosed one of those wicked curving sinkers at her, she lost the flight of it, and it hit her square on the big toe—she was wearing sandals—breaking it and the toe next to it. Shirley swears to this day that was the worst pain she ever experienced, including birthing two sons. As she was rolling on the grass, wailing and crying, Honey tried her best to help, which meant licking Shirley nonstop in the face.

But we also saw that dark side of pit bulls, too. Honey was territorial and fiercely protective of the house and the family. We even had to make sure that she was inside when the postman came around, or our mail couldn't get delivered. And that dark side proved her undoing. Honey had big power-ful legs, and she was perfectly capable of jumping our six-foot fence in the backyard, so when we were away from the house, we kept her on a gener-ous length of chain in the back, making sure she had her water and some shade. One day when we were away, something must have triggered that protective instinct, because we came home and found she had jumped the fence and hanged herself when the broken chain caught between the fence posts—something that none of us ever imagined could happen. Pit bulls are a strange creation, perhaps even troubling, with so much love and so much savagery wrapped up in one animal, all on a hair trigger. I can understand why some people are terrified of them, but if I were called to testify, I would have to put my hand on a Bible and swear that Honey was the most perfectly loving and loyal companion a family could have had. Her death hit Lance particularly hard; I don't think Shirley or I realized how close he was to his dog, and looking back, he never became that attached to an animal again. I don't think he wanted the pain.

★ BABY BLUE, ALICE, AND BABY ★

After we moved to Alpine, Shirley drove to San Marcos and purchased a beautiful blue Doberman pinscher that we named Baby Blue—she also had a long AKC- registered name. We had only had her a couple of months when the owner of the local radio station, Ray Hendrix, ran over her. God bless him, he stopped and took her to the local veterinarian, Ray Allen. He gave Baby Blue numerous blood transfusions, using blood from his personal dog, but nothing could be done for her. My mother was living in Seminole, Texas, about 150 miles north of Alpine, working as a waitress, and she said she would try to get us a schnauzer, as she knew some folks who had a bitch that was about to have a litter. When the time came, I drove up, stopping in Midland, which was on the way, to pick up my sister, Dorothy Gail. The puppy was about the size of a grown cottontail rabbit when I took her home, and all the way back to Alpine she rode between my legs; that was how we bonded, and she was always partial to me. She was the first schnauzer we ever owned—or rather, she was a schnoodle, a cross between a schnauzer and a poodle. We called her Alice, which was my mother's middle name.

Just west of our house in Alpine was that of the Kokernots, with whom

Joaquin with Alice and Baby, Alpine, 1992.

we shared a trash bin, but unknown to me, they had leased their house to a couple I didn't know. One day from my back deck I saw that Alice had gotten out of the yard and was over by the Kokernot's. I hollered at her to come home, but she ignored me, so I hollered again. I mean, I am an old-time Texas Ranger, and I am not accustomed to being disobeyed. I bellowed, "Alice, get your ass over here!" From out of nowhere I heard a righteously indignant woman's voice bark, "I beg your pardon. My name is Alice." I considered myself pretty observant, but I hadn't seen a good-looking blond woman taking her trash to the dumpster.

Figuring I was about to get whipped by this unknown female, who was much closer to six feet tall than five feet and not very happy at the moment, I switched to my most charming personality. "Ma'am," I said, "I am terribly sorry, but my dog's name is Alice, and I apologize." We became friends after this, thank God; having seen quite enough of men not to mess with, the last thing I needed coming after me was a woman not to mess with. She runs a nursery and greenhouse here in Alpine, and her husband, Michael Stevens, is a famous guitar maker.

After we had Alice for about three years, we bred her to a registered schnauzer. She had a litter of four, three of whom we gave away to friends. The one male we gave to Bobby Upchurch, the local Texas Cattle Raisers Ranger, who named him Howie, and he is still alive at this writing. We kept the runt of the litter, which we named Baby. And I mean she was really the runt of the litter. She couldn't even nurse unless Shirley pushed the other pups aside and held her up to the teat. She was only just weaned when we nearly lost her. She had leaned farther and farther into her water bowl until she upended into it and nearly drowned. I got out of bed one morning and found her limp in the bowl. I took her in to Shirley, who laid her beside her and rubbed on her stomach until she revived. She was always small, and people thought she was a puppy, although she lived to be almost fourteen, which is a good age for a schnauzer.

* NO-DOG DEWS *

Readers of my first book will recall my buddy Jake, who was involved in the training of mujahedeen. I continued to work with Jake on various projects after I retired, and one time Jake and I and a friend of ours named Hamp Dews were camping out at the Long X Ranch near Kent, Texas, which is up in the Trans-Pecos, in the Apache Mountains of southeastern Culberson County. Hamp had been in the Special Forces and had served in clandestine ways in Vietnam. We drove into Van Horn, which was about thirty miles from the ranch, one afternoon to have a steak. Jake knew the lady, Eileen, who ran the place, and as they visited, she said she had some puppies she wanted to give away. They were blue heelers, which make good cow dogs, and were about three and a half or four months old, so they were almost half grown. She asked Jake if he would like to take one, and he agreed, and Hamp spoke up and said he would like one too. So we had a few drinks and our dinner, and then we went over to this woman's house to pick up the puppies. We were in my Tahoe, and as we headed back to the ranch, Jake was on my right, and he had taken off his jacket and wrapped up his puppy and laid him down at his feet. Hamp was in the backseat and had his puppy hugged up against his chest, breathing his whiskey breath all over him.

When we got back to the ranch, Jake took his puppy wrapped up in his jacket back over to his truck. Hamp, when he opened his door, loosened his grip, and that little dog jumped out and hit the ground and took off running. Hamp ran after him, calling, "Come back! Come back!" (I was almost waiting to hear the word "Shane" follow), but he disappeared into the night. We searched the next day but found no sign of him, and we left the following day. About two weeks later the dog was found on the ranch, hiding under a culvert, dehydrated and hungry, but he must have found some water somewhere in the draws and waterholes to stay alive. Hamp was called to come up and claim him, which he did.

From my involvement in the episode, I was inspired, if that is the right word, to compose a poem, which I have called "No-Dog Dews":

> Out at the Long X one cold and winter night,
> Was a man and his dog, and Oh! What a sight.
> The dog was a pup the first night they met,
> The man was drunk, and an old Viet Nam vet.
> The ride from Van Horn the two caressed,
> Then at the ranch, things really turned to a mess.
> The truck had stopped for a minute or so,
> And I heard the man shout, "Where'd that dog go?"
> The man was Hamp, who had had him a few,
> Known to this day as No-Dog Dews.

I subscribed it "By the Old Ranger." And while I have never claimed to really be a poet, it just mystifies me how people carry on over this Shakespeare fellow and some others, since with the right inspiration, anybody can write a really fine poem.

⋆ HANK ⋆

There is a wonderful writer up in Perryton named John Erickson, who has made sort of an industry out of his fictional character Hank the Cowdog. Long before he began that franchise, I knew a real cow dog named Hank—actually, there are probably a hundred cow dogs named Hank—who possessed one special appetite worth recording for posterity. My friend Jake was working on a project on a huge ranch, and the manager of this ranch, Dalton, was a rustic old cowboy in his seventies. He had done nothing his whole life but cowboy on ranches in West Texas, and every cowman in this day and time had a good cow dog, or two or three, depending on the number of cattle on the ranch. This is rough, hard country with large rocky mountains on the west and desert hills on the east moving into some large mountains farther to the east and northeast. Jake and Dalton were out on the ranch one day, and it was about five o'clock, and Jake asked Dalton if he would like a drink of whiskey. Now, this is not a question that you ask an old cowhand and expect no for an answer.

Dalton replied more on the lines of "Hell yes, I thought you would never ask." Jake took out his ditty bag—if you don't know what a ditty bag is, then don't ask—took out this quart bottle of Old Turkey brand whiskey, 101 proof, which will burn your gut from mouth to bunghole. Dalton got out of the pickup, reached into the truck bed, and got this old metal coffee cup, one of those that's light blue with white specks on it, and said to Jake, "Well, you know, if we have a drink of whiskey, then ol' Hank has to have a drink. He likes that whiskey about as much as I do."

Jake told me he had never seen a dog drink whiskey—beer yes, whiskey no. So Dalton took the bottle of Old Turkey 101 and poured about three fingers into that speckled blue coffee cup and set it on the ground in front of old Hank. Now, Hank was reddish brown in color and weighed about eighty or ninety pounds, and looked like a cross between a pit bull and a Rhodesian ridgeback. He was not a dog you would want to mess with, and Dalton swore by him as a good cow dog. Hank started gobbling that whiskey up and then licking the cup, then looked up at Dalton, pleading, "Give me some more!" They didn't, of course, because he would have drunk the whole damned bottle and they hadn't even had theirs yet. As they drank, Dalton looked at Jake and said, "That blue cup, it belongs to Hank, but sometimes when Hank's not around, one of the hired hands uses it to drink from—but don't tell Hank." After they refreshed themselves, they drove back to the ranch headquarters, where Dalton lived, and the house was surrounded by a wooden picket fence with a gate. When they all got out of the truck, Hank grabbed that blue cup in his mouth, trotted over to the fence, and hung the cup on a big nail next to the gate. I've often wondered if Hank could do that while sober.

Old Hank died a year or two before Dalton, and Dalton passed away only a year or so ago. He eventually cut Hank off from his whiskey, and that may have been what killed him. (At least he never had trouble with worms.) I remember that when I was stationed in Uvalde, the town was the home of John Nance Garner, formerly vice president of the United States. "Cactus Jack" liked his whiskey, too, and his "spring water," as he called it, and good cigars. When he was ninety-eight, Garner said he wanted to live to be a hundred, but his new doctor, whoever he was, took him off the alcohol and tobacco, and he died in less than a month. It just goes to show you: if it ain't broke, don't fix it.

The West is losing its old cowboys, though, the rough, tough, hell-bent-for-leather type, just as the old-time lawman is a vanishing breed. Sometimes we're just too damn politically correct.

★   WILL   ★

Hank is the perfect example of why I love dogs, but just because I love them does not mean I spoil them. A dog is happiest when he knows his place and what his limits are and what his job is. When he does, he will knock himself out to please and belong, but a dog that is pampered—which really means that he is treated according to his owner's caprices and good or bad humor—gets insecure. He might test those boundaries; he might develop what they call separation anxiety and tear the house apart when the owner is absent. Some people think they are doing a dog a favor by spoiling him, but they aren't. Maybe it's because I've retired now, but I am less exacting of my expectations from a dog, which brings me to my current bosom companion and favorite dog of all time, Will.

Shirley with Will, 4S Ranch, Wimberley, Texas, 2006.

Actually, he is Shirley's dog. He is a Lakeland terrier, and we acquired him from the breeder, Judy McKissick, about five years ago in Pearland, Texas, south of Houston. Shirley had seen a Lakeland terrier win a dog show and said she had to have one. Usually they are light brown and tan, but Will is black with gray—what they call "blue"; in fact, his registered name is Harrington Blue Label. There are only two breeders in Texas that we know of, and Shirley paid some pretty high dollars for him, but they were her dollars. He was the runt of a litter of three, and he had intestinal problems that caused him to be put in a clinic—actually, an ICU in the Houston Vet Hospital—for several days, during which nobody thought he would survive, but his will to live pulled him through. So Judy, his breeder, named him Will.

Shirley does her best to spoil him, but somewhere in growing up he became bonded to me, and now he travels with me everywhere in my Tahoe, where his station is on the console between the seats. He sits there like the RCA dog listening to his master's voice in the talking machine, and he thinks this vehicle belongs to him. In the house, when he sees me pick up my hat, he knows we're going somewhere, and he runs—not walks—for the kitchen door and jumps at it with his front feet, which makes quite a racket. When I get there, he makes a big leap into my arms so I'll carry him to the truck. While we're out, if anyone approaches that he doesn't know, he raises hell about it, and anyone who reaches out to pet him will get bit. Lakelands were bred to pull foxes or otters out of their holes, and they have big scary peg-like canines that would fit on a dog twice their size—in fact, they are the only small-dog breed that has big-dog teeth. I'd like to break him of biting people, and he nearly scared my cowriter, Jim Haley, to death. The first time we met, he came to Alpine, and Will and I drove over to the motel to pick him up. Jim's a city boy, listens to Mozart and that kind of thing, and the very second he got in the passenger's seat, Will was standing on his lap and had him pinned to the seat with his front feet on his chest and his nose flat against Jim's nose, staring him down. He didn't lick him—it's a peculiarity of the breed—and didn't bite him; he was smelling his breath to see what he had been eating. Fortunately, Jim passed the test, and everywhere we went over the next few days, I drove and Will perched on his lap as happy as he could be and even curled up there for a nap or two.

Will has acquired one habit I could do without. I saw this commercial on television where the dog locks his owner out of his vehicle. They use one shot of a dog inside, but then use an artificial limb to show its paw pushing down on the door lock. Will does this gig for real. He could do the whole commercial, and he works cheap; I'm his agent. I don't know if it's play or if he thinks he's protecting my Tahoe, but when I get out, he rolls up the automatic windows and locks the doors. Lakelands are very smart, but they are also very stubborn. I have not figured out how to get him to unlearn this behavior, so I have learned to carry a spare set of keys everywhere I go. It seems he is the only dog that has been smart enough to start training me. I hope he is the dog that outlives me.

CHAPTER 7

The Deadly Duo

LUCAS AND TOOLE

Before I joined the Rangers, the years I spent in the Highway Patrol pretty much hardened me to the sight of death. Having worked high-speed highway collisions, I do believe I saw just about everything that can be done to a body—I came upon them crushed, skewered, decapitated, skinned, and burnt to a crisp. I never liked the sight of it, but I could and did work scenes professionally. The only thing that always affected me was the deaths of children. To see the lives of the young and the innocent snuffed out before they had a chance to experience life was truly hard.

After I became a Texas Ranger, though, there were still times when I occasionally came upon a scene so appalling that I had to stop and collect myself. On Monday morning, April 23, 1979, I received a telephone call from Chief Chisum of the Uvalde Police Department, requesting me to meet two of his officers on Farm Road 117 at a location two miles north of Batesville, which was south of town and well across the line into Zavala County. They had located a blue Dodge pickup truck, whose registration linked it to Lupita Gonzalez, a twenty-four-year-old teacher's aide in Uvalde who had been reported missing by her husband on the evening of April 19. The truck was owned by her father.

I arrived at the scene at nine thirty-five and discovered the pickup stuck in the mud in a bar ditch (a shallow drainage ditch) on the north side of the narrow caliche-surfaced road, which ran east-west; the truck was facing west.

The window on the driver's side was down, the keys in the ignition, the gas gauge indicating just less than a quarter of a tank. Recent heavy rains, five to seven inches the previous night and a half inch the night before that, had completely washed away any evidence or tracks around the truck. The rain had blown inside the truck, also partially washing away the muddy print of a man's shoe on the passenger's side of the cab. There was no blood or sign of any struggle inside the truck. We did find a pillow on the right floorboard, which Ms. Gonzalez used to sit on while driving, since she was only four-eleven. On the road near the truck we found a Miller High Life beer bottle, which appeared to have been deposited there since the rain; it was taken for evidence. We secured the truck, whose interior was later dusted for latent fingerprints, although none were found other than the missing woman's.

The two officers and I searched the brush and pasture in the area surrounding the truck, but found no sign of her. Tracking was impossible because of the recent rains. Still suspecting foul play, I requested a DPS helicopter, which arrived at approximately one. Once airborne, it took only a few minutes to discover a body across the road and about four hundred yards east of the abandoned vehicle. It was on the bank of a small creek, about 150 feet inside the fence line of a pasture. We set the chopper down and approached the corpse, and what I saw still makes the hair stand up on my neck. The pasture led up into a patch of forest, and just inside this wooded area, partly concealed from view by a large fallen mesquite tree, we found the body. Her scalp and hair were in place, but in the five days she had been missing, scavengers had bitten away the fleshy parts of her face, so beneath her ample black hair there was a grinning naked skull, alive with maggots. The position of sexual assault was unmistakable: she was lying on her stomach, her panties, panty hose, and the peach-colored dress in which she was last seen were pulled down to her knees, her girdle discarded a short distance away. One of the few pieces of evidence was the presence of red fibers that did not come from any of her clothing.

Four feet away lay her shoes and purse, splashed with rain and leaves. The mud and vegetative debris on her shoes was all of the type in the surrounding pasture, indicating that the entire incident probably occurred here. The purse appeared intact and not rifled, but inside were only five nickels, two pennies, and a large number of letters from various businesses demanding payment on debts owed by her husband. Some of the letters were two months old, some four. Her driver's license identified her, and her photo revealed her to have been petite and pretty. Later we learned that she worked with children and had two of her own, the younger only seven months old.

We sent for Bert Boxter, the Batesville justice of the peace, to come out and pronounce her dead, which seemed like a silly legal fiction under the circumstances. You really couldn't be much more dead than that. I wondered if she had been a modest girl. Death is no respecter of modesty, and what a sad fate for a person of morals to be discovered in such a state. The remains were taken to Esparza's Funeral Home in Uvalde, which took them over to the Bexar County medical examiner to be autopsied. The finding was that she had been stabbed four times in the chest, two of the blows finding her heart. Off the record, because he could not testify with any certainty to it, the medical examiner, Dr. Reuben Santos, advised that she may have also been stabbed in the vagina. Because of the trauma and the heavy infestation of maggots, it was not possible to determine if she had been raped. The fatal weapon had a blade at least three inches long and from half to three-quarters of an inch wide.

*   *   *

From her parents and coworkers, I learned that Lupita Gonzalez had gone to San Antonio with her husband and six-year-old son on April 16. They spent the night, according to her husband, Rolando, at the El Tejas Motel on South Roosevelt, and returned to Uvalde on the night of April 17. Despite taking this trip together, the couple had separated, and she was living at her parents' home. Gonzalez saw her briefly the next day. He had accompanied a friend to the Dalton School to pick up his friend's child. It was eleven o'clock, and he saw Lupita taking her class to lunch. He waved at her and she waved back, and that was the last time he saw her. At three twenty on April 18, one of Lupita's coworkers invited her out for coffee, but she declined, saying that she had no money and was going home to bake a birthday cake for her mother. Ten minutes later, the school bus driver saw Lupita, driving her father's pickup, turn south from Main onto Camp Street. She was in the truck alone. Sometime that afternoon she was kidnapped from the parking lot next to Casel's Liquor Store. Rolando reported her missing that night, and accompanied by a Uvalde County deputy, he picked up his children from Lupita's parents' house.

Subsequent investigation pointed down many different avenues. I was able to pin down the time of the murder to between six forty-five and seven fifteen on the eighteenth, the time when the Gonzalez truck and another vehicle were seen on the dirt road by roughnecks working on a gas rig a half mile away. When Rolando returned to work on April 20, he told the secretaries that Lupita's parents had accused him of killing and burying her, which was crazy, since he would never have had the courage to commit such an act. Their trip to San Antonio was confirmed by their hosts there, a married couple named Garza, who were attempting to help Rolando find another job, since his present one would be terminated at the end of the month. More importantly, I was able to account for Rolando's whereabouts during the hours when the murder must have occurred. Anonymous information that Lupita was seen struggling with two men in the grocery-store parking lot could not be substantiated, but another tip—that Lupita and a fellow teacher's aide at the school had been seeing a couple of men—proved to have more substance. It developed that Lupita and her girlfriend had been meeting roughnecks from Batesville for about two months. The plot thickened still further when it was overheard in a barbershop that Rolando owed eight thousand dollars to a narcotics dealer and so Lupita may have been killed for the debt.

The Gonzalezes' domestic troubles came into sharper focus when I learned from a former employee of Rolando's that after the separation, Lupita abandoned some of her clothes at her in-laws' house because she was afraid to pick them up; that Rolando's mother wanted to beat her up; that Rolando was always complaining that Lupita would not give him her paycheck; and that he was apparently dealing marijuana out of his place of business. Information from possibly disgruntled employees is always taken with a grain of salt. So are statements from wronged women, and two months after the murder I learned that Rolando was the father of a two-year-old girl living in Great Falls, Montana. I contacted the mother, who was very helpful in answering my questions, but said she did not believe him capable of murder. Other information came in that a self-styled hit man from Batesville had been offering his services, making veiled reference to the Lupita Gonzalez killing as an example of his handiwork.

After several months I reviewed all my evidence. I had a couple who were arguing and had separated; I had in-laws who had joined in the fight; both husband and wife had apparently undertaken extramarital affairs; I had people they owed large sums of money to; and there was a vague whiff of drug dealing. But hard evidence that I could take into court—there just wasn't any, and the case grew cold.

Nearly five years passed, and Texas news came to be dominated by the trials and confessions of an appalling serial killer named Henry Lee Lucas. At the time he was on trial in Georgetown, Texas, north of Austin, for one of his killings, I sent copies of reports on the Lupita Gonzalez murder up to Williamson County, just on the chance that he might have been involved. To my amazement, Lucas readily confessed.

He was by this time already a legend in Texas criminal history. His early life was an Appalachian horror. Henry was born in a rural area near Blacksburg, Virginia, on August 23, 1936. His father, Anderson, was a moonshiner and an alcoholic who lost both legs in a drunken accident with a freight train. Afterward he was viciously abused and dominated by Henry's mother, Viola, a prostitute. Living in a dirt-floored log cabin of two rooms were nine children, most of whom were sent out to relatives or foster care. Henry, however, was kept at home to endure his mother's rages. Sometimes he was forced to dress as a girl and sent to school barefoot, sometimes he was forced to work the still, and sometimes he was even forced to watch Viola turn tricks with strangers. A teacher once gave Henry a pair of shoes, and Viola beat him viciously for wearing them home. Anderson was powerless over the situation, and one night crawled out into the cold rather than watch his wife earn extra money. He died from the pneumonia he contracted. Henry Lee Lucas turned to having sex with a stepbrother, and then the two of them together would have sex with animals after they cut their throats. Henry's brother once accidentally wounded him in the left eye with a knife; Viola denied him medical care until the eye began to wither, and a doctor had to remove it. The orb around the glass eye that replaced it was always prone to oozing fluids and gave him a grotesque appearance.

If he hadn't turned into a monster, you could feel a great deal of sympathy for anyone who endured early years like those. But the fact is, thousands of young people emerge from ugly childhoods without becoming psychopaths, and society is not being unreasonable to expect people to control their sense of betrayal and rage. Granted, though, Viola Lucas pressed the boundary pretty hard of what you could expect any child to emerge from and still be normal; at least there was a small element of justice in her being his first victim.

Blacksburg is about twenty miles west of the larger city of Roanoke, where at eighteen Henry was sentenced to six years in the Virginia State Prison for a series of burglaries. He escaped once and sought out an older sister in Tecumseh, a small town in southeastern Michigan about twenty miles northeast of Toledo, Ohio. He was recaptured after three months, returned to prison, escaped again, but only for a day, and was finally given early release in September 1959. He returned to the sister in Michigan, only to be dogged by phone calls from Viola, who was now seventy-four, demanding that he return to her. His refusal prompted her to come to Michigan to fetch him. Late on January 11, 1960, one of their violent arguments ended when Viola struck him with a broom and Lucas lashed out with a knife, fatally stabbing her in the neck. He raped her dead body before fleeing to nearby Toledo, where he was arrested five days later. A jury, horrified by the victim as much as they were by the killer, convicted Lucas of a lesser charge of second-degree murder, and he served ten years. Because of two suicide attempts, he spent most of his time in a mental facility before being paroled, in 1970. He soon served five more years for attempted kidnapping before leaving Michigan and drifting.

He made his way to Jacksonville, Florida. In a charity soup kitchen there, he met and shared a meal with Ottis (pronounced with a long o) Toole (just like "tool"), a Jacksonville native, an arsonist, and a homosexual transvestite, the product of a history almost as twisted as Lucas's. He was the youngest of nine children born to a mentally ill woman and her alcoholic husband; indeed, mental illness ran strong in the whole family. Teased for being slow in school, Ottis was enrolled in special-education classes, but left school in seventh grade. As a teen and young adult, he exhibited a penchant for cross-dressing, loitering, and lewd behavior, activities that caused him to run afoul of the law numerous times. He also became a prolific arsonist throughout the South, finding that the flames enhanced his sexual fantasies. After meeting Lucas, Toole fell in love with him. Toole was nearly ten years younger, and in his memory the two became lovers; in all probability, Lucas passively allowed Toole to perform sexual favors for him.

But Toole did not take a backseat to Henry Lee Lucas in the shocking nature of his crimes. He was a ghoul—no other word suffices—a cannibal, and a necrophiliac. The year before I met him, he confessed to the gruesome 1981 killing of Adam Walsh, a six-year-old Florida boy, whom he decapitated; he then carried the head around in a sack for several days, sodomizing it for his pleasure. Adam's father, John Walsh, became a strong ally for law enforcement, narrating the popular television show *America's Most Wanted*.

Each of these monsters was bad enough on his own, but when they traveled together, they were Halloween on wheels. After becoming friends, Lucas moved in with Toole and his mentally ill mother. Also living with them was Toole's mildly retarded niece, twelve-year-old Becky Powell, with whom Lucas began a sexual relationship. Lucas and Toole used this house as a base while making their murderous forays across the country. After Toole's mother died, in 1981, they took to the road more permanently, usually accompanied by Becky. Toole would sometimes cruise for men, pick them up, and return with large sums of money, his victims never to be heard from again. At other times Toole would don women's clothing and makeup, then pick up some lonely truck driver, who would come to a grisly end. Lucas never acquired Toole's taste for human flesh, but he was quite matter-of-fact in describing his preference for having sex with people after killing them. "To me, a live woman ain't nothing," he said. "I enjoy dead sex more than live sex." When the two took a woman and Lucas killed her, Toole would often revisit the corpse for more mutilation, fueled by jealousy over Lucas's preference for them over himself.

Occasionally they parted company. In May 1982, Lucas and Becky, who was now a teenager, moved in with a Good Samaritan in Montague County, Texas, a woman in her eighties named Kate Rich. When he was ready to move on, Lucas drove her to an oil field, stabbed her to death, and had sex with her body. After stuffing the remains in a culvert, he later changed his mind, returned, and burned her piecemeal in a stove. Soon after, Becky became homesick and began whining to return to Florida. Arrested for questioning in the disappearance of Kate Rich, Lucas began his confessions, which led officers to the ashes and bones of the old woman. He also confessed to killing Becky and leaving her body parts stuffed in three pillowcases in a field near Denton. During the trial for killing Kate Rich, he offhandedly asserted that he had killed perhaps a hundred more, and the Henry Lee Lucas legend was minted.

* * *

Life would have been easy if we had been able to just accept Lucas's confession in the Lupita Gonzalez killing, but that turned out not to be possible, because in the previous couple of years he had also confessed to just about every Texas killing since the assassination of John F. Kennedy. Once he was apprehended and the shocking nature of his crimes became known, Lucas found himself a superstar of the prison system, and he quickly learned to barter information for time and better treatment. When questioned about his possible involvement in an unsolved homicide, he became a master—and I mean an absolute master—at gleaning just enough information from the questions he was asked to feed answers back in a way that made him sound knowledgeable of the crime. It became a game to him, and inexperienced detectives who tried to jog his memory with facts or photos of a crime scene were actually feeding him the information that Lucas used to convince them he had done it. And Toole, when questioned for corroboration, invariably agreed with whatever Lucas claimed to have done, no matter how outlandish. In fact, the one murder for which Lucas was handed a capital sentence, the killing of a Jane Doe in Williamson County, north of Austin, who became known as "Orange Socks" for the only articles of clothing she was wearing when her body was found, turned out to be a false confession.

That murder occurred on Halloween night 1979, and Lucas went to trial on April 2, 1984. He was convicted and given the death penalty on the strength of his confession, which he had recanted, but over the following months, it became more and more certain that he had been in Florida, employed by a roofer, at the time of the killing. Ultimately, Governor George W. Bush was compelled to commute his sentence to life imprisonment—the only commutation he issued during his six years as governor. Then the *Dallas Times Herald* broke the story on April 14, 1985, that Lucas could not possibly have committed a number of the crimes he had confessed to. One of the reporters, Hugh Aynesworth, got Lucas to admit as much. "I'd go through the files," Lucas said. "I'd look through pictures, everything that concerned that murder. And, when the detective from that state, or that town, ya know, I'd tell them all about that murder. . . . I'd only give them bits and pieces. They didn't care. They wanted to solve it."

One of the county sheriffs who had been interrogating him was forced to agree. "Once you ask him about a murder, you have to give him a certain location, and if you don't watch out, Henry will have you tell him how it happened, where it happened and when it happened. And then, he'll repeat it back to you. He was a nightmare as far as investigators go because he was so street savvy, it's unreal."

"They think I'm stupid," said Lucas. "When all of this is over, they'll know who's really stupid." In the meantime, Lucas bartered information for better food, cable television, cigarettes, and art supplies. "Why would I want to change things?" Lucas asked a defense investigator. "The instant you stop confessing—you're going to death row." Therefore I was wary of him when

I had an opportunity to question him about the Lupita Gonzalez matter. I knew well enough that officers all over the country had open homicides that they wanted off their books, and they may have been too quick to accept a Lucas confession.

The initial interview was conducted at the end of January 1984 by a fellow Ranger, Clayton Smith, who noted in his report that Lucas told him that a woman had been kidnapped from Uvalde and taken to another location, but did not say where. Lucas added that the woman's vehicle was also taken, but did not divulge what it was. Smith then showed Lucas a photo of Lupita Gonzalez. Lucas's initial responses were promising but not conclusive. He described the victim's vehicle as a blue truck, and said that he and Toole had taken her from the parking lot of a grocery store after they had been drinking in a tavern. Upon being shown an area road map, Lucas said they turned right down FM 117 and drove until they pulled off onto a dirt road and had sex with her. He accurately described the field as a rocky one partially cleared of mesquite, and went on to say that Toole then took the girl into a wooded area and shot her; at least he thought he shot her—his memory was hazy.

Still, Lucas's recollection was detailed enough to warrant a trip to Uvalde to walk over the scene, even though we knew that he had been artfully parlaying

Henry Lee Lucas at the Uvalde airport, standing by a DPS aircraft, 1984.

such "information" into free trips all over the country. We felt reasonably confident that we were on to something. DPS pilot Jim Fields landed his King Air at the Uvalde Airport at ten on the evening of February 14, 1984. On board were Lucas, Ranger Smith, and Williamson County deputy sheriff Ray Hardison. Lucas was in cuffs; he wasn't very impressive for a monster, about five-nine, 150 pounds, and rather sad-sack looking. I loaded them into my state unit, with Lucas in the front seat, and drove through Uvalde. I read him his rights at the DPS office and advised him that he was being recorded. He waived his right to remain silent under the Miranda warning and said he would give a statement.

At ten twenty Lucas became alert when he recognized Casel's Liquor Store as the place where he and Toole had bought beer and wine; there was a small grocery store next to Casel's, which many in the Hispanic community favored over the large supermarket some distance away. Lucas said that they had nabbed Gonzalez at this store as she came out with a sack of groceries, and that Toole drove Gonzalez's blue Dodge pickup, since Lucas had her tied up inside their own light-colored old Ford station wagon with red carpet. That rang true, since I remembered the red fibers we found on her clothing, but we were unable to follow up on what could have been a conclusive piece of evidence. Lucas and Toole had sold the station wagon in California, and it had been destroyed, perhaps compacted and sold for scrap. We also could not get information from the only other witnesses to the kidnapping, the niece and nephew; Lucas had killed Becky in 1982, and the nephew had also disappeared.

Rather than give Lucas a chance to polish his story for the next day, I decided to give him an initial run at the scene right away. South of Uvalde, the country is full of ranches on both sides of FM 117 until you get to within two miles of Batesville. It was pitch black outside as we sped along; I was going between seventy and seventy-five miles an hour, and I was determined to give Lucas no clue about our whereabouts. Out of the blue he exclaimed that we had just passed where he and Toole had turned off and taken Lupita Gonzalez. I pulled over, turned about, and followed his directions down the dirt road. He said that from this road he and Toole had pulled into the pasture, to get off the road, and driven a few hundred yards down a *sendero* (an open lane cut through the brush) along the creek. He maintained that there had been no fence there at the time, and indeed this was correct; the fence had been put up in the years since. Lucas remembered traveling with Toole's niece and nephew, and that as they neared Batesville, they pulled onto this dirt road and sent the children to wait by the creek while they undressed and raped the woman on a mattress in the back of the station wagon. He showed us correctly where they had parked, and said that he had stayed in the vehicle while Toole took her out some distance from the car. He was gone maybe ten minutes, then returned without her, having, in Lucas's memory, shot her to death. He guessed that the body was probably across the creek, a couple of hundred yards from where they had parked. He also recalled that Toole had gotten Gonzalez's truck stuck in the bar ditch, and so they had all left in the station wagon. After the whole episode was over, they headed for California.

I suspected that Lucas was starting to play his game with me, since some of these things he could have gleaned from reports shown him to jog his memory. There were also some inconsistencies: in his first interview, he said that he had gone to the body and had sex with it, but denied this in the reinterview two weeks later. Still, the fact that in the dead of night he recognized where they had turned off told me that he and Toole were good for the murder.

A few weeks later, on March 22, I drove to Georgetown, Texas, accompanied by Ranger sergeant and later captain Bobby Prince, to interview the other principal, Ottis Toole, who had been brought over from Florida, where he was serving time for arson. Knowing his sexual proclivities and that he had been servicing Lucas when they weren't having sex with corpses, I was surprised that Toole actually appeared the more menacing of the two. He was considerably bigger than Lucas, six-two and about two hundred ten pounds, and beyond that, the thing that struck me was that his teeth were as yellow as a wild animal's. Even without knowing of his history of having a learning disability, anyone could immediately see that he wasn't nearly as smart as Lucas. This interview was not satisfactory: Toole at first denied having any recollection of the events, but allowed that if Lucas had said they did it, then they most probably had. Items shown him to jog his memory, however, such as a hairpiece belonging to the victim, elicited enough information to justify his also visiting Uvalde.

This occurred on April 3. I read him his rights at ten thirty in the morning and loaded him into my car; in the backseat were Chief Chisum and Ranger Clayton Smith. I drove to Casel's Liquor Store, and Toole seemed to have some recollection of that area. As we headed back toward downtown, we came to the intersection of FM 117, and Toole suddenly said to turn right.

Two miles north of Batesville we approached a dirt road, which Toole identified as the one he believed they had taken with the Gonzalez woman.

Toole also remarked on the fence that had not been there at the time of the killing. Getting out of the car, I instructed him to show me where the body had been, and, again correctly, he crossed the road, walking back to the east through the pasture until he came to a large mesquite log behind which we had found the body. We could still see a stain and where the maggots had been.

After viewing the location where the body was found, Toole began to recall other details of the events, which we recorded on tape. He did not recall much of the actual kidnapping, but did remember buying Budweiser and Miller beer from Casel's. After they grabbed her at gunpoint, Toole drove her blue Dodge pickup, and Lucas followed behind in the station wagon—Toole recalled it being a Ford—with the two juveniles and the captive, Lupita Gonzalez. After they pulled off onto the dirt road, Lucas forced her into the back of the wagon and had sex with her, and then Toole did the same before making her put her clothes back on and walking her out across the pasture and into the woods. He said that she snagged her hose on some brush, and he had her remove them. Once out of sight, he bent her over the mesquite log and sodomized her from behind before stabbing her and slashing her throat. There was no indication from the autopsy that Gonzalez's throat had been cut, but it may well have been; the condition of the body when we found it, and the lack of flesh, made such a determination impossible. Toole said he thought he had had a Buck knife, which has about a four-inch blade, consistent with the weapon that caused the victim's wounds. Following up on what the coroner had said at the time, I asked Toole whether he had stabbed Gonzalez in the vagina. He said he did not remember doing so, but he could have, since he had done that to other victims. Ottis Toole wasn't bright enough to process our information and feed it back to us as Lucas had done, but his memory corroborated Lucas's statements right down the line. Further, Lucas had been unable to remember what Lupita Gonzalez had in her sack from the grocery store; it was Toole who recalled that it contained bread, milk, and cake mix.

Both men gave tape-recorded confessions, but I still had some remaining questions whether they were truly guilty. The crime fit their MO, certainly, and they knew the location. But it was impossible not to be haunted by all those other confessions that had turned out to be false. One trail of evidence

I felt bound to follow was their record of employment, in particular a set of time sheets and pay stubs that showed Henry Lee Lucas working for a roofing contractor in Jacksonville, Florida, during the week of the murder and for at least one week on either side of it. With these time sheets, however, came an affidavit from the head of the company, stating, "It would be very easy for a foreman to add a man to the daily time sheet, without me knowing it. Because of the different locations and size of our jobs this would be easy." I also knew that Lucas and Toole could cover vast distances in only a day or two, and had done so ever since they began living with Toole's mother. The fact that they were traveling with Toole's niece and eleven-year-old nephew suggested that this might have been intended as a fast trip. Further, I noticed that the paycheck dated April 19 was not deposited until four days later, and decided that his pay stubs were not conclusive one way or another as to his whereabouts.

A grand jury indicted Lucas and Toole for the murder of Lupita Gonzalez on April 19, 1984, five years and a day after her death. Lucas was arraigned, and refused to plea—but the case never came to trial. The DA was well aware that both had already been multiply convicted, and thought it would be a waste of taxpayer dollars to prosecute them again. Without a doubt, Henry Lee Lucas was a loathsome serial killer, but he was equally a serial confessor. Despite his claims to have killed hundreds, my best guess is that he actually committed twenty to forty murders.

Henry Lee Lucas died in prison of chronic heart trouble in March 2001, having been preceded in death by Ottis Toole, whose alcoholic liver failed in September 1996. It does not speak ill of the dead to say that the world is better off without them.

CHAPTER 8

The Hunt for Alfredo Hernandez, a *Muy Mal Hombre*

Uvalde is located at the northern limit of the Brush Country, a vast and mostly arid plain that covers the entirety of South Texas inland from the gulf marshes. Originally it was grassland and mesquite savanna with clusters of oaks, but centuries of overgrazing have turned it into a hellish tangle of brush: chaparral, huisache, and guajillo, laced together with a thornscrub of catclaw and prickly pear and other cactus plants. Early pioneers used to say that every plant out here either sticks, stings, or stinks, and they had it pretty much right.

Take U.S. Highway 83 north out of Uvalde for about twenty-five miles, and you'll come to the wide-spot-in-the-road town of Concan, which even today has only about two hundred residents. About ten miles farther on, you cross into Real County, and ten more miles brings you into the town of Leakey. As you make this trip, you climb up the Balcones Escarpment into the Texas Hill Country, and the change between these two regions is so dramatic you might as well have entered another world. Here the high limestone hills are cut by deep river valleys, and apart from the Ozark Mountains of Arkansas and Missouri, which are a very similar kind of country, the Hill Country contains the largest collection of springs and caverns in North America. Concan and Leakey both sit in the valley of the Rio Frio—Spanish for "cold river," which is a dead accurate description of all those clear, spring-fed rivers that come tumbling out of the Hill Country. Once you cross the escarpment, the landscape is as rough and vertical and rocky as the Brush Country is a flat tangle of thorns. There is an abundance of game in the Hill Country; in fact, it has the largest deer herd in the United States. Today it is a haven of dude ranches and hunting leases, and the tourists are the biggest source of income there.

The Hill Country first came to national prominence when Lyndon Johnson was elected vice president, in 1960—he was from Johnson City, which is several counties east and north of Leakey. *Life* magazine did a big story about the area and called it "God's Country," praise that amazed a lot of the locals who had been trying to scratch a living out of those hills for generations. When I was there forty years ago, it was still pretty undeveloped, and the Hill Country's biggest significance to me was that a bad guy could hide out almost indefinitely in those limestone hills. It was a nightmare to have to track one down and bring him to justice—more especially if he knew the country and you didn't, as was the case with the See-More Kid, whom I wrote about in the first book.

That was exactly what happened with one of the meanest coyotes I ever had to deal with: Alfredo Hernandez, a Mexican national by birth, born in San Luis Potosí in 1930, who was in the United States illegally. I first heard of him in 1966, right after I was stationed in Uvalde; he had gained quite a reputation there for a series of robberies and burglaries, and had left the area shortly before I arrived. In September 1966, I went up to the Peck Ranch, near Concan, with my captain, A. Y. Allee. We advised the Pecks that Hernandez had confessed to burglarizing their house back in April 1962. Confessions are always handy to have, even though Ranger Levi Duncan had lifted one of Hernandez's palm prints from the Peck residence at the time. Actually, Hernandez had visited them a couple of times, on one occasion making off with guns, jewelry, televisions, and other quick-sell items that he transported, rather cheekily, by stealing the Pecks' own car to haul them off in. He then sold both the car and the booty in Mexico. I think that's considered adding insult to injury.

Because Hernandez had left the area so recently, I was treated to a full account of his last escapade. The Concan area was rather thinly settled with small ranches, and one of Hernandez's last activities around there before being more or less driven away was the attempted burglary of a grizzled little old banty rooster of a man named Rutherford, who ran a small store and service station right on the highway, not too far from Garner State Park, picking up business from the tourist trade there and from canoeists on the Frio. Rutherford was maybe in his early seventies, and one night in 1964 he and his wife were watching television in their house, which was attached to the store, when Alfredo Hernandez staged what today we would call a home invasion. He wore a mask he had crafted out of the leg of a pair of reddish silk pajamas and carried a pistol and two lengths of quarter-inch cotton rope with which he intended to tie up the Rutherfords.

The old man got up at the sound of the door opening, and Hernandez pointed his gun at him; it was a .38 Smith & Wesson with a four-inch barrel, the Military and Police (M&P) model. Hernandez threw one of the ropes at Rutherford and ordered him to tie his wife up. This area around Concan and Leakey, as you might remember from the chapter about Tom Bybee, is populated with good people who keep to themselves, but who can get thoroughly mean if you mess with them. Instead of obeying, Rutherford jumped Hernandez, starting a struggle with this thug who was maybe half his age. They fought through the room and out onto a small screened porch, which was long and narrow, only four or five feet wide. They struggled through the porch toward the door, where little old Rutherford managed to wrestle the pistol away from him. Immediately he placed the barrel right against Hernandez's stomach and pulled the trigger, twice, but it failed to discharge. Rather than wait around for Rutherford to find a cartridge that worked, Hernandez bolted through the screen door and ran. Hernandez was probably thinking that an old man had just kicked his ass.

I later had an opportunity to examine those cartridges, and the hammer had made deep indentations into the primer on both of them, so they should have gone off. Whomever Hernandez had stolen that gun from had allowed the ammunition to deteriorate, luckily for him. Rutherford called the sheriff, who brought in Ranger Duncan, and they got some prison dogs to track Hernandez, who took off west into some extremely rugged hills and breaks toward Sycamore.

Even though Hernandez managed to escape, this incident convinced him that his Uvalde County luck had just about run out, and he kept going for some one hundred fifty miles, eventually setting himself up again near Dryden. This was a godawful lonely little station of a dozen inhabitants, with a post office and a couple of stores, on the Union Pacific tracks in the desert of Terrell County, seventy miles past the village of Langtry, where Judge Roy Bean once operated the Jersey Lilly Saloon, civilization's last stop

Alfredo Hernandez, prison photo, early 1960s.

before hell. Hernandez took up residence in a cave located up a washed-out arroyo in the middle of nowhere. Working out of this shelter, Hernandez reopened his burglary business, preying on isolated ranches. When he hit the grocery store and post office in Pumpville, he shot the proprietor, Pellum Bradford, who surprised Hernandez during the burglary. Bradford survived, and it wasn't until February 1966 that any information came in that could be used to catch Hernandez. Alfredo Gallego, a ranch hand who worked for Indio Casada, had spotted Hernandez's hideout on Casada's lease. Terrell County sheriff Bill Cooksey, an experienced officer who had been in the highway patrol for many years, was notified.

Cooksey told me later that when he first got the call, he figured it was just another illegal alien trying to make his way into the country. He got in touch with a former border patrolman named Lewis Cash, who lived there in Dryden. Cooksey got in a pickup with Cash and Ben Ross, a local eighteen-year-old who had been finding stashes of Hernandez's stolen merchandise and was attempting to track Hernandez around the area. On November 4, 1965, they went out to the arroyo where Hernandez had been seen, which was east-northeast of town. Cooksey was a careful lawman, and when he went out, he always wore what we refer to as a double rig: a pistol belt that he wore under his pants belt allowed him to have his snub-nosed .38 in his waistband and a .357 magnum in a holster on the right, in the rig. It is important for an officer to have his sidearm always in the same place so he can depend on its being there. On this day, however, not thinking it would be a dangerous encounter, he left his double rig at home and just had a .38 automatic in his waistband.

Gallego showed him where the cave was; Cooksey went down into the ravine, which was fifteen or twenty feet deep, and found and arrested Hernandez. As they were walking out of the ravine back up toward their vehicles, they were almost within sight of the others. Young Ross was carrying a .30-30 Winchester Model 94 carbine.

On their way back up, Hernandez asked Cooksey in Spanish if he could return and get his personal belongings, which were in a bag back in the cave. Cooksey, thinking that he was just dealing with some simple illegal, gave

Sheriff Bill Cooksey, sheriff's office, Sanderson, Texas, 1966–1967.

him permission to do so. Cooksey, who had been following Hernandez up the embankment, stepped aside as Hernandez turned and started down the ravine. After he passed Cooksey, he suddenly turned around, reached under his clothing, and produced a Smith & Wesson M&P .38, like the one he had lost in Concan during the confrontation with Rutherford. Cooksey was a shootist, and had a reputation of being very quick with a gun. Instinctively he reached for the .357 Magnum where it should have been, but it wasn't there. Everybody who knew Bill Cooksey agreed that if the .357 Magnum had been there, Hernandez never would have gotten a shot off.

As it was, Hernandez leveled the gun and fired; the first shot hit Cooksey in the thigh just above the knee, and as he fell forward, a second shot hit him in the back. Cooksey told me later that after he crumpled to the ground, it was the most serene feeling he had ever experienced—that he seemed to be floating away. In the distance, he said, he could hear the train coursing through Dryden; knowing Bill, it must have crossed his mind—hell, the angels are coming for me in a train.

Ross had entered the arroyo and rounded a clump of cedar when he heard the two shots and saw Hernandez running. He figured that Cooksey had fired some warning shots. As he approached, he saw Cooksey on the ground and thought, oh hell, what happened? Hernandez drew a bead on Ross and told him to throw the .30-30 down, which he did, and Hernandez had Ross, Gallego, and Cash go to the top of the ravine. He ordered Gallego to tie Ross and Cash up. Hernandez forced Gallego into his truck to drive him from the scene, having taken the keys out of Cash's truck. Gallego had tied up Ross with baling wire, and once Hernandez was gone, Ross was able to back up to Cash, who untied the wire. Ross then untied Cash, who said he would hot-wire his truck, and Ross entered the ravine again to tend to Cooksey.

Ross heard the same train approach that Cooksey heard after he fell. Bill was still conscious, and told Ross to run and see if he could flag down the train. Ross was just able to reach the tracks as it approached, and to his ut-ter surprise, it stopped. It turned out to be a special freight going from San Antonio to El Paso, and a railroad executive in a business suit got out of the caboose and demanded to know why they had been stopped. Once the situation was explained, they radioed ahead to Sanderson, which was only twenty-three miles away, and an ambulance was dispatched. Ross rode with Cooksey to the hospital in Del Rio, which was over a hundred miles away. In the emergency room, it was discovered that the first bullet had gone through his leg without cutting any major blood vessels. The bullet that entered his back was a .38 wadcutter—a low-velocity round used in target shooting—that had been deflected by a rib and exited just under his armpit. The spent bullet was found between his body and T-shirt. Had it not been for the rib, the path of the bullet would have been directly through his heart. But the Boss Man had more plans for him. Surprisingly, Cooksey was back on the job within three weeks, but he walked with a painful limp for the rest of his life.

It is not shown on major roadmaps, but just east of Dryden there is a caliche ranch road that heads south all the way to the Rio Grande, which is about twenty miles away. Why, having just killed a Texas sheriff—as far as he knew—Hernandez didn't shoot the other three and steal one of the vehicles, I don't know. But it seems doubtful that Gallego took him all the way to the river, because Ross said he began picking up signs of him again within a couple of days.

Area residents soon learned that there was an unwelcome guest in the vicinity. One local eccentric, a laborer named Woody Rutledge, who lived in a little house up on a hill about two hundred yards south of Highway 90 in Dryden, had cooked a pot roast and set the pan on his kitchen table. He then walked down the hill to the store for bread and pickles, which could have taken only a few minutes, and when he returned, roast and pan were both gone without so much as a note reading *"Muchas gracias, señor."* Rutledge was so mad you would have thought someone killed his best hunting dog.

After this, the store and filling station in Dryden began to be robbed every week or ten days. From the list of what was taken—basic provisions such as canned chili and beans, and soda pop—they began to suspect that Hernandez had returned. Any outlaw alive and on the loose after tangling with the Texas Rangers and shooting a sheriff should have considered his ass grass, and it took some first-class machismo for him to return to his old ways undeterred. But Cooksey knew that Hernandez was fond of soda pop, and this was certainly his MO.

Ben Ross missed the final act of the drama, having left to enter the army in July. As soon as Cooksey had healed up, Alfred Allee, Junior, the captain's son and also a Ranger, whom we all knew as "Little Alfred," came over from his station in Ozona, and they began carrying out surveillance of the Dryden store at night. The store was on the north side of the road, facing south; Cooksey concealed himself across the highway to the southwest and Little Alfred took the southeast. After several nights of body-stiffening stakeout duty, they discovered the culprit. On the night of August 19, 1966, Alfredo Hernandez emerged from the store wearing a straw hat, two tow sacks full of provisions tied together behind his neck, the contents hanging in front of him.

Cooksey emerged from his concealment, limping across the highway and armed with a 20-gauge shotgun loaded with buckshot. He declared himself and ordered Hernandez to surrender. Hernandez, with his M&P .38 special within easy reach, as always, dropped to one knee and opened fire on him, and Cooksey returned fire with the shotgun. This took place in the wee hours of the morning, the gun flashes lighting the area in front of the store like a strobe light. Some of Cooksey's pellets carried away Hernandez's straw hat, and what should have been Hernandez's chest exploded in a mess of soda pop and canned chili con carne. The cans acted as body armor and probably saved his life.

Little Alfred had been approaching from the southeast, armed with a .30-30, and he also opened up on Hernandez. This little grocery and gas station was full-service, the kind that hardly exist anymore, and near the pumps was a wringer for squeezing out the chamois skins used to clean windshields. One of Little Alfred's rounds went through this wringer, causing it to flatten like a dumdum and lose velocity. This spent missile struck Hernandez in the jaw, shattering it and causing him to bleed profusely.

When you're involved in a gunfight, time seems to pass in slow motion and the action seems to go on forever, even though it is usually over in just a matter of seconds. In the poor light, Cooksey and Little Alfred could make out Hernandez, who, having jettisoned his spewing cans of soda pop, was running for the east side of the store to reload, fighting his heavy bleeding as he did so. He fumbled with the bullets, several of which we found where he stopped, stained with the blood running down his hands. Trying to keep the building between himself and the officers, he moved behind the store. The owners, who lived in a house behind it, had been awakened by the commotion, and came out on their front porch to see what was happening—not something that we recommend for the safety of the public. Hernandez moved again to the west side, still trying to reload, but that was where he fainted from loss of blood. Cooksey and Little Alfred were approaching cautiously, not knowing whether he had been able to reload. It was the neighbors who called to the officers that the guy was down.

Little Alfred and Cooksey disarmed and secured him, and Cooksey radioed ahead to the hospital in Del Rio that they were bringing him down. Hernandez was loaded into a pickup truck for the hundred-mile trip southeast on U.S. 90. Del Rio was a large enough city that the local police could keep a twenty-four-hour guard on him while he was recovering. The severity of the jaw injury was such that after emergency treatment he was transferred to San Antonio, and, oddly, this was the cause of the one casualty in this affair that really grieved me.

Hernandez had extensive surgery to repair his jaw, which was wired shut, and he required a long hospital stay. Cooksey didn't want this SOB escaping again, but he didn't have the manpower to keep a guard in the room all the time, and the San Antonio police department didn't have any men to spare. Cooksey called down to Uvalde, where Levi Duncan, the Ranger whom I had just replaced, was getting bored in his new retirement. Cooksey called Levi and asked whether he would like to do some guard duty on Hernandez, which Levi said he would be happy to do. According to Levi's wife, Pearl (Captain Allee's wife was also named Pearl; we called them the Two Pearls of Company D), Levi was tickled to be back in action again. He took out his favorite gun, an old .45 single-action Long Colt "Frontier Model" with a five-and-a-half-inch barrel, and oiled it down. In his active days he had always carried it between his belt and his shirt, with the loading gate open so it wouldn't slide on down his pant leg—not exactly regulation, but we all carried our arms in the fashion most comfortable to ourselves. Shortly before making the trip to San Antonio to help guard Hernandez, Levi told Pearl that he felt as though he was maybe taking a chest cold, and that he would lie down for a while first. He did, and he died in his sleep, knowing he was continuing his duty to the great state that he had served faithfully for so many years.

When Hernandez was finally fit to leave the hospital, Cooksey transported him over to the Val Verde County Jail, in Del Rio, since his own jail at the little Terrell County seat of Sanderson had only a couple of holding cells and no twenty-four-hour guard. On October 14, 1966, Captain Allee called and had me meet him in Del Rio, where we picked up Hernandez. We took him over to Dryden and met Sheriff Cooksey. We had the handcuffed Hernandez search through some of his old haunts to see whether we could recover any of the items he had stolen over the preceding months. At the end of the day, we needed to deposit him in a secure place; stealing the pot roast off the kitchen table (which he admitted to) was one thing, but his history of shooting law officers mandated continued full vigilance.

Alfredo Hernandez wasn't really Del Rio's problem, so we drove him up to Ozona, which, although it is in neighboring Crockett County, is a hefty, hundred-mile drive. This is wide-open desert and semidesert country with big landforms covering large distances, and it is rugged—well described in Cormac McCarthy's recent novel *No Country for Old Men*. Little Alfred was stationed in Ozona, and the Crockett County sheriff, Billy Mills, was a good friend and the son of a retired Ranger. We spent the night there in Ozona.

The following day, Saturday the fifteenth, we took Hernandez back to the Dryden area to search again for items he had stolen. It doesn't rain often in those parts, but when it does, the storms can be very destructive—in fact, the town of Sanderson was almost completely destroyed in a flash flood in 1965. Storms wash away any possible signs of evidence, and since Hernandez's thefts, there had been some storms. Some of those arroyos might open out a quarter mile across in some places and then narrow down before opening out again, depending on the geology. We had to navigate our way through the rocks and around some huge boulders down in those dry creek beds. During that entire day, all we recovered was a transistor radio that he had stolen from a residence in Dryden, which was a pretty frustrating return on the time invested.

We knew from the theft reports that he had stolen a lot more than chili con carne and soda pop. Some of it undoubtedly he had been able to fence in Mexico, but some of it had to still be in caches out there in the desert. Hernandez said that yes, he thought he could remember where he had hidden some guns and perhaps some electronics, and he would lead us to them the next day. So we went back up to Ozona for the night and resumed on Sunday. The day was hot, especially in those limestone arroyos, which capture heat like reflecting ovens. It was interesting to watch the men interact: Cooksey limping painfully through this incredibly rocky terrain, and Hernandez lisping answers to our questions through his wired-shut jaws. There was not much love lost anywhere around that circle, and Billy Mills was with us also. Hernandez had moved his hideout from an arroyo north of town to another one south of town, from which we were able to recover some stolen goods.

Little Alfred was wearing his Colt single-action with no tie-down, and I noted that Hernandez, whose hands were cuffed in front of him, not behind, had been eyeing that piece with what could only be called hunger. I had suggested to Cooksey that he cuff Hernandez behind his back, but Cooksey said no, he'd be all right; I guess he was thinking that Hernandez would need his hands in front of him to help him scramble through the rocks. As Hernandez led us farther and farther into deserted nowhere, my suspicion increased that he was planning either a grand escape or a macho death. I warned Little Alfred that Hernandez had been watching his gun, and not to let him get close enough to grab it, since, if he did, he was perfectly capable of shooting us and making another escape.

There was indeed a serious lapse of judgment that day, but it wasn't on the part of Hernandez. After we had been out there several hours, Hernandez led us to one of his caves, which proved to be empty. He said something about perhaps being mistaken, or that maybe someone had found his stuff and stolen it. Maybe it was the heat and the fatigue, maybe it was the frustration—and I know his leg hurt—but Bill Cooksey just hauled off and punched Hernandez right in the stomach and brought him to his knees, gasping for breath. Cooksey was a good man and a fine officer, but even the best of us has a breaking point. I said something mild, like, "Come on, Bill. We don't need to be doing that," and the incident passed.

Alfredo Hernandez did go to the pen, and wasn't released to the immigration authorities until March 21, 1984. Later we received information that he had been killed in Mexico (I sort of hope it was over a pot roast). Cooksey in later years applied to enter the Texas Rangers, but he didn't make it. This disappointed Bill tremendously, and I think the man would have made a good Ranger. In 1970 the Rangers hired ten men, and there was talk that a couple of them didn't meet the qualifications, but one of them was not Bill Cooksey. He wrote some letters to inquire why he had been passed over. Sometime after the whole Hernandez episode passed, Captain Allee called me into his office and asked me bluntly why I hadn't told him that Cooksey had struck the prisoner. I was the newest man in D Company, and I sure didn't want the captain mad at me, so I stammered something lame about not thinking it was particularly relevant to my report. Of all the extenuating circumstances you could name for Cooksey's taking a free shot at Hernandez, and there were plenty, I think that Bill was in more pain physically than he would ever admit to from the wound Hernandez had dealt him. The captain got very direct, as only he could, and said, "Any time an incident of this nature occurs, I expect to be told by you and not someone else."

I don't know for sure who told him about it, but I'm pretty certain that it wasn't Alfredo Hernandez. I took two lessons away from this: first, Captain Allee had a razor-keen sense of justice, and second, when it came to the deportment of the Rangers in his company, the very rocks had eyes, and I better never try to cut a corner or let something slide.

If, after reading this chapter, you would like to know more details about the hunt for Alfredo Hernandez, a very good friend and former chief of police in San Angelo, Russell Smith, has written a full book on the subject, which promises to be very good reading, titled *The Gun That Wasn't There.*

CHAPTER 9

Homicides and Questionable Deaths

A WINDOW INTO THE METHOD

In a rural area in South Texas, where the Brush Country joins the Hill Country, there was a trailer house approximately one mile north of a state highway, halfway between two small towns in Uvalde County. In this area were small hills grown over in mesquite, live oak, guajillo, cactus, and other brush. The trailer had a new, wooden-frame master bedroom attached to it, about fourteen by sixteen feet, the entrance facing south.

Inside this wooden-frame bedroom, in early October 1980, a petite woman—five-two, one hundred pounds—stepped out of the shower, wrapped a towel around herself, and looked up to see her sixteen-year-old son holding a .22 rifle. And that was the last time she saw his face, or anything else, because he shot her in the head.

Because he was a juvenile, I couldn't put his real name in my investigative report; this was before the days when a judge could, within his discretion, try a youthful offender as an adult. The son dragged her body out of the room and out of the house, placed her in a wheelbarrow, and pushed it about one hundred yards west of the trailer. He laid her nude body under a big guajillo bush, cut some limbs, and covered her up. Next he went back to the bedroom, sat on the same bed, and waited like a hunter stalking his prey for his stepfather to come home. Eventually the stepfather returned home, came into the room, and, paying no attention to the boy, emptied his pockets onto the top of a television. The boy shot him in the back of the head. He was a big man, well over two hundred pounds. The boy wrapped his body in plastic curtains, dragged it some fifty to seventy-five feet south of the trailer into some heavy undergrowth, took an axe, cut some brush, and stacked it atop the body to conceal it.

On the following Monday, the boy took the family car and went to school. A day or two later he took his stepfather's company truck into town and gave the keys to his stepfather's employer, telling him that his parents had gone on a world cruise and probably wouldn't be back for thirty to sixty days. He claimed he had driven them to the airport in San Antonio to catch the plane. The employer became suspicious because the stepfather had put in for two weeks' vacation in November, and had not notified him of any change. The stepfather was always punctual to work and very regular in his affairs. The employer notified the local deputy sheriff, who went out to the trailer house, couldn't find anyone, and did not locate the bodies. Evidently he stayed upwind of the bodies, because he did not report any smell; from my experience, that's the worst smell there is. The deputy returned to town and interviewed the boy at school. The boy repeated the same story as before, and said that he didn't know when they would be back.

The next weekend, the boy invited some of his school friends to come out to the trailer, and they drank some of his parents' liquor, killed one of their goats, and had a barbecue. One of his friends noticed the foul odor of the decomposing bodies, but the boy explained that he had shot a javelina and dragged it into the brush. The deputy went back out to the trailer and still couldn't find any evidence of foul play, and again left. The boy told his teachers and school principal the same story about the world cruise.

On Sunday, October 19, the stepfather's boss became so suspicious that he himself went out to the trailer, smelled the odor of accumulating decay, returned to town, and called the sheriff's department; they called me. Sheriff Kelly, game warden Raymond Custer, and I determined to meet there. Custer arrived first on the scene and found two rifles, a .22 and a .35 Remington, and had located both bodies by the time I got there. The mother, who was very slight, had mummified, but the stepfather, who was fleshier, was in an advanced state of decomposition. We got information about where the boy was staying; he had gone over to a neighbor's house, which was where we picked him up.

*　　*　　*

The investigation of a crime scene such as this is more meticulous than what might be gleaned from cop shows on television, although the various versions of *CSI* are built around the careful examination of crime scenes and evidence. It is critically important for a crime scene to be protected. I have been called to many such locations where evidence was destroyed by careless officers or the curious public. (For instance, evidence such as tire treads was destroyed by the mob of morbidly curious who flocked to the 1938 Frome murder scene.) The first officer on the site has the job of roping it off until an assigned investigator arrives, and also of locating and interviewing potential witnesses and keeping them at the scene.

When a corpse is located, one path is used to and from the body to avoid trampling the scene. Nothing is moved or even touched until it is photographed, and a particular regimen is followed when taking photographs. Pictures need to depict the body in relation to all 360 degrees of view, both from a distance and closer in. They need to show the body in relation to the surrounding vegetation, and particular care is taken to photograph any plant matter on the corpse, since this can indicate how long it has been in place. Close-up photos are taken of the body to show in detail the clothing worn, and especially to document any wounds, restraint marks, or other evidence. Insect activity, when present, is carefully photographed. Pictures need to document footprints, tire tracks, any discarded objects, such as cigarettes, and any broken or disturbed vegetation. Videotape is now commonly used either in place of or in addition to still photos.

Interior photographs need to take particular note of any blood-spatter patterns, which in the case of the bedroom in this trailer were pretty dramatic. Interpretation of blood spatter has become a more exact science since the mid-1980s, and often an entire sequence of events can be reconstructed from nothing but a blood trail. One trusting West Texas sheriff, while investigating the death of a college professor's wife, was told by her husband that she had slipped in the tub, and he asked permission to clean the area. The sheriff agreed, and once it was figured out that the professor had beaten his wife to death as she bathed, it was too late to preserve that evidence, and the killer was acquitted at trial. Man, I hate that kind of outcome, the result of failing to conduct a proper investigation.

When it comes to evidence collection, different materials are used for different purposes. I often used 35 mm plastic film canisters for retrieving bullets, because they would not be deformed or affected by the container.

I placed only one bullet, wrapped with sterile cotton, in each container; if they rubbed against each other, it could affect the ballistics examination. Decedents' hands are bagged in plain brown-paper sacks, which protect them from further contamination, but won't collect moisture inside as plastic bags would.

It is equally important to protect the chain of custody of evidence. A successful prosecution can depend upon being able to show that no interested party could have tampered with an item. I always liked to have an evidence officer on the case to keep track of such things, since this practice kept me out of court and in the field, where I could do more good. It also gave me the satisfaction of being able to credit a sheriff's department for work well done (when it was well done), since sheriffs face reelection periodically. I only had to face my captain, the victims' relatives, and my own personal pride in the truth.

The fact that the slightly built mother had mummified indicated that she had been deceased in a hot dry climate for at least two weeks. We assumed that the stepfather had met his end at approximately the same time, and his advanced decomposition led us to estimate the same time frame. Within allowances for temperature and humidity, decomposition happens at a standard rate, and there are many different indicators that are used to determine the time of death. For example, a body holds its normal temperature of 98.6 degrees for up to an hour and a half after death. Peripheral blood, when present, dries within half an hour, or up to two hours if there is an extensive amount. If the eyes are open, the corneas become cloudy within two hours; if the eyes are closed, it takes twelve to twenty-four hours. Eyeball collapse indicates death at least a day before. Rigor mortis is dependent upon temperature: with warmth, it may set in as soon as an hour after death, but in cold climates, it may take up to six hours. A body may be in full rigor from six to twenty-four hours after death, and relaxes after twelve to thirty-six hours. Blue-green discoloration of the skin happens at about twenty-four hours; if it is limited to the abdominal region, thirty-six hours. Bloating occurs from thirty-six to forty-eight hours, marbling at two to three days, purging at four to five days, and skin slippage at five to seven days.

Sometimes corpses that have been in place for a while will not be intact. Pack rats and other small animals such as opossums attack the body. The pack rats will take jewelry, small bones, and even bullets to their back burrows. Canines, such as coyotes or wild dogs, will sometimes take off the head and play with it. Finding a corpse with no head may not indicate a decapitation murder; that's why a thorough search of the scene is so important. Most people have the idea that one way to find a human corpse is to look for buzzards circling ominously overhead. In all my years of rural police work, I have never seen buzzards feeding on human corpses, nor seen any sign that they had been. Animal bodies are often streaked with vulture droppings. Moreover, I have talked to cowboys, ranchers, game wardens, and other law-enforcement officers, and every one of them agreed that the only buzzards they have seen rising from a human body were in a western movie.

Insect activity is also a very useful determinant in gauging time of death. Ants, wasps, and flies begin to lay eggs on a body almost from the time of death, but a lack of larval activity indicates that a body is still relatively fresh, since it takes a couple of days for eggs to hatch. Access into the body is usually through the head, wounds, or bodily orifices. The presence of beetles indicates a death seven to eleven days past, and beetles can remain feeding on cartilage for up to two months. In recent years, larvae have even been used to determine toxicology: when they ingest the victim's tissue, the drugs or alcohol or poison are ingested as well.

All the forensic work in the world can't establish a motive (about the only exception to this is the overkill associated with the murder of homosexuals). In this present case, as it turned out, the youth killed his mother and stepfather because they would not let him use the family car on the weekends. He was placed in a juvenile detention center until he turned eighteen; after his release, he went to Indiana to live with his father. I received information later that in 1984 he was involved in a sexual assault and was a suspect in a homicide, but I never heard a final disposition of those matters. Somewhere in our judicial system, something went very wrong; even a layperson would have known he was a ticking time bomb.

In some states, such as New Mexico, pathologists have investigators working for them, and they are the ones called out to examine death scenes. In Texas, this sort of work is still in the jurisdiction of the justices of the peace, many of whom are not trained, although I have seen some of them attending training seminars, which was commendable. Even in the large urban areas, where a medical examiner's van may show up at the death scene, the coroner still represents the JP, who makes the final determination of cause of death.

While attending a homicide seminar a couple of years ago, I was looking at the crime-scene equipment on display, and everything has vastly improved. For instance, in taking the body temperature of a victim, we had to use an anal thermometer, whose accuracy could be thrown off by other variables, such as the indoor and outdoor temperatures that the body had been exposed to. Now they use a laser; it takes in all the variables and gives an exact read-out of the body temperature as well as an estimate of how long the victim has been dead. From day one as a Ranger, I kept a homicide book nearby for reference on various types of death. The standard work today is *Death Investigator's Handbook* by Louis N. Eliopulos, although at eight inches by twelve and three inches thick, only the Jolly Green Giant could use it as a handbook. But it serves its purpose; Eliopulos was a trained pathologist and investigator, and the book is an excellent resource.

*   *   *

During questionable-death investigations, it can sometimes become very challenging to determine whether a homicide or suicide has taken place. Any homicide investigator will tell you that when you are called to a death scene, regardless of the circumstances, you work it as a homicide, even though the initial findings might indicate suicide or natural death. You still have to ask yourself those five basic questions: who, what, where, when, and how. One case in particular comes to mind, involving a justice of the peace in Presidio County, whom I knew as a friend and a good man when I worked with him during his tenure. However, when audit time came for the county, his office was found to be several thousand dollars short of county and state funds.

I was notified of the missing money, and a request was put in for an investigation by the Rangers. I alerted my captain, who was Gene Powell at the time, of my relationship with this JP, and I asked that another Ranger be sent in. This was the normal procedure because of the need to continue working with local officials in the same counties after an investigation, whether they were found guilty or acquitted. To maintain professional working relations afterward, it always was better to have an outside Ranger.

On June 25, 1989, a few days after the audit findings, the judge's wife, concerned because he had not come home as usual, notified one of the deputies that he was missing. Soon after, I was called to a scene at a local shooting range, located a few miles outside of Presidio. The first officer on the scene found the judge's truck parked at the range, and some fifty to a hundred feet north of the truck, out in the middle of the shooting range, was his body, lying face up, a Ruger .22 semiautomatic pistol at his side. The only tracks at the scene were those showing where the deputy sheriff had driven in, and then mine, and I arrived about an hour after he found the body. There were no other tracks around or going to the deceased. His vehicle was the only one there, and because of the mud—it had rained from half an inch to an inch during the afternoon—we certainly would have seen other tracks, human or vehicular, had there been any.

There were four gunshot wounds to the left side of the chest, all of them within an area two inches in diameter. All shots were contact or near-contact wounds. I was judging this from powder burns on the shirt and the "tattoo-ing" of the skin—which is the term for the mark left by powder that is still burning as it enters the body.

The fifty-five-year-old judge was a large, barrel-chested man, about five-nine, and he was a shootist—a term for a good shot who knows how to handle a weapon. He shot competitively both in the United States and against the police in Mexico, and won most of the time. From what I could see, the only way that a murderer could have inflicted four wounds in such a small area would have been to hold him down as he shot, which would have been impossible while struggling with a strong opponent. The principal question involved was whether he had committed suicide. His wife was certain that he had been murdered, but we could find no motive or enemies, and the only entities that he owed money to were the State of Texas and Presidio County.

All the proper forensic tests were run, including the swab test for atomic absorption, which is a modern replacement for the standard old paraffin test for powder residue on the hands. It was negative because a .22 round does not contain the elements barium or antimony, which this procedure tests for. Urine also contains barium, which can lead to a false positive.

Because of their sheer prevalence, .22-caliber weapons were used in most of the homicides and suicides that I worked over the years—in fact, I would say that 70 percent of the firearms used were .22s. If anyone owns a firearm, the chances are it is a .22, and it is no less deadly than bigger guns just be-cause of the lighter caliber, especially if loaded with .22 long-rifle cartridges in hollow point. Even more devastating is the .22 magnum in hollow point, which fragments extensively. One homicide I worked, which was like an Old West shooting, started as a bar fight over the wife of the victim. He discovered her with another man, knocked her out, and started to work over her boyfriend until he fled outside to his pickup truck. The boyfriend got his .22 rifle and aimed it out the passenger-side door toward the bar entrance. When the husband came out after him and got close, lover boy ambushed him and shot him just below the neck with a .22 long solid point. The husband, however, lived long enough to take the rifle away from him and beat him severely about the head with it before staggering off and collapsing on the sidewalk. He died en route to the hospital.

Back to the judge. The ejected casings found near the JP's body were all matched at the lab to the pistol. The projectiles found in the body were so badly damaged that they couldn't be tested. One of the bad things about .22 bullets is they fragment so easily. Most people wouldn't think of a .22 as being suitable for ending one's own life, but the judge, being a shootist, knew that it was a lethal round because the fragmentation causes maximum tissue damage. Of the four bullets in his chest, only one penetrated; the others were deflected by bone. (In fact, there are no guarantees of success when attempting suicide with a gun. I knew of a woman who shot herself in the chest six times with a short-barreled .22 semiautomatic rifle, holding the barrel to her chest with one hand and squeezing the trigger with the other. She lived to tell about it—that's when you know it just ain't your time.) In any event, why use a .22 in the chest if you're going to kill yourself? We determined that he had sold his .45s to try to help pay off the debt from his office. He sold them to his Mexican police friends in Ojinaga (just over the border from Presidio), and he gave his .38 snub-nosed to his wife—which left him only the .22 Ruger.

Lab results showed that the pistol had been in contact with the victim's shirt, which was another indication of the wound being self-inflicted. Every piece of evidence pointed to suicide, but the unusual manner of it has left his widow, to this day, convinced that this was not the case.

*　*　*

One of the weirdest questionable deaths I ever worked, in October 1989, turned out to be a suicide, but required lots of follow-up legwork. The victim came from Phoenix, had spent time around Alpine in his youth, and loved the country. He drove south of Alpine on Highway 118 about thirty-three miles, to a small roadside park. The pull-off is on a hill with a great view of a large mountain, Santiago Peak, which seems to have a supernatural draw on some people, one of whom I wrote about in *One Ranger*. In the early years there was some kind of gunfight there between Rangers and Mexican bandits; one of the latter's casualties was named Santiago. Perhaps it is his ghost that summons people to their doom—I don't know, but it is a spooky ole mountain. But this guy drove several hundred miles to view this peak and then shoot himself dead. His name was Harold Raymond Cooley, and apparently he had attempted suicide a couple of times before in Arizona.

He used a .44 Magnum called a Bulldog, a snub-nosed revolver, turned the gun upside down, held it behind his head, and pulled the trigger, trying to make it look like a homicide. He had thrown his billfold into the bar ditch with his identification and credit cards inside. There was no cash, but several dollars were found above the sun visor on the driver's side of the windshield.

Little Alfred Allee (a former Ranger and son of Captain A. Y. Allee—we called him Little Alfred), who was deputy sheriff in Brewster County at the time, assisted me in the investigation. We learned that Cooley had just lost his job in Phoenix and was destitute. I took off to Phoenix to follow up, and an old-time Phoenix detective went over my report and photos and said, "Ranger, that's a clear-cut suicide." Sure enough, the swab test for atomic absorption (which, as mentioned, is ineffective on a .22, but works great on a .44 Magnum revolver) came back positive on both of Cooley's hands, indicating that he had used both hands to hold the gun behind his head.

He didn't have any insurance, so there was no question of trying to collect a multiple indemnity. Most likely he wanted to make his relatives feel sorry for him for getting murdered. But for the record, Santiago Peak claimed another victim.

Since I retired, there has been great improvement in forensic methods, such as DNA analysis, which was just coming in a few years before my leaving the Rangers, but was not as good then as now. Most state police labs can process DNA evidence, for instance, whereas in my day there were only two or three places in the whole United States that could do DNA testing. Even then we were standing in line to receive results, which might take several months or a year. These and other advances would have given some of my caseload open-and-closed results, and I wouldn't have logged so many miles with unanswered questions in my mind.

best for growing spinach, and while some of the increasing number of truck farms diversified into tomatoes, carrots, and peppers, Crystal City began to tout itself as the "Spinach Capital of the World." A vegetable cannery was built in 1932, the first annual Spinach Festival took place four years later, and in 1937 a statue was erected across from the city hall, honoring that most famous American consumer of spinach, Popeye the Sailor Man. The town's population reached its high point, just over nine thousand, in 1960, and then entered a long decline that continues to the present day.

Beneath the prosperity that began to grow on this vegetable-based economy, however, serious social tensions developed. It was Anglo investment money that had bought the Cross S Ranch, dug the wells, and developed the town, but as the farms grew and multiplied, it was Mexican, and Mexican American, sweat that produced the onions and the spinach and the rest. Control of the city and county governments and the school board remained unshakably in white hands until the Latinos organized and, protected by Texas Rangers, democratically took control of the county in 1963. In fact, a labor action among the farmworkers in Zavala County in the seventies mirrored somewhat *la Huelga* in Rio Grande City a few years earlier. Rangers found that the strikers were doing nothing illegal and let them go about their business.

But Anglos in Crystal City were used to their status and privileges, and in 1923, John Webster Flanagan was born into this world. He never held a valid Texas driver's license. He was always internally directed; anything he didn't think was right, or necessary, or anybody else's business, he dispensed with without a turn of conscience. He was moderately sized, less than six feet tall and maybe 175 pounds, with a fair complexion, looking as Irish as anyone named Flanagan should look. He didn't start off bad; in fact, he made Eagle Scout in Troop 96 in 1939, but sometime after he went to college and law school, he came to exemplify just how low a life-form an attorney can become. That is not to disparage the legal profession; I have worked with many fine attorneys whose regard for the law equaled my own, but because the residents, and make off with their valuables. These victims came to no physical harm, which was fortunate for them, since some of the guys who ran with James were quite capable of reenacting that massacre from Truman Capote's *In Cold Blood*. (James in fact spent five months on the FBI's Ten Most Wanted list before he was apprehended in January 1968.) Flanagan's contact with such people got him skating closer and closer to the edge of the law until he finally slid off and got disbarred. After this, he returned to Crystal City, where he had started. He was far from down-and-out, however, and rented one of the finest houses in the town. (There were plenty available; after La Raza gained control of local politics, there was a mass exodus of Anglos.) From this outpost, Flanagan continued his association with a veritable who's who of the Dixie Mafia in Austin, supplying them with home-flown dope.

*   *   *

On Tuesday, September 23, 1975, I received a telephone call from a rancher near Crystal City, asking me to come down because he had found an airplane on his ranch, covered up with black plastic and hidden in the brush. When I got there, he led me down a lengthy private road, more of a sendero really, a path through the brush, to what proved to be a low-wing single-engine Cessna. The plane had been landed on this sendero, a maneuver that required a really good brush pilot who knew what the hell he was doing. (Brush pilots are more properly referred to as bush pilots, but most people associate that term with Alaska, and this was the Brush Country, after all, so they're brush pilots to me.)

It didn't take a rocket scientist to know that such an aircraft in this location and these circumstances could only have been about one business, and that was drugs. We didn't touch it or disturb it in any way, lest we tip off the smugglers who had been flying it that they had been discovered. I called in the narcotics division of the DPS and alerted the federal Drug Enforcement Administration and U.S. Customs. We shortly discovered that the plane had been reported stolen in Austin about six weeks before. When the DEA agents got to the scene, they looked into the plane and discovered that the passenger seat had been replaced with a bladder tank—an extra fuel tank—and saw other modifications for running drugs. After they planted an electronic bug in the tail of the plane, we set up a stakeout. We kept the aircraft under surveillance from that day until Sunday, September 28.

Sitting concealed in the brush for hours on end gets mighty boring. Plus,

Stolen aircraft covered with black plastic, in brush near Crystal City, 1975.

Joaquin processing a stolen aircraft in a ranch pasture near Crystal City, 1975.

in South Texas when you move even a little, you get stuck in the leg, butt, arms, and any other body part with some kind of thorn. God only knows how many of them, of all different shapes, sizes, and poison content, are lying out there to entrap anything that dares to move amongst them. And of course, water is needed—which I always had plenty of. We carried C rations, and my military contacts were always ready to lend me extras, and I must say they had rather evil smirks on their faces when they passed these nasty things over to me. Army field rations are now called MREs—meals ready to eat—and they are some improvement over the old C rations. A bedroll is necessary, and with a partner near, you take turns sleeping. If you need nicotine, chewing tobacco has to be used instead of cigarettes or cigars, since the light, smoke, and odor could lead to your being found out.

I don't know why the drug runners didn't return for their plane. Either they were through with it, which would explain the lack of camouflage but not why they had taken the trouble to cover it, or we had been detected somewhere during our comings and goings, which is what I suspect happened. After we were able to tie the plane to Flanagan, it occurred to me that he had a brother living in the area, but he had always been a law-abiding citizen with no tie to any illegal activities. As wily as John Webster was, though, it wouldn't surprise me if he had made us from the day we hid out.

We abandoned that surveillance when we got a call that a small push-pull airplane (one with both forward- and rear-mounted propellers) had alighted on a farm-to-market road west of Crystal City and dropped a large shipment of bundled marijuana into the bar ditch before taking off again and flying on, rather brazenly, to the Crystal City Airport. The occupants of the plane were believed to be Flanagan and his son.

We sped to the Crystal City Airport but missed our quarry. The Customs Service seized his little push-pull airplane, though, and two or three others that he had been using. Further details revealed that the drug drop had been some 300 kilos (around 660 pounds) of marijuana, left on the road eight miles northwest of Crystal City. At that time it was worth about seventeen thousand dollars; today it would be much more.

The following Monday, I went back to process the stolen plane for latent fingerprints, and I was able to lift Flanagan's thumbprint off the yoke, which tied him to the theft of the plane, so I had hopes that we would finally be able to shut this slick bastard down.

Based on the evidence we had gathered so far, we obtained a search warrant for Flanagan's house in Crystal City and also an arrest warrant. By now he knew that we were on to him, and when we got to the house, we discovered that he and his cohorts had fled. We did recover stolen material from the house, though—guns, some office machines, and even a couple of motorboats. (Flanagan used the boats as a kind of currency, trading them for drugs in Mexico.) On Saturday, October 4, we raced up to Austin and executed a further warrant on his house there, but the only thing of interest we found, aside from an M1 Garand rifle, which we seized, was a Texas Ranger badge, which I also impounded. I don't know where he could have acquired it, maybe at some antiques and collectibles show, but I personally found it pretty damned insulting that he should have one. Another of Flanagan's sons was living there, not his reported copilot on some of the dope runs. This boy was apparently not involved in his father's shenanigans.

The following Tuesday I testified to the grand jury in Crystal City, and we got indictments on Flanagan for both the drugs and the thefts. We were prepared to arrest him in Austin, but once again he eluded us, made his way to Mexico using his previous contact, and began life as a fugitive. Not that there was any great deprivation for him associated with that—maybe the term "well-heeled fugitive" would be more appropriate: poolside parties, lots of "interesting guests," music, food, liquor, massages, saunas, and lots of expertise in providing good service to rich gringos—all with no questions asked. Life in Mexico on the lam from U.S. justice was probably very comfortable for him as long as he was in good with the local cartel, which I'm sure he was. He certainly flew enough dope out of there, and continued to do so for some years, just beyond our reach.

Then one day I got a call from a rancher about ten miles northwest of Crystal City: a plane had crash-landed on his place. That is really rough, lonely country up there near the Maverick County line, thick brush and a series of rocky rises separating a whole spiderweb of seasonal creeks. We got out there and discovered an abandoned low-wing single-engine plane that had belly flopped on top of this low rocky hill, a larger plane than the one we had previously seized. This was also a stolen aircraft, and it also had a bladder tank for extra gasoline where the passenger seat would have been. Lying beside the plane were industrial rollers, the kind you see on a loading dock for moving really heavy bundles. The compartment door on the left side of the plane was open; of all the odors associated with airplanes—gasoline, engine oil—and in the middle of all this aromatic brush of sage and greasewood, what hit us in the face when we entered the plane was the pungent smell of marijuana. We found maybe a couple of joints' worth of weed spilled onto the floor.

Concealed in an arroyo maybe a hundred yards from the plane was a stash of quick-opening military parachutes, the kind used to drop supplies from low altitude to troops in hot zones. Not as large as the parachutes people jump with, they are rigged to deploy as soon as the cargo is discharged and are snapped open by the plane's prop wash, so material can be safely jettisoned only a few hundred feet above the ground. And in this plane, the whole apparatus was operated by a nylon rope that extended up to the pilot, so that all he had to do to unload his dope was bank the plane steeply and pull on the rope. The bundles of marijuana would roll toward the door until they fell out, then the chutes would open and they would float to the ground. It was ingenious; the capacity of the plane was perhaps four or five two-hundred-pound bales. The irony was that this pilot had run out of gas only two or three miles short of a clandestine landing strip that was operated by some guys he had ties to. Having crash-landed, he removed the marijuana, concealed the attached chutes in the arroyo, and made off with the dope.

It didn't take long to get information from a couple of people in Crystal City that they had seen Flanagan in town shortly after the plane would have crashed. One of them saw him making a call on a pay telephone and observed that Flanagan had a cut on his head. Probably he had not had an opportunity to release his cargo where he needed it before running out of fuel; the rollers were outside the plane, as though they had been used to reload the bales onto another conveyance. The likelihood was that he had crash-landed with the dope on board, then walked into town and telephoned one of his people for assistance. In either case, the grass was gone by the time we got there, since the rancher had not discovered the wrecked aircraft for several days after the crash.

We quickly had a line that Flanagan was involved. I processed the crashed aircraft for latent fingerprints, but all I got was smudges and glove marks. This almost made me smile: I had heard that after losing that first plane, Flanagan had said he would never fly a plane again without wearing gloves. Good, I thought; anything that causes a criminal to take notice and is an inconvenience makes my day. And looking around the scene, I realized that there were not many brush pilots who had the skill to fluff a plane down on this rocky hilltop and walk away with only a bump on the head.

Eventually, like most criminals, he slipped up, and we got our hands on him. We had prepared four or five good, solid state cases against him. But then there occurred one of those incidents that can really ruin your day and make you question why the hell you try to enforce the law. We got Flanagan arraigned on theft of the first aircraft and the equipment, plus the dope—it was enough to put him away until he got too old to stay in business. But then, the United States Attorney called the district attorney in Uvalde and asked us to drop the state charges and let the feds have him. The DA asked me about it, and I said that as long as he got a good sentence out of it, I didn't particularly care, since I wasn't crazy about having to take time out of the field to go to court and testify. As it turned out, Flanagan used some of those law school horse-trading skills to cut a plea bargain with the feds, and he got something like five to eight years on federal charges. But then it got even better: we heard that he had escaped federal custody. The story was that he had been standing in the receiving line at the federal pen in Florida—and he just walked off. So the feds claimed. You've got to be kidding me!

Now, even allowing for federal incompetence often and amply demonstrated, that simply doesn't happen. I worked for the U.S. Marshals Service for a while, and they deliver prisoners cuffed and chained. I believe to this day that they let him take a hike so they could use him as a snitch. I worked with a number of DEA personnel over the years, and I could never get one of them to admit to me exactly what had gone on with Flanagan's "escape." But then the DEA can be almost as high and mighty as the FBI about what information it will share with lowly state police officers, even when they wear white cowboy hats. I doubt that it got much useful information out of Flanagan, though, since we got a call later that he was back living in Mexico, playing both ends against the middle.

It does seem possible that the feds got tired of playing games with him, because Flanagan eventually graduated from marijuana to cocaine, and when he got caught flying some into Kansas somewhere in about 1986, he was sentenced to ten to fifteen years. Despite the vigorous exercise of his litigious skills, none of his appeals were heard by the courts. He also filed on me in federal court to get back that Texas Ranger badge I had seized from his Austin house. I had to tell him the truth, that I had taken that badge out to the dam on the Nueces River near Crystal City, and if he wanted to dive into twenty or thirty feet of water to recover it, he could keep it. I did still have the guns seized from the houses in Austin and Crystal City, and since they could not be tied to any crime and were apparently acquired legally, I had to return them. That was a very strange feeling, handing over firearms to a character like that—at least I delivered them to his attorney and not to Flanagan personally—but that is a Ranger's job, to serve the law, and sometimes you just have to hope that you're serving justice along with it.

The best thing I can say about Flanagan is that he was maybe the best brush pilot I ever knew or heard of. Eventually he finished paying his debt to society and returned to Crystal City a free man. The last I heard of him, he was living on a farm near town, and his one remaining ambition, he claimed, was to run a small airport.

That's just what we need. Talk about the fox managing the henhouse.

CHAPTER 11

The Fall of the Champ

When I became a Ranger, one of the first things Captain Allee told me was that statutes were on the books to outlaw offenses against the peace and dignity of the state of Texas, but the people in the community would back us up only on laws that they agreed with. Gambling and prostitution were two areas of law where a lot of people thought that the state had no business sticking its nose, and I discovered on my own that the Captain was, as usual, right about that. Today, of course, the state still looks down its nose at prostitution—it's legal only in certain counties in Nevada—but many forms of gambling have become almost a spectator sport. Poker games are all over television; betting on horse races is widely legal; casinos support Indian tribes that otherwise would be stuck in poverty; and the Texas lottery has contributed billions to the state school fund, though some school personnel would question this amount. Forty years ago Texas and the rest of the country were more prudish.

Much of what I have written about up to now has concerned events in my home county of Uvalde, or Real County to the north, or Zavala County to the south. The following events took place to the east, in Medina County, which separates Uvalde from San Antonio and Bexar County. Like Uvalde, it sits on the border between the Brush Country and the Hill Country, and its northern parts contain some of the most spectacular scenery along the southern escarpment. Near the center is the county seat, the ranching community of Hondo, which at that time had a population of about five thousand.

On October 23, 1968, I received a telephone call from Medina County sheriff Charles Hitzfelder, an old-time lawman who bore a grand old German name and who liked to run, as they used to say in the westerns, a nice, clean town—which is a polite way of saying he could be pretty controlling of people. The citizens must not have minded, because they elected him to several terms as sheriff. He was an experienced officer; in fact, he had FBI training, which he passed on to his deputies. He was so honest that according to Alvin Santleben, a deputy who later succeeded him as sheriff, he used to tell them, "Don't take a penny. That way, if somebody accuses you of taking it, you can look them in the eye and call them a damn liar." I liked Charlie, and he needed my help with a homicide that had some puzzling aspects. The deceased was one Henry C. "Champ" Carter, whose body had been discovered two days earlier, having lain, decomposing, beside his private road on Medina Lake for perhaps a week.

The location alone told me this was going to be an interesting ride. Medina Lake, in the northeastern part of the county, near Bandera County, was a playground where San Antonio's rich and popular maintained weekend houses, but like the whole history of Medina Lake, many of them partied on inflated expectations and make-believe. The area's first settlers were a colony of Alsatians—Hitzfelder's stock—led by a pioneer named Henri Castro, who founded the town of Castroville, on the Medina River, in 1844. About fifteen miles upstream from the town, they noted a great bowl in the hills, a box canyon, and it became a popular hunting spot. Being German, they were always looking for ways to master the landscape, and early on they conceived of damming the entrance to the box canyon. Aware of the terrifying floods that periodically roar down the Medina valley, they believed a dam would harness the river and provide irrigation for thousands and thousands of acres of farmland.

Capital was scarce, however, and not until 1910 did an internationally known engineer, Fred Stark Pearson, convince some British investors to back the dam. Its waters, he said, would irrigate 150,000 acres of rich land, and farmers who leased the land and bought the water would pay a handsome return on the investment. Fifteen hundred laborers, the majority of them Mexicans who had worked on Pearson's projects in Mexico, took two years to pour nearly three hundred thousand cubic yards of concrete. At the time, it was the fourth-largest dam in the United States, 1,580 feet long and 164 feet high, and the largest irrigation project west of the Mississippi. Its lake is eighteen miles long and up to three miles wide, covering at spillway level over 5,500 acres. Then the trouble started.

It became apparent that the engineers, having been awed by the volume of water carried by the Medina River during its floods, had grossly overestimated the normal flow. The gravity-powered canals would not irrigate 150,000 acres—more like 35,000, if the lake would ever fill. But it sat there nearly empty year after year, without a flood to top it off. Then World War I came and shut off further investment from Great Britain. In 1915, Pearson saw the need to travel to England and encourage investors; sadly for him, he and his wife sailed aboard the *Lusitania*, so that was the end of them. (The sinking of the ship by a German U-boat was one of the events that led to the United States' entry into World War I.) Subsequently the company went into receivership.

With its irrigation potential scaled back into reason, Medina Lake began to be marketed as a recreational paradise. In the twenties, advertisements touted automobile excursions to the area to inspect that marvelous dam and the property for sale. The boosters conveniently forgot to tell people that it had taken seven years for the lake to fill up. They also neglected to tell people that because of the way the land had been acquired and because of the irrigation contracts that had been signed, these new property owners had no guarantee that there would actually be water in the lake at any given time. During dry spells, Medina Lake looked about as pathetic, and was about as much fun, as a nearly empty bathtub.

But when the lake was full it was a paradise. Land was bought and weekend getaway homes were built, and Medina Lake evolved into a kind of secluded haven where San Antonio's well-to-do could retreat and indulge in some of those victimless crimes that drove the morality monitors—the local police and county sheriffs—crazy. This was Champ Carter's world, and his place in it was to cater to those needs.

He was not a violent man—in fact, he was never known to carry a weapon—never got into fights, and never risked getting into situations that could get out of hand—although he often consorted with violent men. But Carter was also a pimp, with a large stable of girls working for him, and a gambler, into dice, three-card monte, and other games. He leased a large house on Medina Lake that the locals called The Castle; he intended to turn it into a casino with ladies of the night working there, just across the line from the San Antonio Police Department's and Bexar County sheriff's jurisdictions. In its architecture, the house did resemble a castle, and Carter set to filling it with expensive furniture and gaming equipment. It was on the east side of the lake, which was convenient to San Antonio, but it was shrewdly located where prying eyes could not see in. To get there, we turned off a paved road, drove along a dirt road for a distance, and then turned off again onto a long, narrow one-way trail along a barbed-wire fence line.

The body was found by a neighbor named Schott, whose property shared the fence line. Carter was lying on his back along the fence, and his car, a fancy new Thunderbird, was abandoned in the brush off from the track. Having suffered some kind of massive trauma and having been dead for about ten days, he was a mess. We did a meticulous crime-scene investigation to recover any evidence that could be found—which wasn't much. Then we released the body to a funeral home, which took it to the renowned longtime pathologist in San Antonio, Dr. Vincent de Mayo. He gave us the cause of death as a shotgun blast, loaded with buckshot, to the face and chest.

Starting the investigation, I worked with a DPS officer in San Antonio who was a friend of mine and an ace criminal-intelligence investigator, Vince Ramirez. We brought the San Antonio Police Department into it, since it had had a long relationship, as it were, with Champ Carter. The SAPD man we worked with was Detective John Smith, a top hand at his job. Almost immediately, we interviewed a woman named Lillian Mahavier who said that yes, she was with Carter on October 13, which was the date on which we surmised he had been killed, and she gave us the names of those she said were his murderers. She was given a polygraph at the San Antonio Police Department, which she failed (with no trouble at all), but in the absence of any better information, I followed up for months on the leads she provided us. We should have believed the polygraph; none of her leads went anywhere. This cautioned us that some of Champ Carter's friends had enemies who would make up stories about them. Lillian hung around bars and knew a number of these characters, but as far as we could determine, she wasn't working for any of them. So why she threw me a red herring, I couldn't say, unless it was just for her personal amusement. If it was, I sure as hell hope she enjoyed it. I didn't.

I had my own list of some of Carter's less savory associates whom I wanted to question, and ran down that roster. At eleven thirty one day I interviewed a

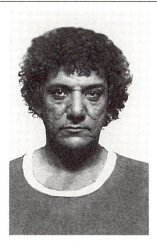

Bunny Eckert, 1970s.

gambler named Fernando Fernandez, who, according to my information, had procured girls for Carter's establishment in the past and was involved in the new operation at The Castle. I failed to hear anything likely from Fernandez, and then at one I sat down with one of Champ's fellow pimp-gamblers, a lowlife named Bunny Eckert. He was about six feet or a little taller, with a ruddy complexion, and weighed roughly 190 pounds. At the time, he was in his late thirties and was the kingpin of San Antonio gambling—three-card monte, crooked dice, and the like.

That was a name I remembered, and not just because you don't hear of many men being named "Bunny." I had some previous history with him. Ever since pioneer days, Uvalde had had a little fly-by-night seasonal horse track out at the fairgrounds, and events were held maybe two Sundays a month during the summer. On those Sundays when I wasn't called away from my family to stop a dogfight or a cockfight, I often had to go out to the fairgrounds and make sure no one was organizing any betting. Of course, you can't stop people from making wagers with each other, but this was before the days of legal parimutuel betting, and I was supposed to keep a presence out there and keep a lid on anything that looked illegal. About six months before the Champ Carter killing, Vance Chisum and I were out at the fairgrounds, and we stopped this seedy-looking character with a couple of henchmen following him around, and there was a female with them.

I knew it was pretty common for underworld types who couldn't afford to be caught with a gun to deposit it in their girlfriend's purse, and, sure enough,

I discovered a 9mm automatic in this woman's handbag. She claimed that it wasn't hers and that she didn't know how it got there. Eckert denied any knowledge of it, as did his two cronies. So I said to Eckert, "Well, I guess it must belong to the chief of police," and we confiscated the pistol. Chisum took it down to the Uvalde Police Department property room, and I marked Bunny Eckert as a man who was capable of violence, which was a good thing to remember for future contacts with him and his henchmen. I wanted to make sure I dealt the winning hand.

DEA agent Jerry Rice and other agents raided Eckert's place in San Antonio and found his briefcase full of crooked dice. Some of the dice were missing certain numbers and some were loaded, ensuring that Bunny would win more than he would lose. Rice turned the dice over to me, since he knew I had him under investigation. Eckert sicced his lawyer on me to get them back, but the legal office at DPS advised me that I didn't have to return them. After finishing with Eckert, Vince Ramirez and I went back out to The Castle and worked the premises. We discovered drug paraphernalia stored in the garage, so unless it had been for his personal use, the Champ seemed to have graduated from gambling and girls to dope—which would have introduced a whole new array of persons and circumstances that could have cost him his life. He was stacking the deck pretty bad against himself.

On about October 30, we received information that a woman who had once been Carter's favorite girl, his "old lady," as they call them in the underworld, his combination girlfriend and most productive employee, was serving time in a state penitentiary in Florence, Arizona, southeast of Phoenix. Her name was Jean Ann Peoples; she was also the daughter of Lillian Mahavier, who had sent me on one wild-goose chase already, so I was guarded whether to believe anything she might say. A carload of us drove out to interview her—me, Chief Deputy Ralph Chancey, and Chris Christianson of the Bexar County district attorney's office. We were seeking background on Carter's activities and on who might have had a motive to kill him, and for two hours she was very cooperative. She seconded what we already knew about his being a peaceable and nonviolent person, and she gave us a long list of names of his past associates, but no direct information that might lead us to his killer.

Once Jean Ann Peoples started talking, she figured if she was in for a dime, she'd go in for a dollar. Jean Ann said that Carter had developed ties to the syndicate in Chicago—which would explain the narcotics gear in his garage—and she volunteered information on the disappearance of a prostitute three years earlier. She said that Bunny Eckert had killed her, and she gave us directions to where she was buried. These accusations did not pan out, but I damn sure did recognize Eckert's name when it surfaced again. As I said earlier, not many male human "bunnies" were running around my work area. I would have liked to pin something on this rabbit, but there just wasn't any case to be made.

★   ★   ★

On November 7, Trooper Jim Fields, who worked the San Antonio area and was a good friend of mine (and later became maybe one of the best pilots DPS ever had), developed a lead on a woman who claimed she and another girl had been with Carter and another local gambler and San Antonio bar owner on the night of October 11. This also turned into a blind alley, except for letting us know that Carter was alive on that date, and we soon developed other witnesses who had seen him alive on the twelfth.

Champ Carter may not have been a violent man, but he certainly had no problem in running with those who were, and by now we had an extensive list of characters from the unsavory side of town, men who had convictions for armed robbery, burglary, safecracking—a whole cop show full of the San Antonio underworld, plus a roster of tough women, hookers, and strippers. If it's true that hell has no fury like a woman scorned, and I think the writer was talking about a normal, decent woman, God help you if you get one of these gangster molls pissed at you.

The following spring, in May 1969, Lieutenant Dave Keene of the SAPD developed a lead that a lady by the name of Jeannie Piper had been a witness to the murder and had given an oral statement to that effect. Piper had now relocated to New Orleans. At the time of the killing, she had been Bunny Eckert's woman for a short time, but also living with them were two more underworld types, named Arnold McCoy and Donald Wiemer. Just what all was shared in this happy household was not an image that I wanted in my head. At that time, the inspector of detectives was a fine officer named Hutton, and I went in on Tuesday, May 7, to gather information from him on where in the New Orleans area Jeannie Piper could be located. From what I learned, if she had fled Texas for safety, she jumped from the frying pan into the fire, since she was living with a capo in the Marcello crime family. (Carlos Marcello was the longtime New Orleans don who was implicated, in some minds, in the assassination of President Kennedy.) There was nothing else to do but make the long drive to New Orleans, find out where she might be in the Big Easy, and then try to get an honest interview from her. Honesty in the criminal world is not a virtue.

At the New Orleans Police Department, I worked with Detective Peter Hand, who set me up with the Jefferson Parish Sheriff's Department, where I met up with Detective Clarence Schaltz. We located Jeannie Piper on the morning of May 28, living in a trailer park. Although she and Eckert had supposedly been steady for a couple of years, she was not the woman I remembered seeing with him back in Uvalde at the fairgrounds. Piper was a beautiful—in fact, she was dazzling—brunette, calm and self-possessed. Our interview with her was surprisingly simple. With all the trouble we had had finding her, I figured it was going to be a "push-pull" situation. We knocked on the door of her trailer and she answered. I told her that we had information she'd witnessed Champ Carter's murder. She was a bit slow to answer and looked very apprehensive, so I quickly added that she had the choice of being either a witness for the prosecution or a defendant. She said, well, that's a choice that's not hard to make, and then admitted she had been present.

On the night in question, she had gone out to The Castle in a pickup truck with Bunny Eckert and Arnold McCoy, intending to break into The Castle and burglarize it. Their intention wasn't to seriously cripple his business, but since Champ Carter was competing in their field of enterprise, it was just more or less a nuisance visit to mess with him and maybe delay his opening a bit. Jeannie Piper's part in the burglary was to be the "jeeper," the lookout who would alert them if anyone came up the long dirt track toward the house. Having broken into the house, they proceeded to steal some furniture, including a marble-topped table.

Jeannie said this was all she wanted to say at this point, but she agreed to come down to the Jefferson Parish Sheriff's Office at two and give a statement. She failed to show. I wouldn't have known where to begin looking for her, but Detective Schaltz was very familiar with the Marcello hangouts, and in his company we visited a string of bars, pleasantly inviting ourselves into the back rooms and offices where law-enforcement representation, not to mention a six-five Texas Ranger, was not particularly welcome. This was the Sicilian Mafia we were dealing with, and I really felt as though I had moved up to the big leagues. Local outlaws in Uvalde, and even union enforcers like Magdaleno Dimas, were small-timers compared with these people, whose don was the top dog for the Mafia in much of the South. We raised enough of a ruckus among the Marcello crowd that they undoubtedly told her to take care of her issue with us and keep us the hell away from them. She called at one the next day to give us her location. She said her attorney had told her to make a statement if the DA would grant her immunity, and she would come in where we wanted if we'd just stop looking for her. I said, "We already told you where to go—the Jefferson Parish Sheriff's Office." I wasn't really happy having to chase her all over town. The immunity was arranged, and at six thirty that evening we took her statement, which we worked on for about three hours.

According to Jeannie Piper, Eckert and McCoy finished loading the stolen goods into the back of their pickup and headed down the fence-line track. Eckert was driving, McCoy sat by the passenger door, and she was between them. It was getting pretty late, perhaps eleven, when they saw Champ driving up the other way in his new Thunderbird. Carter pulled off the one-lane drive, toward the pasture and away from the fence line, stopped his car, opened the door, and stood between the door and the body of the car. Then, out of the blue and without any warning, McCoy threw open the passenger door of the pickup, leveled the twelve-gauge double-barreled shotgun at Carter, and blew him away. McCoy and Eckert then rolled Carter's body up against the fence to clear the road, then moved the Thunderbird out of the road and into the brush so they could get by. The murder made it impossible to keep the marble-topped table or other furniture, so it was dumped—she didn't recall where. She did say they then went to Mexico, and Eckert married her to prevent her from possibly testifying against him.

I got back home on the 30th and gave testimony to the grand jury in Hondo on June 2. Indictments were returned against Bunny Eckert and two others, Earl Hunter and Donald Wiemer, the latter known to be a close associate of Eckert's. There was no need to seek an indictment of Arnold McCoy, since he was already dead, shot in the head with a .45 in a bar in Austin. (So again goes the old saying "Live by the gun . . .")

Eckert was arrested in San Antonio and returned to Hondo; Hunter was arrested in Temple on the 6th, and I went up to fetch him. His name had actually surfaced during the second day of the investigation, but he now stoutly claimed that he had had nothing whatsoever to do with the killing and wanted to take a polygraph test; eventually he was cleared. Wiemer was similarly ruled out of the case after his indictment, although he did admit to going out to the murder scene and cleaning it up on October 14. At least we finally learned for certain that it had happened on the thirteenth. He had removed two shotgun shells from the scene and obliterated footprints, but he refused to give a written statement. The circumstance of McCoy's death did not indicate that it had any connection to the Champ Carter murder; he seemed merely to have finally run up against someone meaner than he was. But the upshot of it was that now the only one left under indictment to answer for Champ Carter's murder was Eckert. We tried to interview him on June 10, but he had nothing to say, and that was certainly no surprise to anyone.

We never recovered the shells or the gun, but according to Wiemer, the murder weapon was a double-barreled side-by-side twelve-gauge shotgun, and Arnold McCoy was the actual shooter. Wiemer's statement backed up Jeannie Piper's in all the other important respects, but he had not been present at the killing and only knew what they had told him before sending him out to clean up the scene.

After I and numerous other officers spent six months investigating this case, Bunny Eckert was never brought to trial. While it was true we didn't have a murder weapon, and it may have been true that Eckert took Jeannie Piper to Mexico and married her to keep her from testifying against him, murder cases in Texas have been made with less than that. I have always suspected that some of Champ Carter's more powerful connections intervened to make the case just "go away" rather than have his sordid life, and their ties to him, bandied about in open court. The whole mystery was certified several years later with the disappearance of Eckert himself. He had been living in San Antonio with his mother when their home was broken into, his mother was brutally murdered, and Eckert and his truck wound up missing. Searches were fruitless; police divers combing area lakes found nothing. To this day, Bunny Eckert and his pickup have never been found.

I am pretty sure that law officers in the San Antonio area and myself know who got Bunny, but we can't prove it. The guy was an archenemy of Eckert and an ex-con as well as a professional hit man. I think he got him hanging around the Pearsall area, southwest of San Antonio, where the country is sandy loam. The killer was raised in the area, knew all the people, and could have had access to a ranch or smaller property where they could have buried Bunny in his truck.

Today when I visit San Antonio, I like to enjoy its history—the Alamo and the cathedral, the River Walk and the King William District. I try not to think about the city's seamier side, and those who pander to its vices. But I know they are there, that a younger cast is now playing the same roles, and with even greater violence than Champ Carter and Bunny Eckert did. If you break off the veneer of the society, you will find them, busy as termites. They stay busy because vice is as old as mankind, and the demand for illicit pleasure has not diminished. But, thankfully, that is someone else's fight now.

The one person who came out well from this whole story was Jeannie Piper, who later married an honest, hardworking man, settled down to a respectable life in Del Rio, and stayed happily married for twenty-five years. She telephoned me a couple of years ago to say hello and express her appreciation for my conduct in the investigation. That was a complete surprise and really nice to hear. I had no idea that six weeks later her husband would call to say that Jeannie had passed away. The best I can recall, he said it was from a heart attack. She was the one who broke the Champ Carter murder case, and I was glad that she escaped that life and found some happiness. Jeannie took the difficult steps to make a better life for herself, and she deserved it.

CHAPTER 12

The Valadez Kid

Back in frontier days, the West was a place where social misfits, juvenile delinquents, and the marginally crazy could disappear and live their lives less restricted by social convention. A lot of times it was to their advantage to forget their old identities, and they were known by their nicknames, such as Billy the Kid. (A lot of people are unaware he started off in New York City.) Many of these desperadoes were very young—Billy himself was charged with a dozen murders before he turned eighteen, and he was only twenty-two when Sheriff Pat Garrett gunned him down in New Mexico. Today, of course, humankind still produces delinquents and misfits, but there is no longer a West to disappear into, or perhaps run amok in, and society has to take steps to protect itself. But now as then, those of us who have the job of upholding the law and catching lawbreakers are left struck by the fact that, now as then, a lot of them are just kids, in their minds even if not physically, mentally impaired but short of barking insanity.

The conditions in the Old West also made it easier for incompetent fools or petty autocrats to become lawmen, and I wish I could say that those days have passed, but just as those two equally misfit personality types occasionally collided back then, just so they still do today, and when it happened around me, it could certainly complicate my job.

On April 17, 1989, police were called to the home of Antolina Rojo, an Hispanic woman, eighty-four years of age, in Alpine. Officer James Johnson arrived at her house on South First Street just after six in the evening and found an ambulance already on the scene. Johnson was a spit-and-polish officer, who always looked like a cop should—very athletic, six-two, 200 pounds, about thirty years old at the time. As he approached the house, a neighbor named Daniel Celaya told him that "she" was in the kitchen. Inside the dwelling, he encountered the next-door neighbor, Augustina Chavarria, who was Celaya's grandmother, and another neighbor from a few blocks away, Joe Frank Valadez, who was behaving erratically and almost incoherently.

In the kitchen, Officer Johnson found the EMS technician attending to an elderly woman lying on her back in the middle of the floor beside an over-turned chair. Her slippers were displaced and her dress had been lifted above her waist, exposing her, but she had been covered by another garment laid over her pubic area. Her glazed eyes were not responsive to the pen light, no pulse could be detected, and her arm was cool to the touch.

Johnson had just put in a call to the police dispatcher to have the justice of the peace come to the scene of an unattended death when one of the EMS technicians drew his attention to apparent stab wounds in the woman's up-per abdomen. Immediately Johnson put in another call, this one for a camera and an evidence kit. Closer inspection of her dress revealed as many as nine small slits located over matching punctures in the skin.

When the justice of the peace, Chester Wilson, arrived and approached the house, Valadez told him, "I didn't do it." Wilson related this to Johnson, who had not told any of the gathering neighbors about any apparent foul play; as far as they should have known, she had passed away of natural causes. Johnson took a close look at Valadez, who had fresh scratches on his face and neck. His hands were shaking uncontrollably, and he was drinking water continu-ously, pacing from the living room to the kitchen repeatedly. Johnson had to order him to leave the kitchen five different times, and finally told him to wait outside the house. At six thirty, one of the neighbors came in and told Johnson that Valadez had gone. Leaving the body with the JP, Johnson jumped in his car and two blocks away overtook Valadez, who said he was going to get a priest. During this brief foray, Valadez had also stopped at the house of another neighbor, Irene Valenzuela Johnson, asking to borrow some cigarettes. He told her that Antolina was dead, but that he didn't know what had happened. Johnson took him back to the house and ordered him not to leave again, since he needed to answer some questions when they were through processing the scene.

In the kitchen sink, Johnson found reddish puddles, which he blotted up with toilet tissue and bagged as evidence, and also removed and bagged the sink strainer. He found four white-handled steak knives in the kitchen drawer, which he noted for comparison to a murder weapon if one could be found.

As Johnson interviewed the bystanders, it became apparent that Valadez had spent part of the afternoon in the Rojo home, along with Celestina Gomez, who had come over to help the elderly lady thread her sewing machine. When she left, around five, Valadez was alone with the victim, Mrs. Rojo. He was seen leaving ten or fifteen minutes later by the next-door neighbor, Augustina Chavarria, who had been preparing dinner and stepped outside for a cigarette. Valadez returned to the Rojo house at close to six o'clock, then ran over to Chavarria's house, yelling for her grandson, Danny Celaya, to help. The latter had just driven up in his pickup truck; neither he nor his grandmother saw Valadez enter the Rojo house before calling for help. They were well acquainted with Joe Frank Valadez, whose birth name was Jose, but whom they had nicknamed El Gordo (Fat Guy) in consequence of his weighing about 230 pounds while standing only about five-seven.

Augustina, who was seventy-eight, asked Valadez what had happened, and he responded cryptically, "What happened is what happened." They entered the house, and Valadez blocked the door to the kitchen with his body, his hands up on the doorframe, saying, "She fell down." When they saw the scene in the kitchen, Celaya told Valadez to call the police.

"Why?" he asked.

"Because if you don't, I will."

As the ambulance was being summoned, Augustina entered the kitchen. Although she and Antolina were both elderly and lived next door to each other, she had not been in the Rojo house for a couple of years. She told Johnson she checked for a pulse and, finding none, went into the bedroom for a second dress, with which she covered Antolina's exposed privates, and lowered her right foot from where it was elevated on the chair.

Officer Johnson completed his careful processing of the scene; it wasn't until eight fifteen that a hearse from Geeslin Funeral Home arrived to take charge of the body. As it was prepared for removal, Johnson noted fluids dripping from her upper thigh into one of her slippers, onto which she had fallen, and he took the slipper as evidence. As the body was being removed, Valadez wept and clung to the gurney, crying, "My old lady! My old lady!" While

Johnson was securing the residence, neighbor Arnulfo Urquidez volunteered that Valadez had a key to it. When asked to surrender it, Valadez refused, insisting, "This is my house. I do not have to give the keys to anyone."

All suspicion pointed to the distraught twenty-one-year-old Joe Frank Valadez. During the evening, Johnson had given Valadez permission to use the bathroom three different times, and since he had never flushed the toilet, Johnson took a urine sample from the stool for whatever evidentiary value it might have. When Johnson questioned Valadez, he told him frankly that he didn't believe his story, and that he believed Valadez was responsible for the death. The troubled youth made no mental resistance; he broke down and admitted killing her. Later in the evening, Valadez led police to an old white porcelain stove in a vacant lot behind his mother's house, opened the oven, and produced the murder weapon. It was a steak knife, a match for the other four found in the Rojo house.

At ten forty-five that night, Joe Frank wrote out a confession that was almost illegible from his shaking hand. After Celestina left, "Antolina went to the kitchen to start supper. She was sitting on a chair. I lost my head & started strangling her. She fell back in the chair onto the floor. While she was lying on the floor I started stabbing her with a knife I got out of the kitchen drawer. . . . After Antolina was taken away, I went to the police department and made a voluntary statement to James Johnson. I told him that I stabbed Antolina. I voluntarily took the police to get the knife from the stove behind my house. I am a very cooperative person." Valadez did make mention of Augustina Chavarria's covering Antolina's naked lower body, but did not admit to a sexual assault, and indeed there was no forensic evidence that he had raped her. Apparently, her dress became disarranged during the struggle, and she happened not to be wearing any underwear. Sometimes crime scenes are not what they so obviously appear to be. Antolina's body was taken to Lubbock for an autopsy, which revealed that she had suffered nine stab wounds: one had punctured her abdominal aorta, and three had pierced the inferior vena cava, resulting in massive internal bleeding. Alpine being a small community—about five thousand people at the time—homicides are a rarity, and this particularly gruesome one shook the town badly.

According to Valadez, after the killing he walked north to the Prescription Drugstore to get some blood pressure medication. This was confirmed by Betty Hill, who had been on duty but had had to refuse the prescription because the pharmacist was not there and because they did not have authorization from the indigent-care program to fill it. She described Valadez as agitated and belligerent, but he did leave after she gave him three diuretic pills, which seemed to satisfy him. He then walked to his mother's house, where he hid the knife. He telephoned Antolina's house, and getting no answer, said he returned to check on her. His mother told him to return a saw they had borrowed, and he took it with him. When he got back to the scene, he called for help. Valadez's story had contradictions, and in places it didn't make sense, but considering his known mental problems, it fit the facts pretty well.

Still, the search for more evidence continued even after getting the confession, and it was soon learned that almost exactly two years before the attack, a social worker had visited Antolina Rojo at her home, investigating a tip that she was being victimized by Valadez, who was then nineteen, and his mother, Carolyn, who lived together close by. The information was that Antolina had largely raised Joe Frank since boyhood but was now afraid of him, that he and his mother would go to Antolina's house and expect her to cook for them, and that they would make long-distance telephone calls, which she would have to pay for. Joe Frank had been reported as having struck her, taken her money, and locked her in the bathroom. His mother sometimes did Antolina's laundry, but was said to have thrown clean clothes at her, calling her *vieja sogrosa* (nasty old woman).

The social worker found Antolina's house and yard neat and well kept, but her physical state poor. She did not see or hear well, and she moved about painfully with the aid of a walker. Her mental faculties appeared adequate, however, since she passed the basic questions about time, place, and day. The social worker suspected severe codependency, however, since Antolina denied all the allegations about Valadez and his mother. The worker noted in her report that "the client appears to be over protective of the alleged perpetrator and said that she would not know what to do without him." But since the elderly woman refused any intervention, there was nothing further that the Health and Human Services Department could do.

In jail after the killing, Valadez complained of suicidal thoughts, and precautions were taken. On August 19, he was given a psychiatric evaluation by the director of the Texas Department of Mental Health and Mental Retardation's drug and alcohol program, Dr. L. Arden Gifford. He described Valadez's demeanor as polite and noted that he had a history of pleasant and goal-oriented behavior. He was aware and remorseful of what he had done; despite his problems, he had not considered himself dangerous, but now realized that he was. Valadez was diagnosed as schizophrenic, with a history of hearing voices that said they were going to kill him. They did not tell him to kill Antolina, whom he had loved all his life and addressed as "Mema," but when he did kill her, the voices told him he "had done well." For months Valadez had been taking a daily regimen of antipsychotic drugs, whose effect was known to be dangerous when mixed with alcohol. After approximately two years without drinking, Valadez on the day of the murder consumed four beers. Gifford recommended a full medical and neurological workup, but declined to take Valadez into the El Paso State Center because of the safety risk he posed, so he was remanded to the Brewster County Jail to await trial. As in many of these cases, people talk a good game about what needs to be done, but they don't want to be part of the solution—the actual "doing," the follow-through. I've seen it my whole career.

On August 15, 1989, Valadez escaped from jail by climbing over the perimeter fence. He didn't make much of a flight, going straight back to his mother's house. It was locked and she was inside; since she didn't know who was trying to break in, she called the police. It didn't take long for the house to be covered by the county sheriff, who was Jack McDaniel at that time; James Johnson; and the constable, Solomon Ramos. Valadez had gotten inside, so Johnson opened a window and called to him that the house was surrounded and that he should come out. In response, Valadez raced from the back room into the kitchen and seized a knife, threatening to kill himself as he held it to his chest. There is a fine art to talking would-be suicides out of their intention, and McDaniel and Johnson, after crawling through the kitchen window, convinced Valadez to return to the jail with them.

On December 24, 1989, still awaiting trial in the Brewster County Jail, Valadez assaulted one of the guards, Ken Clouse. He had been taken from his cell to take a shower, and on the way back an argument erupted over the towel, which Valadez was not permitted to have in the cell because he had attempted suicide before. Valadez suddenly turned and began choking Clouse, screaming, "Don't ever touch me! Don't ever touch me!" It was another inmate, Gary Ball, who coaxed Valadez into releasing the guard, and then assisted in getting him secured back in his cell. But no sooner was this done than Ball alerted Clouse that Valadez was trying to hang himself. That effort was prevented. (This was the same Gary Ball whom, as I wrote in *One Ranger*, I had to shoot after he escaped from the Brewster County Jail.

Sometimes even in a low-populated rural area, things can get interesting.)

The matter was finally scheduled for trial in February 1990, when Johnson's carefully prepared case met with a sudden disaster. In a ruling that would have won a gold medal if there were an Olympic event in logical gymnastics, Judge Gonzalez of the 83rd District Court ruled Valadez's arrest invalid and his confession inadmissible, and all the evidence obtained by it, including the murder weapon, was declared to be what they call "fruit of the poisonous tree," and so was thrown out. The court said Johnson erred by getting in his car and going to fetch Valadez after he left the Rojo house while witnesses were being interviewed. Bringing him back to the scene of the crime and making him wait to give a statement amounted, said the court, to an arrest without probable cause. Well now, really! Everything the boy had said, every element of his behavior, would have indicated guilty knowledge to any experienced officer. Johnson had conducted a good investigation (he is now a deputy U.S. marshal in Austin), but the upshot of the ruling was that the DA had to drop the case and allow Joe Frank Valadez to walk away a free man. He spent the subsequent months either at his mother's or at the state mental facility in Big Spring.

On March 26, I received a request from Officer Johnson to help reinvestigate the case and try, if possible, to come up with enough new, admissible evidence to get a fresh indictment. Ever since the first case was dismissed, he said, he had to see Valadez free in the community, going about his not-always-lucid business. Knowing what Valadez had done, Johnson believed the safety of the community warranted a fresh effort to put this guy where he could do no more harm.

Like everyone else in Alpine, I had been aware of the Rojo killing, and I might have thought it a bit strange that I wasn't asked to help at the outset, but the police chief in Alpine was pretty definite that he did not want Rangers or anybody else messing in "his business." Well, it wasn't just his business—it was the people of Alpine's business. By early 1990, that chief of police was gone, having been dismissed, and, I hear, he narrowly escaped indictment for misappropriation of Crime Stoppers money—which may offer one collateral explanation of why he didn't want Rangers around his office. It was only after this roadblock was removed that I was called in, and it was only after I had reviewed all the records that I realized this case was now in about as good a shape as the victim lying on her kitchen floor.

Johnson wasn't happy that Valadez continued to slink around the streets in his belligerent and half-crazy way, but there was nothing we could do to justify holding him on the murder count that had been dismissed. We discovered, however, that he had never been charged with the August jailbreak, which was a felony, so we filed a complaint on him and arrested him about noon, again at his mother's house, on May 1, 1990. We got him arraigned before the justice of the peace, Chester Wilson, the same judge who had declared Antolina Rojo dead. (You would never guess this from his JP duties, but Chet Wilson was a retired Border Patrol supervisor and a crack pistol shot. I competed against him many times, and we're still good friends.)

I took Valadez to my office at the DPS headquarters, and there we got a fresh confession to the murder; we Mirandized him fully, and he said he understood his rights. This statement largely repeated the first, although he added that shortly before the attack, "I started feeling sick and confused, I felt something in my brain, I was confused. I remember all the sudden [sic] on top of Antolina on the kitchen floor." He related being arrested by Johnson and leading him to the murder weapon.

Sheriff McDaniel was present for the statement, as was his chief deputy, Little Alfred Allee, who was now a former Texas Ranger. I asked Valadez twice whether his statement was truly voluntary and given without any coercion, and he replied that it was. The confession was witnessed, and notarized by the DPS secretary, Marsha Lavallee. Later that afternoon I got a call from a lawyer in Fort Stockton, Steve Woolard, who had gotten Valadez off the first time. He told me that he had been hired by Carolyn Valadez to represent her son again; I told him that was fine, that his client had given a statement, and that I would bring him a copy.

Taking Valadez into custody again really set off his mother; she even made a few irate phone calls to my house, and while I don't think she was hitting on all cylinders either, I quickly laid down the law to her about that. With Valadez safely put away where our renewed investigation couldn't send him over the edge into some new spree of violence, Johnson and I started again from square one.

The time elements of the crime were pretty well established by now, but having to begin with no murder weapon and a judge who seemed determined not to let him confess, we wanted everything else to be picture-perfect, so we decided to retrace Valadez's movements of that afternoon. We knew that Celestina Gomez had left the victim's house about five and that Valadez had stayed a bit longer. The next-door neighbor and her grandson had seen him leave between five ten and five fifteen, walking north. On April 2, Alpine police officer Bryan Ward and I paced off his route and timed it. We figured it would run a bit long, since we walked at a normal pace, and witnesses said that because of his constantly agitated state, Valadez walked everywhere he went at a very brisk pace. From the Rojo house to the Prescription Drugstore took six minutes. We allowed five minutes for his belligerent exchange with Betty Hill. From the pharmacy to the Valadez residence required nine minutes, another five to ten minutes to the abandoned stove in the back lot where he hid the murder weapon, made the call to the victim's house, and talked to his mother about returning the borrowed saw. The seven blocks from the Valadez house back to Antolina's took seven and a half minutes, which placed Valadez back at the scene of his crime in a half hour to thirty-five minutes after he left, and indeed it was close to six o'clock when he arrived at the victim's house and ran out again calling for help.

When he telephoned Antolina's house, of course nobody answered because he had just murdered the woman. That might have indicated the extent of his derangement: maybe he believed that he hadn't really done this, and that she would get off the floor and answer the phone. However, since we got a jailhouse source to tell us that Valadez had told him he intended to beat the rap by acting crazy, the greater probability was that he was just laying the groundwork to return to the house and make a big show of his distress and surprise. (If he thought an insanity defense would get him off in Texas, he really might have been crazy. It almost never works.)

Fortunately for us, he couldn't keep his mouth shut when he was in jail the first time for the murder, and former inmates virtually lined up to tell us what he said. In a series of interviews, Guadalupe Garcia related that Valadez said he had committed the murder and that "he was sorry for what he did to her." This he said two days after the killing.

On March 26, I interviewed a former inmate, Joel Hernandez, who had been incarcerated with Valadez, but was free and at home when I talked to him. He indicated that Valadez told him he had killed the old woman, went home to hide the knife, and then returned. I also enlisted a fellow Ranger, Clete Buckaloo, who is now the captain of Company D, to take a statement from a county jail trusty who was still incarcerated, Joe Richard Gonzales. He stated that Valadez told him that he had killed an older lady because of his medication and alcohol and depression, and claimed that he was going to get out of the charge by playing like he was crazy. Felipe Cobos, who occupied the cell next to Valadez for four months, said that he often heard Valadez weeping and having nightmares during the nights, and that in one of them, Antolina was "coming after him and trying to kill him." He also had overheard Valadez on the telephone, raging at his mother and threatening to kill her for having sold some of his things, and telling his lawyer to "take any kind of plea bargain" that might be offered on the murder charge.

In all we interviewed over twenty inmates for knowledge of what Valadez had said while in lockup (both times). Nor did he limit his confessions to other inmates. Former guard James Casey related to us that one day during exercise period, Valadez approached him and asked whether he, Casey, had been told of his murdering an old woman. Casey told him very curtly that he really didn't want to hear about it, but if it would make Valadez feel better, to go ahead. Casey knew that Valadez had attempted suicide a couple of times. Valadez told him of the slaying in considerable detail. When he finished, Casey asked him why he left and then returned, to which Valadez replied, "So they wouldn't know it was me that killed her." In putting together this part of the case, it also didn't look good for him that he had escaped from the county jail once and assaulted a guard.

We reinterviewed those who had given statements before, such as Arnulfo and Teresa Urquidez, who lived directly behind Antolina Rojo. Arnulfo said that during his comings and goings in previous years, Valadez would cut through his back yard via a hole in the fence. This made him uncomfortable, so he repaired the fence, but Valadez made a new hole and continued to cut through his back yard. We spoke again to Betty Hill, the pharmacist who had refused the prescription for blood-pressure medication. She reiterated that Valadez had been very belligerent and had said, "I am in no mood to be hassled." The physical evidence for the case was weak. We still lacked the actual murder weapon, which the judge had thrown out, and the remaining steak knives had since been sold in a rummage sale. The knives we were able to track to a woman in Fort Stockton, who turned them over to police. They matched the wounds, and she swore out a statement about where she had obtained them.

Finally, in October 1990, I had to go to Fort Stockton and testify in Joe Frank Valadez's trial for the murder of Antolina Rojo. Valadez's second confession was crucial to our case but his lawyer, Steve Woolard, made a good college try to get the second confession thrown out, on the grounds that I had denied Valadez access to counsel. I'd had no idea his mother had called and retained him, the Brewster County DA had in fact advised me that Woolard no longer represented Valadez, and we had Valadez's statement that Woolard did not represent him, even though Woolard was advising him to keep silent. This time it didn't work, and Judge Alex Gonzalez (the same one who had thrown out the first confession) let this one stay in. That second confession was the largest factor that led the jury to convict him. He got ninety-nine years, so he won't be back for a long time. Justice has been served.

Was the Valadez kid in his right mind when he stabbed Antolina Rojo to death? Of course not; I doubt that the man has ever had a right mind to be in. But was he criminally insane? In Texas, that is a narrow and particular legal definition, hinging on whether he knew the difference between right and wrong, and whether he could appreciate the consequences of his actions. I doubt whether there is a psychiatrist in the state who could tease out with certainty whether, when Valadez telephoned the victim, he didn't understand that she was still as dead as when he had killed her, or whether he was cleverly setting up a defense. The fact that he was sane enough to tell other inmates that he was going to beat the rap by pleading insanity would tend to suggest the latter. In Texas, this highly difficult question is left to a jury of lay people, who rely on their common sense and experience. They hear conflicting testimony from dueling expert witnesses—if the defendant has the money for an expert witness—and try to do the right thing.

More than half the people in prison today are not mentally right, so the adequacy of criminal defense and the fairness of the system are matters that I leave to the conscience of the voters and the legislature. My only job, along with Officer Johnson's, was to put Joe Frank Valadez in a place where he could not endanger the public anymore. Thank God we got it done, even if we did have to jump through the hoops.

CHAPTER 13

Rio Bravo

Ever since Texas joined up with the United States, in 1845, the Rio Grande has formed 889 miles of the international border. The Mexican name for it is Rio Bravo del Norte: the Wild River of the North, and compared to the other streams in that watershed, it truly is the Rio Bravo. Or it was, before irrigation sucked it dry. There are many years now when no water at all actually reaches the Gulf of Mexico from the mouth of the river. El Paso, at the northern end of the Rio Grande boundary, is a teeming city of about six hundred thousand—at least, that's how many want to be counted. An accurate census at the edge of the Third World is not possible. El Paso's sister city, Ciudad Juárez, is three times larger. South of El Paso, though, the river winds through the Chihuahuan Desert, arid and sparsely populated, for the first half of its Texas journey. Del Rio marks the point where the land begins to flatten out and become more fertile, and the population increases, and increases again geometrically below Laredo as the stream enters what is called the Lower Valley.

To say, however, that the Rio Grande is just the border between two countries doesn't begin to address what has to be talked about if you want to understand this region. For a hundred miles, in some places for two hundred miles, on either side of the river, the Valley is an economic and cultural unit, an entity of its own where the fact that the stream is also an international boundary is purely incidental. In fact, it probably doesn't go too far to say that the Valley is in effect a third country, one whose economy takes place largely off the accounting books of both Mexico and the United States. That is because the mainstay of this economy is the illegal trade in narcotics, characterized by an underworld of bribes, official corruption, suitcases of cash, torture, and murder in riverside hooches—to all of which the U.S. law-enforcement apparatus has been only a partial barrier.

Also important to this economy is the illegal trade in human beings, of impoverished Latinos, the large majority of them Mexican, but many also making their way up from deep in Central America, seeking ways to cross into what they imagine is the paradise of the United States. Driven by their want and lacking visas or other papers, they are easy marks for "coyotes": guides who, for ruinous fees, often six to twelve hundred dollars a person, offer to transport them into the United States so they can disappear into the shadow economy of one of the major Texas cities. Just as often, they are abandoned en route and left to die in the desert. If they do reach their destination, they are crowded together in small apartments or cheap houses while their handlers get them jobs in construction or menial labor. They are kept there until their debt is paid off—or long after. The women, if they're lucky, become maids or domestic servants; if they're not lucky, they end up in white slavery. Often the coyotes are paid by the people who are going to hold the illegals in a kind of indentured servitude, and by the time food and housing is deducted from the immigrants' pay, it can be several months or even a year before they earn their freedom. And the illegal immigrants caught in this trap have no recourse to the law, because reporting the coyotes would only call attention to themselves and lead to their own deportation. It's a little slice of hell, existing right in the cities of Dallas, Austin, Houston, San Antonio, in the suburbs surrounding them, and even in small towns.

Monetarily, the traffic in human beings is small potatoes compared to the commerce in illegal drugs. Since I retired, the open and savage drug war fought between competing cartels in Nuevo Laredo and Juárez for control of the narcotics trade has increasingly spilled across the border into this country, forcing the United States to acknowledge that a serious problem exists. Yet even now we are not willing to face up to what must be done to curtail it. People have asked me many, many times over the years how this hellish trade in narcotics can be stopped. Mexican police and judicial officials have given me the standard line, that as long as there is a demand for it in the United States, Latin America will fill it. What most people on our side of the river don't understand yet is that American industry, those giant corporations that have outsourced their manufacturing to *maquiladoras* (assembly plants) in Mexico, are also not keen to see the drug trade crushed. Make no mistake: the United States has the power and the resources to stop the traffic cold, but we lack the political will. The intractability of the problem, the fear of giving offense to the Mexican government, and American investment in Mexico, which doesn't want that boat rocked, have all made it seductive to pretend that it is not a fifty to seventy *billion* dollar a year enterprise, which my sources tell me it is. But then, big money has been winning out over justice for many centuries.

★   ★   ★

Much of my time in the late 1980s was taken up with vigilance against the narcotics trade, providing a vantage point from which I observed the whole alphabet soup of the federal drug-enforcement apparatus at work. And what I saw was incompetence that had to be seen to be believed. For just one instance, when I first arrived in the Big Bend country in January 1987, the national government had just launched what were called "aerostats," big balloons that were lofted up as high as fifteen hundred feet. They contained electronics to carry out air-traffic surveillance on drug-smuggling planes coming out of Mexico. It was not a bad idea; if they had been around earlier, they could have made short work of people like John Webster Flanagan. They were the brainchild of a senator from Arizona; General Electric got the contract to build them; and fifteen aerostats were floated along the border from San Diego, California, all the way to Brownsville, Texas.

The one that I became most intimately familiar with was floated up eighteen miles west of Marfa, which is about twenty-six miles west of Alpine. (This aerostat was big enough and high enough that I could just see it from the deck of my house in Alpine.) It was dedicated in April 1987 by a high-powered congressional delegation with all kinds of hoopla. Of course, the Mexican drug smugglers had already figured out how to evade them.

The aerostats were under the command and control of the U.S. Customs Service, so when a plane was detected humming its way in from Mexico, the crew in Marfa would call customs headquarters in Sacramento, California, which would call the customs sector in Houston, which would call air intercept in San Angelo, Texas, which was over three hundred miles from the border and halfway to freaking Houston. The fastest aircraft the service could use for intercepting smugglers was a Beechcraft King Air, which can fly approximately three hundred miles an hour. So from detection to any possible intercept, at least an hour and a half or more—reasonably, two hours—was required, during which time the smuggler had set down on his desert airstrip maybe fifty to a hundred miles inside the United States, disgorged his marijuana or cocaine, and gone merrily on his way back to Mexico. Those interceptors should have been stationed no more than a hundred miles from the border, and it's not as though they were B-52s and needed two-mile runways at some major air force base.

The customs guys in Sacramento and Houston and San Angelo were just following their instructions, as they had to. The fault lay with the bureaucrats sitting on their thrones in Washington—trying to justify their high positions and high salaries—who waved a pointer at a map and issued decrees on how it was going to be, and exercised no more common sense about how to enforce the law than a South American dictator. They should have listened to their agents on the border and local law enforcement in order to get the job done right, but they didn't do it. Never have, and most probably never will.

Moreover, a good brush pilot—there are plenty of those around, and I always think of Flanagan, who was the best—could evade the aerostats altogether. This is mountainous country, where peaks reach over seven thousand feet, separated by vast flats and cut by deep canyons. By keeping in the canyons as they came out of Mexico and keeping a low altitude, pilots could often go undetected by radar. As it was, the only plane—and I mean the only plane—that I ever heard of being intercepted as a result of detection by an aerostat was a homemade job that came chugging and wheezing out of Mexico, loaded with four or five hundred pounds of marijuana. Customs tracked this airborne jalopy all the way to New Jersey, where it crashed of its own accord, but I guess you have to count it a success. The pilot walked away.

*   *   *

Most of the drugs that come in through the desert country now are brought in on foot by hikers in their backpacks. They move in groups of, say, five for a small group and as many as a dozen in a really large group, each one carrying thirty-five or forty pounds of marijuana. After the Rio Grande cuts that big arc from southeast to northeast—that's why they call it the Big Bend—it gets progressively closer to U.S. Highway 90 as it runs east from Alpine to Marathon and Sanderson and finally skirts the river itself near Langtry.

Most commonly, these hikers will trek toward a predetermined point on the highway and meet a vehicle there to unload and get paid, perhaps a thousand dollars each, depending on how far they had to walk—fifty or sometimes seventy-five miles. Sometimes these "mules" are illegal aliens who then get into the vehicles to be transported on to join the ranks of the millions of other *indocumentados* living and working in the United States.

In both drug and human trafficking, it is the Lower Valley that is the most active, and the most dangerous for American lawmen. In the upper reaches of the river—my territory—the problem of overwhelming numbers is replaced by the problem of isolation. There was one incident I worked that took place around the tiny town of Lajitas. I wrote about it briefly in *One Ranger*, but it bears retelling in more detail here because it is a window into the complexity of the campaign to stop the flow of narcotics, which is another sort of river, one that seems to slide around every effort to block it.

Lajitas sits on the river, right on the border between Brewster and Presidio counties, just at the western edge of Big Bend National Park. Virtually every town in Texas on the Rio Grande is mirrored by a corresponding town on the Mexican side, and directly opposite Lajitas is the village of Paso Lajitas. Living in a hooch (a tiny house or hovel) near Paso Lajitas and within a hundred yards of the river was a smuggler named David Rosenthal. (Actually, that was an aka. His real name was David Marrufo.) In previous years he had been a schoolteacher in northern New Mexico (perhaps if teachers were paid a living wage, he might not have turned to something so dramatically more profitable). Rosenthal had a couple of outlaw confederates who supplied him with semiautomatic weapons that they acquired in the United States, such as AR-15s and AK-47s. Rosenthal would pay for the guns with dope, and then with the application of a little know-how and some readily available hardware, he would turn them into fully automatic weapons. These he would trade to the boys in the drug cartels, who found automatics indispensable and couldn't be bothered with anything less, and Rosenthal would then be paid off in more narcotics.

His thriving little enterprise was well known to the sheriffs of both Brewster and Presidio counties. One night shortly before I arrived on station in Alpine—cold weather had already set in, and since I got there in January 1987, it must have been just before I arrived—those two officers had a conference in Lajitas. Brewster is the largest county in Texas and Presidio is the fourth largest; together they cover an area about half again bigger than New Jersey.

The one route west from Lajitas, State Highway 170, crosses into Presidio County within half a mile and reaches the town of Presidio fifty miles distant, opposite its Mexican sister city, Ojinaga. About two-thirds of the way up the route is the only other settlement, the tiny hamlet of Redford, with a population of barely a hundred, and across the river from Redford is the village of Mulatto, which is a very heavy smuggling area. For most of its length, SH 170 commands a view of the river, with a range of mountains behind it.

After leaving the meeting in Lajitas, Presidio County sheriff Rick Thompson and his deputy stopped at a point opposite Rosenthal's hut, and perhaps as much for devilment as to spy out any activity, fired a couple of parachute flares across the river to light up the area. Outraged, Rosenthal opened up on the sheriff from his hooch, aiming high and intending only to scare him, which he thoroughly succeeded in doing, since the rounds spit and pinged off the rocks above them.

This in turn got Thompson's blood up, and he got in touch with his friend Robert Chambers, who, as you might remember from *One Ranger*, was a veteran of cross-border smuggling operations. Chambers contacted the Chihuahua State Judicial Police in Ojinaga, which captured Rosenthal at his hooch and had him sitting on the banks of the river as Chambers confiscated a small arsenal of automatic and semiautomatic weapons. At an opportune moment, Rosenthal leaped up and made a run for it; Chambers fired two or three shots after him, thinking that he missed (but he actually did hit him). Rosenthal made good his escape. What Rosenthal probably knew, but which I had no clue about until later, was that Sheriff Rick Thompson had waded up to his ass in the mire: he was working with Chambers, who was working with the cartel. Thompson was later busted and sentenced to life in prison without parole, which, in my view, he deserved as much for courting and betraying my trust and that of other lawmen as for running dope.

A couple of weeks later, the FBI got a call from the park rangers in Big Bend National Park, advising that a body had washed up on the American bank of the Rio Grande inside the park, which is downstream from Lajitas. The federal agents who inspected the body found it to be pretty well decomposed, and concluded it had been in the water for a couple of weeks. Being the new Texas Ranger in the district, I was called in to consult, and opened my own investigation.

From a cursory look, it appeared that fish and turtles had eaten away some of his viscera, and the body had picked up river-bottom debris as the current had rolled it along. On closer inspection, however, it was discernable that the body had been slit open and its organs removed, and then weighted with stones before it was sunk in the river, where the powerful current had rolled it along, weights and all. This was not the mark of some ghoulish cult, but of a Colombian gang execution.

The involvement of Colombians was unlikely, however, considering the reach and power of the local drug lord, a *cabrón* named Pablo Acosta Villareal. In Mexican culture, that term denotes a man who is unattractive but too manly not to admire. Scar faced and butt ugly, Acosta held American citizenship, centering his operation from the Mexican side in the village of Santa Elena, directly across from the American town of Castolon, which is located within Big Bend National Park and populated mostly by concessionaires. The two towns are located near the mouth of Santa Elena Canyon, which is the most dramatic one in the park, barely fifty yards wide at the river but more than fifteen hundred feet deep. Published accounts differ whether Acosta was a hundred-tons-of-marijuana-a-year guy, or, as he is more frequently described, a sixty-tons-of-cocaine-a-year guy. The latter is more probably the case, since he was surely a billionaire, and he shed enough of his generosity among the local poor people to be hailed as a kind of Robin Hood and celebrated for his macho defiance of the gringo law-enforcement apparatus.

Acosta could not have stayed in business without the cooperation of the state judicial police, and he became outraged when he learned that his nephew had been picked up by some Honest Abe in the Federal Judicial Police and tortured for information. And believe you me, they know how to torture in ways that will make suspects say anything. For vengeance, Acosta had his people pick up some hapless *madrina*, or reserve officer of the federal police, and haul him back to his lair at Santa Elena. Acosta's men tied this officer to a chair in an eight-by-ten adobe hooch near the river, and then began to "interrogate" him for information on exactly who was responsible for the torture of Acosta's nephew. One of the guards at the door of the hooch was carrying an AK-47, and, standing easy, he had the muzzle resting on his foot, which was a stupid thing to do. One of the interrogators had an AR-15 pointed at the officer tied in the chair.

Acosta was present, as was Chambers, who had just squatted beside the *federale* to question him when the guard at the door accidentally pulled the trigger, shooting himself through the foot. The eight-by-ten hooch acted as an amplifier, and the loud report of the AK-47 so startled the guy covering the officer that his gun went off too, popping two .223-caliber AR-15 rounds into the officer's chest and killing him instantly. Incensed that his henchmen were carrying on more like Keystone Cops, Acosta administered a short beating, pressing his pistol under the nose of and threatening to kill one of them, who was another nephew. After calming down, Acosta ordered them to take the dead officer up into the mountains and bury him. Too lazy for that, they cut him open and partly eviscerated him, weighted him with rocks, and rolled him into the river below Santa Elena. If federal judicials were going to start getting killed, they figured it was better to make it look like the work of Colombians.

The current kept him rolling downstream and across, and this was the body that surfaced farther into Big Bend Park. After I was called in, we traced through dental records and were able to learn through Wayne Wiemer, who was a U.S. Border Patrol intelligence officer, that he was in the reserve in Mexican federal judicial. Naturally, I passed this information on to the FBI, which accepted it without so much as a thank you or a kiss my ass. We had a good idea that Acosta was behind it, and we got hold of a couple of his henchmen. When we interrogated them, we showed them a photo of the reserve federale, and they admitted that he was the one who was killed and thrown in the river.

As for Marrufo/Rosenthal, once he realized his services were no longer needed in Lajitas, he returned a couple of days later, unearthed a cache of guns he had buried as insurance against such a day, and drove off into the interior. I had two confidential informants working for me in the Lajitas area, and they told me later that federales had trapped Rosenthal as he was camped in a canyon, killed him, and confiscated his arsenal. I think he probably should have stuck to teaching near Albuquerque. I couldn't get any official confirmation of his fate (no surprise there), but Rosenthal never surfaced again, so the chances are my information was accurate—one story among many, many, many.

The loss of one of their reservists drew the attention of the Federal Judicial Police, which decided to take some action. The *commandante* (which can be read as chief hit man when someone had to be eliminated) at that time was a little short guy named Guillermo Gonzalez Calderoni; I first met him when he was in charge of the judicial in Reynosa, across from McAllen, when Captain Allee had detached me from Rio Grande City for a week's scout in 1967. Now, twenty years later, our paths crossed again, when he was in a much more powerful position. He came chopping across the river in an American-donated Huey and set down at the headquarters of Big Bend National Park. He and an FBI agent and the DEA began laying an ambush to take out Pablo Acosta.

The strike was set for April. Surprise was of the essence, and Santa Elena was too spread out, with too many houses and outbuildings, to hit without knowing exactly where he was. FBI agent Farris had a confidential informant who was very close to the Acosta clan. The CI went into Santa Elena and emerged after a couple of hours, telling Farris which house Acosta was in at that moment. Farris relayed this information to Panther Junction, where the Mexicans' Huey was. Carrying numerous armed men, it swooped in on Santa Elena and opened a gun battle lasting an hour. At the conclusion, one Mexfed was wounded, and was flown to Alpine for treatment; Acosta was dead, his body flown back into the United States and left with Big Bend Park rangers, who had to buy all the ice in the store in Panther Junction to chill the body pending autopsy. The raid was led by Calderoni, who had taken the same FBI training as I had at Quantico. That he was a Mexican national made little difference to the impoverished locals of Santa Elena, whose Santa Claus, they needed to believe, had been cowardly assassinated by the jackbooted gringos.

Calderoni posed for honors and photos at the presidential palace, and my sources tell me he received $90,000 from the U.S. government for his services. Only later was it learned that he had really bumped off Acosta to make way for a new narcotics *jefe* (boss), Amado Carrillo Fuentes, chief of the Juárez cartel. Calderoni, like so many others, was dirty. Calderoni later fled Mexico for residence in the United States, but was gunned down in his attorney's parking lot in McAllen in 2003.

And by the way, I later received information that the guard who had shot himself in the foot when the *madrina* was killed later had a shootout with Robert Chambers south of Candelaria in Presidio County. Chambers managed to wound him, so I drove over to the hospital in Odessa where he was being treated, and sure enough, there was the old bullet wound in his right foot. I couldn't get Chambers indicted, and the Acosta lieutenant was later found crushed to death beneath a car on which he had been working, supposedly the result of an accident. I have a different opinion.

* * *

Inevitably, some part of all this mayhem gets carried out under the flag of some bogus popular-resistance movement. In western Chihuahua there is an organization, the Comité de Defensa Popular (Popular Defense Committee), that goes under the acronym CDP, whose members pose as resistance fighters to give some justification for the presence of Cuban and Salvadoran advisers. They are generous to local peasants, who are in turn loyal to them, but the bulk of their financing comes from the drug smuggling. At one time there was an isolated camp of them in a bowl-shaped canyon about twenty-five miles south of Lajitas and about two miles distant from a two-acre field of marijuana.

During 1988 and 1989, I began assembling information on Ruben Chapa, who, after the death of Pablo Acosta, had begun carving a large niche for himself in the cross-border narcotics traffic, especially in the area from Lajitas to Presidio. He built a nice house on several acres in Redford, Texas, and tried to establish the cover that he was an alfalfa farmer, although I've never heard of anyone smoking alfalfa—but they might. He also supposedly had a brother in New Jersey who owned a restaurant that was a front to launder money. When I first became aware of him, he owned a trailer in a park near Study Butte (both pronounced with a long *u*), which is a popular resort stop for Big Bend tourists. The trailer was located right on a creek near a restaurant. While doing some old-time cowboy tracking, I cut sign several times on mounted riders heading up the creek bottom right to Chapa's trailer, where they could unload. It had a combination lock on it, whose combination the smugglers knew, and they could leave the dope there for Chapa to send for at his convenience.

This went on for years, and was organized enough that Chapa established a staging area on the Mexican side of the river, about thirteen miles above Lajitas. His suppliers could bring drugs from down out of the mountains and stockpile them there until a buyer was found. They could then cross into the United States with the contraband. The DEA finally got a bellyful of Chapa and "targeted" him, which in their lingo means pretty much the same thing as putting him in a bombsight. I worked closely with an agent named Dale Stinson, made copies of everything I had on Chapa, and was present when they arrested him. Chapa was accustomed to being able to bribe his way out of any jam, and got some extra time tacked on for attempting to bribe his way to an escape, so he's out of circulation for good.

★   ★   ★

In Greek mythology there was a multiheaded beast called the Hydra, which, when you cut off one head, two more would grow in its place. That is what it is like to fight drugs on the border, like fighting the Hydra. The rewards of corruption are so vast that we come to expect it, in a slightly racist way, from the other side of the river. Then we have it thrown in our faces that some of our own people have also been corrupted. Betraying the trust of the people is unforgivable, and the law cannot deal with those who do too severely.

And then layered into all this was the management of Big Bend National Park, whose rangers once spent 80 to 90 percent of their time in antidrug activity. Beginning in the early eighties, however, park superintendents tried mightily to reestablish a "good neighbor" kind of policy, and replaced law enforcement with "cultural sensitivity." From their standpoint, the Acosta killing was a public relations disaster. And then the FBI stepped in, in its usual imperial manner, and told park officials that state officers (that meant me) had only limited authority to operate within the park. The twelve hundred mostly empty square miles of Big Bend National Park are a drug smuggler's dream. I had to make a trip to park headquarters and tell them that according to the Department of Public Safety legal office, under the terms of the agreement that transferred Big Bend to the National Park Service, state officers could still exercise their full legal authority in that jurisdiction. In my polite but firm way, I informed the park administration that I intended to do exactly that, but would keep them informed whenever I was operating within their boundaries. In most cases they proved willing to assist me.

I have my doubts about how the park rangers' "sensitivity training" affected their abilities, though. In 1990, I got a call from a vacationing police officer from Missouri, who had gone parking with his girlfriend one moonlit night inside the park; they found a romantic spot at San Vicente Crossing, overlooking the river in a grove of salt cedars. Without hearing anything, he looked up and saw that they were surrounded by a number of armed and mounted men. They didn't say a word to him, and he didn't say a word to them; he just cranked up his vehicle and got out of there. I don't know how he found my number, but he was pretty upset. "What in the hell is going on down here?" he demanded. "That was an armed invasion of the United States."

I said, "I know damn well it was."

He went on, "Scared the living hell out of me and my girlfriend. Looked like that damned Pancho Villa and his army."

I had heard for years about what they called the San Vicente Cavalry, which was a group of mounted *caballeros* operating around a low-water crossing on the river southeast of Panther Junction. It was a lively spot for transporting stolen vehicles out of the United States. When the river was down, it was only about bumper deep, and when it was higher, they could pull the vehicles across with horses.

Bill Fort, U.S. Customs agent; George Barala, Jr., U.S. Customs agent; my Ranger lieutenant Bob Favor; and I went to park headquarters. I asked the park ranger if they had had any reports of armed riders known as the San Vicente Cavalry coming across the river.

They said, "Yes, we've had reports of them for a long time."

"Then why in the hell don't you do something about it?"

"Well, they're armed."

I couldn't believe my ears. I asked, "Well, what the hell is that on your hip, a slingshot? You're armed too."

I guess that went against their sensitivity training, and my remarks didn't bring any friendly smiles to their lips.

So we all drove down there, and since two of us were U.S. Customs officers, there was no question of the Rangers' jurisdiction. We didn't have to announce ourselves; the San Vicente Cavalry is always vigilant and looking for business, and presently a few riders approached. When they saw we were officers, two riders hung back and a young Mexican boy of about seventeen came forward. I went over to meet him, and told him we needed to speak to his *patrón*. He didn't ask what about, he just said, "*Sí, señor*," and all three recrossed.

About thirty minutes passed, and I wasn't real sure that anyone would show, but then we saw a dozen or fifteen riders crossing, led by a big man—six feet, maybe 225 pounds—of about fifty-five on a big sixteen-hand horse, a hell of a lot better-looking animal than the little Mexican ponies the others were riding. I could tell right off who the boss was by the mount he was on.

My Spanish was not fluent enough to carry on this myself, but our Hispanic customs officer translated what I told them: We've had complaints from U.S. citizens of riders coming from across the river at this crossing, armed with long guns and handguns. You are in violation of both state and federal law when you do this. I'm going to assure you, if this happens again, we will get you, your horses, and your weapons. You might eventually get back to Mexico, but your horses and weapons won't.

He nodded, and said in Spanish, "We will honor your request."

I had the agent emphasize that this was not a request but a lawful order, and again the *patrón* nodded and said, "*Sí, señor,*" and they departed. That was not the end of drug smuggling through the park, but from that time on, reports of the San Vicente Cavalry ended.

*   *   *

One of our recent candidates for governor in Texas, Kinky Friedman, asked me what I thought could be done to stop the flow of drugs into this country. I told him that across the frontier in Mexico, from Baja California east to El Paso and then southeast down the river to Brownsville, there are five to seven districts, each of which is controlled by a general. I wrote in *One Ranger* that if I died and discovered that there is reincarnation, I wanted to come back as a Mexican general. They are the most powerful people in the country, and that damned sure is no exaggeration. They control the federal narcotics police, they control the federal and state judicial police, and they control the city municipal police; nothing happens in their districts without their knowledge and approval. If we want to get serious about stopping the influx of drugs into the United States, we should pay each of those generals more than the cartels pay them—ten million, twenty million, whatever it takes, deposited in Swiss bank accounts. Then we should inform each general that for each illegal alien that crosses the border from his district, he will be fined five or ten thousand dollars, and for each load of drugs that is seized coming from his district, he will be fined much more heavily. I guarantee you, the flow of illegal narcotics and undocumented people would cease. There wouldn't be a pissant crossing that border.

This is not as cynical as it sounds; there are precedents for bypassing the supposed government and dealing with the real powers. During World War I, the Wilson administration mandated a total embargo on arms and ammunition shipments from Texas to Mexico. The weapons were used to arm various factions in the revolution—or more accurately, the protracted coups and countercoups and insurgencies and shifting alliances that are now all lumped together and called the Mexican Revolution. The Texas Ranger service was highly politicized at this time, and when word came down that this policy was to be ignored, those Rangers who had a conscience about such things figured that a deal had been struck somewhere and that money had changed hands.

Frank Hamer—who, as I will explain in detail later, was one of my heroes—announced that he would continue to obstruct the flow of arms through his area. He was not dismissed or even disciplined, since the higher authorities knew that if they did, Hamer might expose whatever foul dealings they had been up to. Instead, the politicians transferred Rangers out from under him until he was the only one left to patrol half the length of the Rio Bravo; undoubtedly they hoped he would get killed. I guess politics falls into the same category as love and war—anything goes. Undaunted, Hamer crossed the river and had a discussion with local *rurales*, who stood to suffer from the continued smuggling of munitions. For the next several months, shipments that should have been interdicted before leaving the United States were intercepted by the *rurales*, who acted on information supplied by Hamer, who was tracking the smugglers. And instead of going to prison and paying fines, as they would have done in the United States, the traffickers were usually stood against a wall and executed as a sword fell and someone cried, "*¡Fuego!*" It worked, and it would still work if we had the guts to do it.

Less dramatically, information gets more done than anything in stopping crime. Federal agents should develop informants along the river, paying good money for information found to be true, and paid only after arrests are made or contraband is seized. I kept a string of informants in my territory along the river, most of them on the U.S. side. I didn't have, and the Rangers didn't have, money to pay for information, but U.S. Customs and the DEA would help us out on that end. And a lot of my information came from U.S. citizens of Hispanic descent who passed along what they knew without asking for payment. They wanted the smuggling and killing and mayhem to cease, which would make their life much better on the Rio Bravo.

CHAPTER 14

From Ranger to Private Eye

I wrote in my first book of the circumstances under which I left the Texas Rangers, but neither that nor all the talking I've done since has dispelled the belief that I am that guy who quit the Rangers because they began admitting women. My reasons for retiring are still the same: the hiring of unqualified females in the Ranger service, which I knew was coming; being called out at two to four in the morning; and all the political rights affecting the job. I began this book with the United Farm Workers' strike and the notion that history puts together its story based on what people feel they need to hear rather than on what actually happened; there's only so much I can do to change that, regarding either the strike or other stories.

I took off my Ranger badge a few seconds after midnight on October 1, 1993. Believe me, I had stayed up that night to do just that, and I didn't sleep well the rest of that night. Removing my badge with only myself to witness it, for my own reasons, had no legal effect of course, but there was something satisfying and, well, western about it. Any good mythical figure, whether Alan Ladd in *Shane* or Gary Cooper in *High Noon*, answers to his own code, which must be higher than the one governing most people. It didn't matter when my letter of resignation was dated: I quit the Rangers when I took off my badge for me.

★   ★   ★

While I had pondered that decision far too deeply to second-guess myself afterward, I still had then to consider what to do next. I began to adjust to the phone not ringing in the dead of night—which was bliss, because that was one of the reasons I quit—but the best part was that I got to be around Shirley more. She was still working as a counselor at Alpine Middle School (she retired on June 30, 2004). I had worked and been active outdoors all my life, and even if I'd had any mind to adopt a sedentary lifestyle, Shirley would never have allowed me to sit around driving her crazy. A Special Ranger commission is automatically given to you upon retirement, but you have no powers of arrest except those allowed any other citizen: you can arrest someone only for a felony or a breach of the peace committed in your presence and view, and the commission has to be renewed every two years. I no longer held the Special Ranger commission, and so I took a reserve deputy sheriff's commission in Jeff Davis County with my good friend Sheriff Harvey Adams, then later in Brewster and Presidio counties under Sheriffs Dodson and Dominquez, both top-notch lawmen. I was available to these sheriffs if they needed me.

I continued in this familiar area of work until I received a telephone call from Reese Harrison, a former assistant U.S. district attorney with whom I had worked before. He had gone into private law practice, and currently had a situation on his hands for which he had recommended me to act as a private investigator. This held instant appeal for me. I had seen enough private-eye shows on television to have taken a little shine to the genre, and as long as I didn't have to work infidelity or domestic stuff, I was game. They also offered me two hundred dollars a day, which was something I sure as hell wasn't used to.

Reese had been contacted by Charles Tate, a very successful Dallas businessman, a principal of the former Hicks, Muse, Tate & Furst investment firm. Charles certainly had a couple more dollars than the old Ranger did, and he bought a beautiful Texas ranch they called the Escondido, a ten-thousand-acre spread in the mountains about twenty-five miles southeast of Marfa. It came with a great old adobe house from the late 1800s or early 1900s, which he immediately set to renovating and expanding, as well as adding a number of other amenities for his pleasure, like a shooting range for trap and skeet. He bought this place in the early '90s and got married out there, busing guests in. It was quite a hot affair, especially after the caterers knocked one of the Sterno warmers over, setting the grass on fire and burning down the tent and

do chores on the ranch, and when I became the overseer, I suggested that he might want to make a clean sweep and just let everybody go. Charles said he liked the fellow, who was Hispanic, knowledgeable about looking after the cattle, a hard worker, and a good cowboy. So Charles thought he would keep him. It turned out that the fellow was later busted for possession of a large amount of dope. The ranch was only about thirty-five miles, as the crow flies, from the Redford-Mulatto area on the river. This area is not an official crossing point, but is a heavy drug-smuggling area. The backpackers had been bringing across drugs for him to sell. Charles is a generous man, and sometimes too kind for his own good—but he is also a man you don't want for an enemy. Lucky for that crooked manager that he dropped dead when he did. He had wealthy relations in San Antonio who tried to buy him out of trouble. Charles was inclined to be lenient until he found out he'd bought the same guns twice. That really pissed him off. After that the guy was headed to jail big time.

⋆   ⋆   ⋆

I enjoyed the investigative work enough that I sat for my PI (private investigator) exam with Sid Merchant, another retired Ranger, from Abilene. Sid was one of the best Rangers I ever knew and a good worker, his long suit being oil field investigations. Having hung out my shingle, as it were, I wondered how much business I would get in lonely little Alpine, population six thousand. But once word got out that I was available, many of the lawyers I had worked with over the years started calling, beginning with Jim Darnell of El Paso, a top attorney, a good friend, and a true Texan, even if he is from Oklahoma and has a ranch in that state. Jim and Mike Myers of San Antonio have kept me working steadily on accident lawsuits involving the major tire companies. Often these suits are a couple of years old by the time I get them. It makes running down witnesses more of a challenge, but most of the state troopers who worked the accidents remain available, and that makes it easier, since we talk the same language.

One of the more satisfying PI cases I worked was for my good friend and, in my opinion, the best criminal lawyer in the United States, the famous and flashy Dick DeGuerin of Houston. Dick and his beautiful wife, Janie, also have a place in Marfa. Dick is a straight shooter and, I am told, "one hell of a cowboy." In his spare time he works on some of the big ranches in Texas, like the 6666, but he makes his living as a lawyer. A few years ago Dick called me and said that he had been retained by a civil law firm in Houston to investigate a state district judge who seemed to be in cahoots with a large law firm in Dallas. The Dallas law firm had opened an office in the judge's small town northeast of Austin. The judge had been hearing lawsuits over asbestos poisonings; the defendants were some large manufacturers. Those suits amounted to millions of dollars, and the manufacturers were almost at the point of bankruptcy. However, if the judge did not win an upcoming election, he had only a few months left in office. In this town I saw full-size billboards touting his candidacy; I had seen smaller signs in many judicial elections, but here it was obvious that someone was spending big money to keep this judge in office.

I met Dick at a restaurant in this little town, and he laid things out for me. A case had just been tried in which the plaintiff, who was represented by this large Dallas law firm, won a huge settlement, and there were rumors of foul play by the judge. Dick wanted me to interview the jurors in the case.

My first chat was with one who lived on a farm in the area. He said that the judge would overrule defense counsel, representing the manufacturers, but never objected to testimony by the plaintiff. He admitted into evidence everything asked for by the plaintiff, but nothing for the defense. Other jurors told me that they had sent a note out to the judge to answer some legal questions during their deliberation. The judge and his bailiff came into the jury room and answered their questions to the advantage of the plaintiff, which is a huge breach of judicial ethics. Every juror I talked with told me the same story.

To shorten the story: as a result of our investigation, the judge had to recuse himself from an upcoming trial, and he didn't win reelection either, although I was told he then went to work for this same Dallas law firm (as if he hadn't been working for it already). I have done other work for Dick DeGuerin, but this case was the most satisfying because I helped bring down a crooked judge. Now I suppose he's just a crooked lawyer, where, I hope, he can do less damage.

*　*　*

One kind of investigative work I always said I would not do was domestic trouble. It is a losing battle. One day a few years ago, however, I received a telephone call from this lady who suspected her husband, who was going to school at Sul Ross State University, in Alpine, of having an affair there. I was not doing anything at the time, and she told me what motel and room number he was staying in. So I went over and kept watch, and shortly I saw him come out of his room with this woman—by habit I almost said "lady." They had a dog on a leash, which they walked for a bit, and then went back into the room. I sent photos to the lady who had called me, and a few days later I heard that she had committed suicide. My God, that was a bad deal. I have stuck to my convictions ever since. There are some kinds of trash I just really don't want to play in.

⋆ ⋆ ⋆

Some parts of the new job aren't that much different from parts of the old job. Joe Fitzsimmons (his father, Hugh Fitzsimmons, was a good friend, and I worked some cattle thefts for him when I was stationed in Uvalde) was one of the owners of the family ranch, called the San Pedro. The ranch is southwest of Carrizo Springs, in Dimmit County, about a third of the way downriver from Eagle Pass to Laredo. It is such an isolated stretch of country that the only human beings you might come across are a local vaquero, an illegal alien, a Border Patrol agent or an occasional USDA river rider trying to keep cattle from crossing. The San Pedro is only a mile in from the river, and separated from it by only one other ranch.

Joe called one day and asked if he could hire me to help remove, or redirect the flow of, the mass of illegal aliens streaming through his ranch. His wife was homeschooling their three children, and the *indocumentados*, coming by in bunches of twenty-five or thirty, were scaring them pretty bad. Joe, being a man of middle age and having been raised on the San Pedro Ranch, was very aware of the influx of illegal aliens over the years, but there had recently been a large increase, and their attitudes seemed to be less friendly than in other years. He knew we couldn't stop them, but maybe we could exert enough pressure that the word would extend back up their grapevine that they needed to pass north or south of his ranch.

I took the job on. They had a place for me to stay on the ranch, and I would work there several days, go home for a couple of days, and then come back. I had a couple of guys fill in for me when I was away: my buddy Jake, whose adventures I have often written about, and Ron Stewart, another former Texas Ranger, who was a top hand and good friend. Bobby Hasslocher, a friend of mine from San Antonio whose family owns a chain of restaurants, came down and kept me company and often helped with tracking. This is rolling-to-hilly brush country, and when I say brush, I mean brush as thick as the hair on a dog's back, maybe a wire-haired terrier. I would leave my cabin before daylight each morning and cut sign for illegals; upon finding it, I'd determine their direction of travel and notify the U.S. Border Patrol by cell phone. They always responded promptly—great men who do an incredibly difficult job. If the undergrowth was almost impenetrable, they would call in an aircraft, either a helicopter or a Piper Cub flying low and at very slow speed. The latter were more effective because they are much quieter than the choppers; the illegals wouldn't hear a little plane until it was right over them.

One of the Border Patrol agents I worked with a lot there was Agent Sweeten, the son of Lewis Sweeten, a former sheriff of Zavala County, which is right next door to Dimmit County. (Odd how much law-enforcement tradition is carried on in families, including my own.) He is retired now and living in the Carrizo Springs area. In the six months I worked on the San Pedro Ranch, we took into custody more than 600 illegals. I remember one particular bunch of about thirty that we caught one day: the Border Patrol processed them, put them on a bus to Piedras Negras, and later dropped them at the port of entry in Eagle Pass, about forty miles from the ranch. The next day we caught the same damned bunch, except they were being guided by a different coyote. We did succeed in diverting the stream around the ranch for a short time, but they came back as soon as we left. It's a never-ending job. God bless the Border Patrol.

*   *   *

That work was hot and lonely, and it was high time for a change of pace. I wrote in *One Ranger* about my dabbling in the movies, so I won't repeat myself here except to say that after working with some big names and sometimes entertaining them in my home, it was a nice surprise to discover what truly nice people many of them are, especially James Garner. I was ambitious enough at one point to hire a talent agent in Dallas, but he never got me a job. I guess in justice that's a little revenge for Shirley, for that agent in Nashville I set her up with who never got her a job—although she probably still has more of a beef than I do because she actually has talent.

Oddly enough, it was Charles Tate who was also responsible in good part for my other little career, writing books. Shortly after I retired, I received a call from *Texas Monthly* magazine, which was planning an article on the Rangers, since some fifteen or twenty others had retired at the same time

I did. There was nothing conspiratorial about that, but great minds think alike, I guess. Robert Draper was to write the article and Dan Winters was to be the photographer—both men are top guns in their fields. The Draper article appeared early in 1994, entitled "Twilight of the Texas Rangers." I appeared on the cover, in the same photo you see on the jacket of *One Ranger*. Several other Rangers' photos appeared in the article, all done by Winters. Draper's piece was fantastic, and we became good friends. I am told it was the top-selling issue in *Texas Monthly*'s history. In fact, the magazine had posters made of it and a couple of other pictures—one featured my Ranger boots, made by T. O. Stanley of El Paso, and one showed me on horseback at twilight with the West Texas mountains and brush behind me. That poster of me must have sold one hell of a bunch of copies, just based on the number I have been asked to autograph over the years.

After the article came out, I received a phone call from Jim Hornfischer, a literary agent in Austin. He came to Alpine and visited with me, saying that I needed to write a book and that he would find a cowriter to help me, since I had never written anything more involved than my Ranger reports. Besides, I would rather talk about good Rangers other than myself. As I mentioned, Draper and I had become friends, and he agreed to make a run at writing my memoir. Robert is one hell of a great writer, and he prepared what they call a proposal, which Hornfischer sent to a number of New York publishers. Well, his treatment began with my reflections on my career as I drove to Austin to turn in my resignation. The publishers reached the quick-draw judgment that the book would have to be about my objections to having women in the Ranger service—there we go again—so there were no takers. Disappointing, but like Shirley and her singing career, I had other fish to fry, and so forgot about writing a book.

Sometime in 2003, Charles Tate called me up and said he had found just the guy to cowrite my book. His name was David Marion Wilkinson, but I was not to contact him until I had read his book *Not Between Brothers*, which was a finalist for a Spur Award from the Western Writers of America. Shirley and I both read it, and it was just one hell of a wonderful piece of work. David and I got together, and *One Ranger* was born.

So now we have another kind of business. Shirley, Will (yes, Will), and I sign books and give talks. Shirley takes the money, which she loves, and best of all I get to see more of my old friends than I ever would by sitting on my ass in Alpine. And I don't have to go through people's trash anymore.

CHAPTER 15

Stand By Your Ranger

⋆ SHIRLEY JACKSON ⋆

I've been married to a lawman for forty-four years, and I guess some people have it in their minds that I should have spent a good deal of time worrying about his safety, even being afraid for him, dreading that knock at the door to find the captain and a minister bearing terrible news. But the honest truth is that has just never been the case. I have always had complete faith in Joaquin's ability to handle any situation, and I have always thought if any criminal tried to carry out some evil intent, God help him if he got in Joaquin's way! Yet I know that many other lawmen's wives have answered that awful knock at the door. Have I been whistling past the graveyard? Perhaps. But it has gotten me through. Life has never held many terrors for me; most of what can happen, I meet head-on.

Most of my childhood was spent in El Reno, Oklahoma, living with my mother after my parents' divorce, which occurred when I was two. I have to smile at all the attention given these days to what are called "blended families," as though they were something new. In fact, family troubles and hard economic times have always caused families to get by with unconventional arrangements. My sister, Yvonne, whom I adored, was only two years older than I, but she went to live with my father when she was ten, while I stayed with my mother.

Some of the best times were down at my maternal grandfather's farm, where my best buddy was Uncle Harold, who was only a year older than I was. My sister would team up with another uncle, Johnny, and we'd play war games and romp. I was an absolute, bona fide tomboy. In fact, when we played at war—we were children as World War II was being fought—Harold would be the Germans and I was the Americans, and once he hung me up by my thumbs to force me to tell America's secrets. My mother caught him just as he was playfully switching me with a small tree branch for torture (I guess hanging by your thumbs wasn't torture enough), and she was furious with him. But America's secrets were safe with me.

Of all the places we lived, my favorite was the little town of Prague, Oklahoma, about fifty miles east of Oklahoma City, where my stepfather raised Black Angus cattle. I was pretty popular at Prague High School—I was a cheerleader, the school song leader, class officer, band majorette, and most importantly, my boyfriend was a school jock—but otherwise I never was a girl that you could fit into a mold. In that day, most girls were fated to be housewives, and the one class that I hated the most was home economics. My sister was an excellent seamstress, but I was hopeless, and made a mess

*Shirley with her mother, Vera, and her sister, Yvonne,
in Oklahoma, around 1948.*

of my sewing project, which was a simple straight skirt. I never could follow a pattern, in fact. I should have taken the hint and figured that my life would be the same way. I learned to be an excellent cook, but not in home ec; I learned because I love to eat good food. Fortunately, the teacher was lenient with me because she was also the faculty sponsor who took students to choral contests, and if there was one thing I could do, it was sing.

Too young to know or care, I didn't understand until years later that it's truly God's gift. I never had to study for it; it was just there. My sister, Yvonne, studied: she played the piano, she sang soprano—she had a tremendous range, and I mean she could get up there to those high notes—she had breath control, she could sing harmony, and she was even a finalist in the state rounds of the high school music competition. I sang chest, that familiar country sound, I didn't have Yvonne's range, and my harmony left much to be desired. What I had going for me was an absolutely free and natural vocalization. Even when I was as young as five, my voice was pretty much what it is now, and people wanted to hear me sing. I guess I was considered a novelty.

During the war years (when I was a little thing), Yvonne taught me how to jitterbug. I don't know where she learned it, but she had it down pat, the real honest-to-goodness, no-messing-around jitterbug. In that era, parents didn't use babysitters the way they do today. Many children would accompany their parents to dances. Everybody would dance. Usually Yvonne and I danced together. We were so different that most of the time other people would get off the dance floor to watch (this was a happy time, when military folks and civilians enjoyed themselves together—lots of patriotism), and some people would throw money—in fact, quite a lot for that day and time. Money went a long way, and people didn't just give it up easily. Yvonne and I even began singing with the bands; I was around six and Yvonne was eight.

At around nine years old, I took steel-guitar lessons. In retrospect, learning the steel was something of a handicap; I wish I had learned acoustic guitar, which is portable. A steel guitar is a cumbersome sucker to have to move around. If there is one thing I love to listen to, it is good guitar picking. My mother played the acoustic guitar, and we often performed together on a radio show in Oklahoma City. I sang everywhere. I just saw it as a natural thing. I'd hit my key and we would take off from there. And when you think about it, many country-and-western singers had a similar history. A lot of them grew up singing in church choirs, which I never did, but they can tell much the same story of having had unique voices early in their childhoods

Shirley, age nine, onstage in Oklahoma.

and being urged to perform. Consequently, I skipped that student stage that everybody seems to go through, of forming bands with school friends and practicing in somebody's garage. I was singing with professional groups from the very beginning. They had to arrange the songs to fit my range, but once we got in the same key, we could rock a joint.

Before my senior year, the bottom fell out of the beef market, and my step-father, a rancher, was forced to rent land on his sister's farm near Plainview, Texas. My mother, of course, went with him. They recovered their wealth and stability by farming maize and cotton. For some reason, their relocation plans did not include me; my stepfather was accustomed to doing well for himself, and perhaps because of this failure, he really could not afford to finish raising me. I was always too proud to ask. I had arranged to live with the family of one of my girlfriends so I could finish my senior year at Prague High School, and her parents had agreed, but my folks would not allow it. I was shipped off to live with my father in Weatherford, Oklahoma, which is about seventy miles west of Oklahoma City on the famous old Route 66, which is now I-40. My father had also remarried.

I was not happy about the home situation. I spent my senior year in Weatherford, and while I made senior cheerleader, it wasn't the same. I did not feel as if I fit in with the new school crowd—a statement (I have learned) made by thousands of transient students. Daddy and his wife, Opal, treated me well and didn't fuss at me, and I know now I should have tried to be more loving and fit in, but I was resentful, and so I didn't. I did not ask anything of them, and they didn't demand anything from me. I didn't want to have to ask for money, so I got a job after school waiting tables in a small restaurant. I also sang with a band on Saturday nights. Singing was always in my life. The bandleader just happened to be a good-looking cowboy—actually, he was probably what they call a drugstore cowboy. Joaquin definitely would not have been impressed. I was hardly ever home, but I made enough money to pay for my own things, including my prom formal and a suit, complete with hat, gloves, and a purse, for a tea they gave for graduating seniors. Both outfits were pink, by the way, and I thought they were smashing. I was too young to know that, as a redhead, I am not flattered by many pinks. But selecting my own clothes and spending my own hard-earned money on them represented an important step toward independence.

Weatherford was in the heart of what had once been the Cheyenne-Arapaho Indian Reservation, but we only knew one Indian family that had children in my school. In what was perhaps an early indication that I would eventually have a career in teaching and counseling, it struck me what a difference it makes for children to have the right kind of education. This family lived in a house just like ours, apparently shared our values, and seemed well adjusted or assimilated. Most of the native children went to the reservation school and lived a completely different life. One of the native students at our school was Yvonne's best friend, and I saw her only in that regard, not as a member of a "minority."

Yet in El Reno, I remember seeing signs in bars and barbershops that said "No Indians Allowed." They said the Indians would drink the hair tonic or aftershave lotion, anything that had alcohol in it—I'm just telling you what I heard as a little girl. And I would see the Indian women sitting on the street curbs around town; they weren't begging or holding their hands out or selling anything. I never knew, nor thought to ask, what they were doing. It almost makes me think of Willie Nelson's song "Pretty Ribbons," which I love. Just as in the song, it was crowded streets and busy feet hustling by them, and they were never really noticed. I was just one of those hustling by.

In Weatherford, my father and his wife never socialized much, so after Yvonne moved in with them, she missed out on a lot of that experience of singing with bands, although she was a wonderful vocalist. And then she married very young and moved out. When I graduated, there was no discussion of my going to college anywhere, but I had saved enough money to go out on my own, and I moved to Oklahoma City. I got a job and what they now call an efficiency apartment, just a living room–bedroom, kitchenette, and bath. I was a waitress in a swanky Chinese restaurant—I still love Chinese food—and the job provided a glimpse of a culture other than my own. I had just turned eighteen and was none too worldly, but something in the way that the owner treated a tall Chinese woman who worked for him, abrupt and domineering, made me uncomfortable. I learned in later years that many Chinese immigrants are bound in servitude to sponsors who pay their way into the country, and I suspect she might have been one. She made telephone calls in secret and was terrified that the owner would hear her; her calls were in Chinese. Needless to say, I wasn't going to repeat anything I heard (I'm still having problems with Spanish after being in Texas nearly half a century, let alone Chinese), but it was all very dark and secretive.

On my walk to work every day I had to pass by the courthouse. This was at the end of the Korean War, the services were taking people, and there was a recruiting poster outside for the WAVES (Women Accepted for Volunteer Emergency Service), the female branch of the U.S. Navy. (The acronym WAVES was superseded by WIN, Women in the Navy. I don't know why, but that's now a defunct title.) "See the world," they always said about the navy. Women didn't serve on ships in those days, but who knew where I might be sent—I really didn't care. After a month in Oklahoma City, I had had enough of waitressing Chinese food, and one day on my walk home from work, I regarded the woman on the poster pointing her finger and saying, "The Navy Wants You," turned my steps into that courthouse, and enlisted. Boy, did my life change after that!

★ ★ ★

Boot camp was at the U.S. Naval Training Station in Bainbridge, Maryland. Maybe it was because I'm a country girl and can adjust to just about anything and get along with almost anybody, but I loved it. The work was hard, but we were all in it together, even when cleaning the head (that's the navy word for "toilet"), and there was a great spirit among the women there. When we were finished with boot camp, one of my new WAVES friends invited me to go home with her to Boston. This was indeed a world away from Weatherford, Oklahoma; I was young, pretty, and single, and I had a ball in Boston. In the parks, they even had hot chestnuts sold by vendors. I ate my first pizza in Boston—a world apart from my early life.

My duty station was at the Naval Correspondence Course Center in Brooklyn, New York, and the living facilities were at a hospital in St. Albans, New York. Finding it seemed to require the helpless country girl to ask directions of just about everyone, and it involved toting the heavy white Samsonite suitcase that my mother had given me down into a subway station. Eyes wide at the experience, I could hear the train coming, and when it stopped and the doors opened—they are not very wide—there suddenly appeared this tremendous rush of people pushing off and on. My suitcase was wrenched from my hand and lost in the jumble, the doors shut, and the train rocketed off again, leaving me there to gather up my Samsonite and wait for the next train. I was always a pretty quick study, and, by God, we were at war again (in Korea), and I elbowed my way onto that next train with the best of them. When I got off, I walked back up into daylight and resumed asking directions for which bus to take to St. Albans, and then learned the daily commute from there to Flushing Avenue in Brooklyn.

I know a lot of people join the service to give their lives structure and discipline, qualities that I already had in abundance. But as a broadening experience, and for the satisfaction of serving our country and turning a child into an adult, it was wonderful in every way. I highly recommend it. And those veterans' benefits later paid for the college education I had been lacking until then. I also found a husband. I had met a young sailor from West Virginia, and he had all the qualities that mamas tell you to look for in a man—a loving nature, steady habits. He was in every sense of the word—and I know this is the curse of millions of young boys who can't get dates—a "nice guy." We married in Oklahoma, and after we got out of the navy, we moved to his home area, in the very tip of the West Virginia tea spout.

I got a job at some hush-hush government installation in Shepherdstown; officially I worked for Western Union, but the facility was some miles underneath a mountain so that it would be safe from a nuclear blast, and we had orders to report there if the United States ever suffered any kind of attack. We sent the teletypes to government installations around the world—some encrypted, but most in plain English. (Just as when Uncle Harold hung me up by my thumbs, America's secrets were still safe with me!)

I never gave up singing during all that time. Every Saturday night, all the country-music fans listened to Jimmy Dean host *Town and Country Time*, which was produced in Washington, D.C. One feature of that show was a talent search, and I didn't have a tape, but I sent in a list of the bands I had sung with and where, and sure enough, I got a call to go in and audition. I got on the train and went to Washington, which was fifty-five miles from Shepherdstown, and I was amazed to see how many contestants wanted to try out for that show. I had been sought after by professional bands in Oklahoma since I was in primary school, but this was absolutely a cattle call. We all took our turns, and when we sang, the audience consisted just of Jimmy and the people who put the show together.

Only two of us got picked to be on the show that night, me and another young girl. She went on first, and I don't know whether she had practiced her song so long in one key that she couldn't switch, or whether she told the band to play in a key other than the one she was prepared for, but her performance was a disaster from beginning to end. She sang her entire song in one key while the band played in another. I'd never seen anything like it before, and haven't since. In the back room (I guess it's called the green room now), we couldn't believe it. We just stared at the television in shock. Thank goodness my song went smoothly. She was not asked to return.

I was asked back, and eventually I became a regular and sang on the show for a little over a year. That was a heady crowd for this Okie girl to be running in—not just Jimmy, but Hank Thompson, Roy Clark, and Patsy Cline. Later they all became more closely identified with the Nashville music industry, and they became hugely famous. I also remember George Hamilton IV, who was very preppy like a college boy and wore white shoes; he didn't sing country music, but he sang around that scene. He never became hugely famous, although he had a big hit with "Abilene" in the early '60s, but he was quite good, and a real heartthrob for the bobby-soxers. Even back then they were trying to get the younger teenage girls interested in country music.

This was the time that I got to be good friends with Patsy Cline. She lived in Winchester, Virginia, which was only twenty-four miles from where I lived in West Virginia. I still reported to work every day under the mountain— I may have gotten on Jimmy Dean's show, but this conservative Okie was not about to give up her day job! Patsy's career had started its rise; she had just sung "Walkin' After Midnight" on *The Arthur Godfrey Show*, and he had her back many times. Patsy had just cut a record with Decca, and she had a big red convertible with "DECCA" on the license plates. She wasn't on *The Jimmy Dean Show* every Saturday, because she had gotten big enough that she had to keep other commitments, but when she was in town and I had taken the train in from Harper's Ferry to be on the show, she would offer me a ride home.

I never will forget one day: I wasn't feeling well, and when she saw me, she insisted on calling the Winchester pharmacist at home on a Sunday afternoon, and she got him to open up the drugstore for me. That's the kind of person she was, open and generous. I'm pretty sure that Cline was her married name, and there was some gossip among the others that she had had a child or two who had stayed with their father, but I wasn't about to repay her friendship by coming across as some snippy little hick asking a bunch of personal and judgmental questions. I don't know to this day about her children. That might come from a "mind your own business" attitude that Middle America still espouses. I know that the rest of the country remembers Patsy Cline as a legendary country-and-western singer, but my memory of her is of an incredibly kind and genuine person who would use her star clout to get doors opened for others—even if it was just to get a prescription filled for a friend. And I remember that her mother just adored and encouraged her throughout her career. When I heard that Patsy had been killed in a plane crash, my first thought was, "Oh, my God! I hope somebody is there with her mother."

There were some ways in which at nineteen I was still a naïve Oklahoma girl. The hall where the TV show was telecast had arena-like seating. In fact, it was an arena, where the rows get higher the farther back you go. The performers would come out of the dressing room and down the aisle—like the football players that you see now coming out through a tunnel to the football field—to a place just to the side of the stage. At times we would hang out below the stage until we went on, and we had a chance to visit with some of the audience. Many of them were regulars, and we got to know them quite well; I thought of them as a sort of second family. One night I heard one of the singers, very well known and now deceased, and his road manager talking pretty nasty stuff about some of the women whom they would like to—well, go out with, let's say. I took it pretty unkindly that they were so disrespectful of people who came to hear us play; they were always there and we knew them by name and they were big fans and supporters of ours. However, I found out as time went on that's just the way it is. Poor fella, I probably held a grudge against him for many years because I thought he was tacky to my fans and friends. However, it is just a common understanding, I guess, between artists and the many fans who clamor for their, well, affections.

At one point the show moved from Washington to New York to be syndicated as *The Jimmy Dean Show*, and they asked me to go with them. I never will forget our meeting in D.C. to discuss this change. Connie B. Gay, the big man in this operation, said, "Shirley, the only thing wrong with you is that you're married." I was wide-eyed. Did they want me to say, "I'll get a divorce"? I was from rural Oklahoma, and there you don't just change your husband the way you change your hat. I hated the thought.

I knew I was good enough to share the stage with these performers, but I wasn't sure if I had what it took to break through to major stardom. People don't realize how tremendously competitive the music business is. If you ever go to Nashville, you will find people singing on every street corner who are just as good as the ones who are recording. Who knows what they are lacking to break through—a unique sound, a competent manager, being in the right place at the right time? And sadly, most never do make it big. Professional music is a romantic's dream but a fool's reality. One thing the producers were really looking for at that time was songwriters, not people who could just sing. One who filled the bill was Johnny Rodriguez, with whom I toured and who became a dear friend. Joaquin wrote in his first book about finding Johnny at Garner State Park in Leakey, Texas, and helping him with career connections. Johnny was one of the first singers to translate country-music songs into Spanish and sing in both languages. This was his "really big hook" into the music industry, although being single and nineteen didn't hurt either. He was the biggest find in Music City.

Johnny wrote his own music and had a unique sound as well, as did Patsy and some of the others during their musical reign. Along with all these thoughts, it was mostly because of my personal life at that time that I decided not to go to New York with them. In later years, I felt as though I had made the right decision, because the big stars that sang with Jimmy Dean in New York were already big stars when they went there. Of the other singers like me who went up with him, not one of them ever really broke through. But still, of course, I have to wonder.

Plus, I don't think I was pushy enough. It is true of so many people in the music business that success is what drives their lives, and they will do absolutely anything to get there. But I had sung all my life; it wasn't as if I got to be twenty and discovered I could sing and had to wring everything out of it that I could. People had always applauded me and paid me money. Perhaps my decision was related to the phenomenon that makes it easier for actors who have been child stars to walk away and try something else. But I just didn't have the killer instinct that you seem to need. There is a lot of

Shirley in the recording studio, Nashville, 1975.

politics on the management side of the music business, and you have to be able to fight tooth and nail.

For instance, during our marriage and after Joaquin had discovered Johnny, I was singing a lot with Johnny and his band. I cut a record called "Easy Lies" for Mercury Records—Johnny produced it—but Mercury did nothing to support it. They didn't want him going off to be a producer, because he was their hottest singer, so they kept him on the road a lot—in his place, so to speak. I also remember the guy who was supposed to be my agent (I use the word "agent" loosely), and after we had cut the record, they had an opening to get me onto the Grand Ole Opry, but he turned it down, saying that he wanted the record to come out first, which was goofy beyond belief! I later realized his main interest was an attractive young protégée he was grooming for the big time, and I felt as though I was being railroaded out of her way. Nashville executives, managers, and agents blow so much smoke up your rear end that you look like you're on fire. If I had been a killer, I would have raised holy hell. This agent was also supposed to be a friend and tied in to Johnny. I felt handcuffed, but I just thought, fine, you horses' butts, my plate is running over anyway with (by then) Joaquin, two kids, and getting my teaching degree. I had my own idea about what my ass of an agent and the record company could do with it, but I'll forgo passing it on.

*   *   *

The irony was that after all this stew over letting *The Jimmy Dean Show* move on without me, my first marriage fell apart anyway. Who can say how many factors go into a marriage failing, but I certainly came away feeling as though it was my fault. Maybe in some way I held a subconscious resentment about my singing career. And I was affected by the stigma that was attached to divorce at that time. It was so frowned upon and such a blot on your character that in later years none of my friends or children knew that I had been married before Joaquin. My younger son, Lance, was in his twenties before I told him. So after all the disruptions in my own childhood, and after making the conscious decision to escape from Oklahoma, here I was, just as divorced as my mama was. Years later, when I took courses in counseling, I learned what a powerful impact childhood experiences have on our beliefs and actions, and having seen those forces at work in my own life, I realized what huge responsibilities parenting—and counseling—are.

After leaving West Virginia, I got a job on the flight line at Reese Air Force Base in Lubbock, Texas. My stepfather had drowned, and I moved there to be with my mother. I also got to reconnect with my sister, Yvonne, and we went on a trip to New Orleans together. Yvonne's husband, Bob Kahn, was a jeweler, and he had business there. My uncles had an offshore oil-services company in Grand Isle, and we'd go down there for big shrimp boils. (One of them was Uncle Harold, of World War II childhood games.)

I remember we were with Uncle Buddy, in the Roosevelt Hotel in New Orleans, and he asked the bandleader if I could sing in the Blue Room, which was a pretty famous lounge venue. Even with my background, they didn't just wave me onto the stage, but the bandleader took me into another room with a piano and had me sing for him privately first. It was pretty cool getting to perform there. Tony Arden, a popular singer during this time period, was their featured act.

The hotel where we stayed turned out to be the hangout of a large social

Shirley and Joaquin at a recording session in Nashville, 1975.

group of local people. One day when I had no particular plans, I was sitting in the bar and restaurant, looking my worst —my hair was up in curlers, hidden by an always-present scarf —and reading a magazine. The waiter served me a drink that I had not ordered, and when I looked over to this group, the guy who was smiling at me was a gorgeous young Italian man. His parents, it turned out later, owned a chain of cleaners in New Orleans, and they had a big yacht on Lake Pontchartrain. We dated, and boy, was I impressed. My sister and I went out on the lake and went swimming off their yacht. One night we went to the Club My-Oh-My on the West End lakefront, and there were men dressed up as women, and Big Eyes here from Oklahoma had no idea what that was about. We left there and hit some bars, and when we came out, it was daylight. And I was thinking, good gosh almighty, what a place! His family had a couple of jobs lined up, and I was a quick study, so I told Yvonne to pack up my clothes and send them when she got back to Lubbock, because I had decided, "I'm staying." I thought I had found paradise. I could call the people at Reese Air Force Base and tell them I wasn't coming back. But she wouldn't do it.

Reluctantly, I went back to Lubbock, but I still thought about New Orleans. One day on a lark a girlfriend and I consulted a palm reader, and she predicted that I would marry a man in uniform, which was safe enough, since I worked on the air base. In fact, I was dating an officer, although his name was Bierwinkel, and the thought of going through life as Mrs. Bierwinkel was not the loftiest fate that I could imagine for myself.

My mother had always told me that if you're going to dance, you have to pay the fiddler, so I almost never went out on a weeknight. When I did, I never, ever was late for work because I had been out partying. Once, a crop duster who had heard me sing with some local bands pestered me to death for a date. He finally wore me down, and we made a date for a Thursday night, which was unusual for me, the next day being a workday. This goofball and I went to what they called a private club. In much of Texas, including Lubbock, it was illegal to buy alcohol by the glass, but there was a loophole in the law that let people buy memberships in private clubs, where you could buy drinks. These clubs were sort of like legalized speakeasies.

Two guys came in, one of whom knew the crop duster. They came over to say hello, and they joined us. The other fellow was a highway patrolman named Joaquin Jackson, tall as a cliff, brownish hair, piercing blue eyes, and a nose and chin that could have been modeled from a Roman statue. The band that was playing was one I had sung with before, so I got up and performed with them for a while, little knowing the effect this was having on that patrolman. We all got ready to leave, and while my crop duster date was at the cash register, Joaquin took me by the elbow and steered me out into the parking lot. As my poor date was paying the bill, Joaquin was making hay, or, I guess you could say, "making a date." I guess fate does work in mysterious ways.

Joaquin wrote in his first book about our first time together, parking at Buffalo Lake, and about how he struck out swinging in short order. That was completely factual, and I was sitting there thinking what in the world am I doing sitting in a car with this wolf. But what was even more remarkable was that after we got back to my apartment, he wouldn't leave. I had to go to work the next day, and at three o'clock in the morning he was still talking. Trying to show good manners, I didn't tell him to get lost—I suppose a liberated woman today would kick him where it pains a man most—but then it was four o'clock in the morning, and he was saying he would not leave until I agreed to go out with him again and give him another chance. I finally said yes just to get rid of him, and I was at work right on time the next morning, just as I was brought up to be.

I suppose that to set a good example, I should say that I continued to go out with Joaquin because he possessed some list of admirable qualities that you look for in a man— intelligence or spirituality or something. The truth: he was just devastatingly handsome in that Highway Patrol uniform. Sorry, kids. And my Lord, he was persistent. He had duty on the weekends and could go out only on weeknights, so whenever we arranged a date, I depended on a short, thirty- or forty-minute nap after I got home from work to keep me fresh during the evening. It also helped with getting up early the next morning. I don't know how he did it, but every time I got home from work, there he would be in the parking lot, and I'd think, "Damn! No nap today."

I tried to pour some cold water on his ardor by telling him that I was dating an officer at the air base, but he was not about to lose me to anyone named Bierwinkel. I told him about my Italian dreamboat in New Orleans, and he almost got me to believe that the only way to be Italian in New Orleans and have that kind of money was to be in the Mafia—an organization, not to put too fine a point on it, that often used cleaners to launder money as well as clothes. As he got to know me better, naturally he had to make some kind of witticism about wanting to join the navy and ride the WAVES. I suppose a prissy girl would have been offended, and a proper girl should have at least acted offended, but I thought it was pretty funny. Somehow I knew he meant no harm, and I'd never count off on a man for being able to make a joke.

On our third date we went over to Raton, New Mexico, where Joaquin introduced me to a horse-raising friend of his by saying, "And this is the girl I'm going to marry." I was too ladylike to contradict him at the time, but I was absolutely thinking, *I . . . don't . . . think . . . so!* He certainly didn't have enough money to woo me with anything that was monetarily impressive, and I was used to being shown a pretty good time. But somehow or other I never made it back to New Orleans. Joaquin got my sister on his side, and he needed an ally because my mother was unequivocally opposed to him. You may have read in *One Ranger* that she cried for three days before the wedding, and I was dragging my feet. So Yvonne was his big ally. We dated three months—*barely* three months, from July to October—and we got married in Yvonne's house. And I think about that palm reader who said I was going to marry a man in uniform, and so I did, just not the uniform that we were all thinking she meant. I was twenty-five, and I had had a lot of fun.

It was nice being married to a man who wanted to take care of me (I want you to know that as I write this, Joaquin has a couple of words to throw in here, really funny but definitely R rated, so I'll pass), but I come from fiercely independent stock. My mother always worked and was frugal and saved so that if a husband proved unsuitable, she knew she could rely on herself. It was a good thing too. She eventually was married five times, nice enough guys mostly, although a couple of them drank too much. (She had to bury two.) In Mother's day, young couples didn't get to try out "keeping house"; things had to be legal in the eyes of society and the law from the get-go. But she instilled in us girls to never have to depend on anybody. That streak runs deep in my family. My grandfather lost the use of an arm and shoulder in a cotton gin, but after that terrible accident, he built a two-story house with his one good hand. Not out of fear that Joaquin would get killed on the job, or out of dissatisfaction with his income, but I have always worked. I guess it is a throwback to my senior year in school: I don't like to have to ask for money—or, as my counseling classes would have it, "give up control."

When we settled in Uvalde, I got an associate's degree from the local branch college and a BA from the Uvalde branch of Sul Ross State University, looking toward a career in teaching. The first eight years of my career were spent teaching sixth graders in Uvalde, and I loved, loved, loved it. During those years, my sister remained an enormous presence in my life. She had borne two daughters from her first marriage and a son from her second, and

Shirley's sister, Yvonne Conder Kahn, Wichita Falls, 1969.

she and her second husband had settled in Wichita Falls. The fact that 350 miles separated us presented no obstacle. Just as in home ec class, she was still the supreme Suzy Homemaker. Holiday gatherings were always held at her house, and the planning, cooking, entertaining, and cleaning up—all her. When my boys were born, she came down and took care of me until I was back on my feet. She was also extremely brainy, and competed successfully in many bridge tournaments. She chauffeured her son, Bill, to Boy Scout meetings and her younger daughter, Renée, to tennis practices and tournaments.

Yvonne was driving down to our house on the night of January 6, 1970, when she missed her turnoff and headed down a dirt road that somehow led her out onto a frozen playa lake. Her car broke through the ice, but it was not deep. Yvonne got wet getting out of her car. She walked to high ground; she sat down among some cattails to wait for help, and she froze to death. She was only thirty-four. Joaquin would be the first one to tell you that underneath all our civilization and modern amenities, nature in Texas is just as harsh and unforgiving as it was back in frontier days. But for my brilliant shooting star of a sister to end in such a way is something that I have never, ever been able to accept. Even as I write this, the emotions take control and tears come. It was just so very wrong, so wrong. Joaquin wrote in his first book that having to come to my office and tell me that she had passed away was the hardest thing he ever had to do, but that didn't begin to cover the depth of my grief. To this day, and it has been over thirty years, it is the one family death that I cannot talk about. Despite that inability, I want the rest of the world to know what an amazing and giving human being she was.

Renée, her daughter, was a junior when Yvonne died, and she came to Uvalde to live with us and attend school. Her older sister, Debbie, was married and had her own family. She picked a good group of friends and was doing well. Her stepfather, however, said he needed her to return to Wichita Falls and help with her younger brother, who was Bob's biological son. We did send her back, but I am not sure we made the right decision; I think Renée resented it to some extent. I understand that feeling, and what a strange circle to close in my own life, looking back at my own disrupted high school years.

* * *

Of course, in its correct place, I must tell of the most important accomplishments of my life: the births of our two boys. This seems to be the place. For some reason, I decided early in our marriage that it was time for me to be pregnant. Whether a good attribute or not, I am not quick to forget a chosen goal. We consulted a specialist, and were advised that I would need to have my fallopian tubes "blown out," so to speak—for want of the proper medical terminology—which I did. I became pregnant with Don Joaquin almost immediately; Joaquin picked out his name. We were very happy: a boy for Joaquin, bearing his name. As you may have read in *One Ranger: A Memoir*, there is sometimes pain with your offspring, and it is covered most eloquently in that book. I think Joaquin conveyed the extremes of our emotions. I can add nothing more. From time to time we have information about possible parole dates. The last one was so disheartening that I almost didn't want to know; it's just so long, so long. I wonder if Joaquin and I have that much time left on this earth. But neither Don Joaquin nor we were like O. J. Simpson, or so many of the rich, who could afford the best counsel and now are free, or were never convicted. That type of leniency is not for the common folks or ordinary people. At these times, you just have to dwell in your grief for a time and then say to yourself, "I'm not going to continue to think about this or I'll go crazy." And you go on. We do have Don Joaquin's son, our grandson, Adam Michael, and he is a wonderful young man. He looks so much like his father. He lives in California with his mother, and we do not see him much. In this book, Don Joaquin has written part of a chapter along with his younger brother, Lance Sterling. You can read his thoughts as he wrote them.

Lance Sterling was born in 1969, after I once again had the medical procedure mentioned above. I had trouble with both pregnancies, but because of some bad blood transfusions, with Lance my recovery was much longer, and I was told not to have any more children. I guess it's not possible, but I always felt Lance must have sensed this vulnerability, even as an infant; he was always happy, never any trouble. He followed that pattern all his life—just a joy. As a student, he worked hard and excelled both academically and athletically. He had all the virtues that we were taught in older times: don't lie, work hard, be respectful to your parents, your elders, and people in authority. As a young man, he still epitomizes these characteristics. Lance has one child, Tyler Joaquin Jackson, named after his grandpa. He is the spitting image of Lance, who is the spitting image of Joaquin. It's pretty cute to get the three of them together. "Cute" is my word, not theirs, I'm sure. Tyler Joaquin lives in El Paso with his mother, Laura, and her new family.

We get to see him on holidays and during the summer. At least we have that. Lance is close; he works in Marfa, and lives in Alpine with his new family. They are both very busy with successful careers and with making a life of their own. But I have the satisfaction that he will always be a good boy who has become a wonderful young man. (I'm using a mama's words again.) The words of endearment I used when he was a child and young adolescent will always be the ones that come to my mind. I am grateful for those times. As you read Lance's chapter, I hope you get an understanding of what I am trying to say. It is so like him.

*   *   *

When Joaquin was transferred to Alpine, we bought a house on the east side of town, with a mountain behind us, a view of the town in front of us, and all the classes I could ever want to take at Sul Ross State University, whose property literally abuts our back fence. I took two master's degrees, in education and counseling, and then received accreditation to become a

Joaquin and Shirley at home in Alpine, 2007.

principal. I taught for fifteen years, and then was a school counselor for nine more before retiring. We still live in the same house, as settled in as two old cats in a basket, except for the occasional row, and I guess they can be pretty colorful. Joaquin has some very expressive language, and he can be short tempered, but I'm not bashful about taking up for myself either. I'm still very independent minded. People who don't know us well may wonder why we've been together all these years, and the short answer is: he usually comes over to my point of view. But then, come to think of it, he doesn't hear as well as he used to (too many gunshots), and sometimes he seems to just look at me when I'm talking to him and nod his head yes in agreement. He may be a bit deaf but he is definitely not dumb, and this has sure saved a lot of disagreements. Still, while we occasionally have a good battle, we're even better at making up. It's always been that way. I still see him as the sexiest man alive.

CHAPTER 16

Sons of One Ranger

★ DON JOAQUIN JACKSON, B. NOVEMBER 10, 1963 ★

I'm sad to say that I don't have many recollections from before the age of eight or nine. I'm not sure why. From what I understand, the average person is able to remember events going back to ages five, four, or earlier. The memories that I do have are few; it seems as if I should be able to remember more.

Two things stand out from my earliest awareness: the times my father spent teaching and coaching me in baseball, and the first time he took me deer hunting. My father coached a Little League team, which I believe was called the Giants. Before I could have even thought of becoming a member of that team, my father spent hours and hours with me, either in our front yard or on the baseball field, playing catch and helping me learn the fundamentals of the game. How much I enjoyed those days, just he and I, forming a bond.

Certainly the most memorable moment came during a Little League game. I was playing second base, and as I remember it, there were runners at first and third. It was the ninth inning, and there were two outs. My father was in the dugout to my left, and he was yelling at me and the other players to stay on our toes and to remember where to go with the ball if it came to us. My mother was in the stands, cheering her lungs out (as always), and I was focused on the batter and what I would do if the ball was hit to me.

Don Joaquin playing high school baseball, Uvalde, 1974.

Well, the ball was hit to me, a hard grounder to my left, so I ran in that direction and dove for it, stretching my left hand out, and as I hit the ground, the ball rolled into my glove. I could hardly believe it, and I could hear my father yelling, "Throw it to first, son!" I quickly jumped up and fired that ball to the first baseman. The runner was called out and the game was over—we won!

The next thing I remember, I was looking toward my team's dugout, and they were all streaming out of it, heading my way, led by my father. I'll never forget the joy of that moment, of my father lifting me up in the air, hugging and congratulating me, and I will never forget the smile on his face. He also umpired games. As I reflect back now, I can appreciate more fully his love for the game, but most of all I think it was his desire to teach and coach young boys and then see the fruits of his labor. He was giving of his time to the community as a whole, and the only reward I think he looked for was witnessing the positive impact he made on the lives of so many.

Besides the baseball, I think that my times with him hunting together were the most enjoyable. I am still in awe now, as much as I was then, at how alive he seemed to become when he ventured out into the wilds. He was so much in his element, so in tune with the subtle forces of nature. I'm still amazed at how he was able to know which direction was north, south, east, or west after having walked several hours through thick sagebrush and cactus, going up and down hills, stopping intermittently to listen and observe our surroundings for any movement. The best way I know to describe it is to say he had a built-in compass.

Besides hunting and baseball, my father also taught me basketball and golf. I am very athletic and have a love for many sports. In basketball and football, I regret that I wasn't as aggressive as I should have been. I believe I would have excelled in basketball, particularly, had I been more so. But I loved golf. When I was about twelve or so, my father gave me my first set of clubs and taught me all about the game. I carry such pleasant memories of walking long fairways, hitting, chasing. Of course, he was not a professional, and when some of his shots didn't fly in the intended direction, he always had a few choice cusswords for that poor little ball. While every boy should have such memories, for me there was a dark side as well. To have been a "hero" even once on the baseball diamond, or been the center of my father's attention, fueled the fact that I was very self-centered. I put myself first in just about everything, putting my family and other responsibilities in a secondary role. I am aware now that it's not all about me, that I am just a tiny part of this vast planet, that others are searching for answers to life's questions, seeking peace and happiness in their own way.

Home life was pleasant overall, although there were moments that were not. My father worked very long hours, and many times he was gone for two or three or more days at a time. I missed him tremendously then, and always asked my mother when he would be home. And as that time got closer, I would go to our front living-room window, peering out to see if he had arrived yet. When that wonderful moment came, my brother Lance and I would run out to greet him. We would embrace him, exchanging kisses, and most times my father would have a gift for us that he had purchased at some point during his travels throughout the state. These gifts for my brother and me were usually toys, and we would run back inside the house and begin playing with them.

Lance and I were for the most part pretty close growing up, but there were times that I wasn't very nice to him at all. I think it had to do with my jealousy toward him and what I perceived to be more attention being directed toward him by my parents. I might have been too self-centered to see truly whether this was the case.

My father has a temper, and when he got angry and spanked me with his belt, I would see a different side of him. I'm not saying that I didn't deserve the spanking, but I was a very emotional and sensitive child, and I think I had a hard time distinguishing between those two sides of him. He came and apologized to me after every spanking, saying how much he hated to do it, that it hurt him more than it did me. I always resented his telling me that, because those scenarios would repeat themselves over and over again, and I became somewhat afraid of him. But I know that my father's relationship with his father was not very warm, and I think that he strived to do his best to not repeat with his sons those negative experiences.

The worst moments were when I witnessed my parents fighting between themselves—not physically, but through verbal assaults that would last for an hour or more. My mother also has a fiery temper, paired with a reluctance to admit when she is in the wrong, and that was bad chemistry to mix with my father when he was angry and stubborn. I absolutely hated those times, and I don't think they realized how much they affected me. But, thank God, they always resolved their disputes, and I am so thankful they have remained faithfully married all these years.

In school I was never pressured by my father or mother to excel. They always stressed that I should do or try to do my best at whatever I did, but inside I always wanted to live up to what they expected of me. When I failed, I took it pretty hard. I was always extremely critical of myself and my abilities. My mother was a teacher, and she devoted long hours to helping me with my homework and coaching me through spelling bees.

My life took an irreversible turn when I was in high school. My best friend, Carlos Alvarado Gonzales, Jr., and I were in the kitchen in my house. As I was preparing large glasses of iced tea to take back to a school pep rally, Carlos took my mother's revolver from atop the refrigerator. He removed all the bullets but one and pointed the revolver at his temple, as I think he had seen in the film *The Deerhunter*. I was only three feet away when he shot himself, and the event shattered me in ways I can't even describe.

One Ranger leaves the impression that Carlos and I were playing Russian roulette, and that my subsequent problems stemmed from my inability to accept responsibility for my part in his death. That is not true. I have blamed myself endlessly for not knocking the gun away from his head, but we were not playing Russian roulette and had never even talked about it; it was a random, thoughtless act. I loved him like a brother, and after this I became increasingly withdrawn, enraged at a God who could let such a thing happen. My parents reached out to me, but without much success. I remember my father asking me so many times to talk to him, and I wouldn't, or I didn't know how. He had taught me sports and hunting, but no one ever taught me how to express feelings. He was always closed about his own feelings—that was the culture we were both raised in—and the pain and the silence drove a wedge between us. My mother also tried to get me to open up, but I had always felt that she was secretive about her own life and feelings. To be asked at that age to trust without being trusted was more than I knew how to do.

It has only been in recent years, while I've been in prison, that those relationships have been healing, and now I can thank God so much for my parents and their love and support. I see my parents now in such a different light than before, and now I understand more fully how they did their best to provide a safe and comfortable home for my brother and me to grow up in. Lance and I have also grown closer since my incarceration, particularly over the last couple of years. He reflects so much of what my parents tried to instill in both of us; I am so proud of the person he has become, and I love him dearly.

How common it is for men to say they found religion in prison, and whether anyone accepts this about me is beyond my control. But one of the things that finding God has taught me is the need to take responsibility for my own feelings and actions, including the pain and suffering I have caused, and to continue to search for ways to make amends.

* LANCE STERLING JACKSON, B. MARCH 26, 1969 *

People who know that I have had a long career in the U.S. Border Patrol seem to assume that I determined upon a career in law enforcement because of my dad, and they are correct. My earliest memories from kindergarten are of drawing pictures of him, his gun, his holster, and his cowboy hat. Who more than the son of a Texas Ranger grows up with an awareness that the good guys wear white hats?

In a way this is odd, because my dad never brought his work home with him, never talked about the cases he was working on, even when he returned after an absence of several days. There were times when I would see him at parties or with other Rangers and he would tell a story about something he was working on, but that was rare. Nevertheless, his character, his code of conduct, and his sense of ethics for what was right and wrong were so much a part of his personality that even when he wasn't wearing his gun and badge, their presence was still felt. And I also couldn't miss the sense of respect that my parents' friends and other Rangers had for him. If that's what being good got you, I wanted some.

My being a second son—I followed Don Joaquin (D. J.) by six years—I had the advantage of his example. I knew to be aware of what my parents expected of their children, and what would disappoint them. D. J. was always a bit of a rebel and would push the envelope, but like so many second sons, I was the one who never got in trouble—I always tried to color between the lines. I grew up listening to their admonitions to him: If you go looking for trouble, you're going to find it. Never lie. No matter what you've done, lying about it will only get you in deeper.

When I was a small child, there were times that I wished my dad had been at home more. He worked long hours and was often gone for days at a time. But even then I was aware that this was how the house got paid for and food found its way to our table—not that we were rich, by any means—and I accepted it.

When I was older, and a more fit companion for a man of his active nature, he made up for it. How many kids get a chance to fly in a DPS helicopter, or accompany dad when he goes out tracking bad guys? With his obligations to his job, I don't know how he found the time to coach and umpire Little League, but he and my mom were always at our games, and he was always a Ranger. At six-five and 230 pounds, he absolutely towered over all the little kids, and even when crouched behind the catcher to call strikes and balls, the bulge at his waist covering his .45 was always visible. One mother complained about his coming armed to Little League games and started to raise a stink about it, and he told her squarely, "I've put a lot of people in jail, and I never know when one of them is going to come for me or my family. I'm always going to be armed." Be polite, be plain, and never, ever lie.

My best quality times with him were when we would go out fishing—or even better, hunting for arrowheads. His skill out in the Brush Country near Uvalde at spotting where ancient Indian campgrounds would have been—the presence of water and a rock shelter, or a vantage point where the surrounding country could be observed—was unnerving. We would set to picking over the ground, and almost inevitably we would find arrow points and flint artifacts. I remember we were out once with a cousin of mine; I was about thirteen, and he was maybe seven or eight. With the blind stupid luck of the beginner, this child picked up a museum-quality arrow point, showed it to my dad, and asked whether this was what we were looking for. My dad got so excited for him, told him what a great job he had done, what skill he had, and sent him rejoicing back on the hunt. Quietly to me he said, "I should have told him it wasn't nothing, and he would have thrown it back for us." His sense of humor has always been sly and ironic—and often devastating.

Even on such trips, he was always the Ranger. Once we were going to Carrizo Springs in his car, and a call came in for 645—that was him—and he answered; he was needed at the scene of a bar shooting. We took off, and when we got to this Mexican bar, he told me to wait outside. On discovering that there was a fatality inside, he came back out for his tape and camera, then went back in and worked the scene for an hour and a half before the hearse showed up from the funeral home and collected the body. It was the first time I ever saw someone under a blanket, which was sobering, that first eerie awareness of death. I heard him telling others that it was an apparent suicide with a high-powered rifle, and that there were gore and tissue everywhere. And when he was finished, we went hunting arrowheads as we had planned from the beginning. My father always had the uncanny ability to put issues aside, whether it was murders, robberies, or any other felony case he was investigating. Family time came first when I was with him.

When I was thirteen, I had the opportunity to go on a manhunt—an immigrant worker on a ranch near Uvalde had shot a man in self-defense over a woman and then taken off. I'm sure if my mom had known what was going down, it would have been an early trip home for me. But we raced to this ranch at breakneck speed, and when we got there, a full posse was waiting to track this guy. It was apparent from the first word that my father was in charge. He asked the rancher for a map, and he asked where the waterholes were, since it was summer and it would be over a hundred degrees. It turned out that the quarry was sleeping at the first tank we came to, a .357 Magnum in his waistband. I still remember the ride home that day: the immigrant was sitting in the front seat with my father, smoking a cigarette, not handcuffed. Dad conversed with him in the best Spanish he could manage. At one point he looked at me in the rearview mirror and said, "If you're going to keep going on these manhunts with me, I'm going to need to take you to the pistol range and make sure you can shoot." And he did.

I also remember seeing a sheriff and deputies dragging the Nueces River for a body, and there was a sense of cooperation and camaraderie among the officers that was very attractive.

Aside from never giving him any trouble, I matured late—didn't start dating until I was almost out of high school—so there was little trouble for me to find. Especially since I had baseball. As I discovered in Little League, I had a crazy curving slider that just came natural to me—even my fastball had a natural outside-in hook to it. I played varsity in high school as a junior, then we moved to Alpine for my senior year, and I played on the team at Sul Ross State University for three years until I graduated.

★　★　★

The town of Carrizo Springs always held special as well as disturbing memories for me. At first it was playing sports against its teams. I still remember that after every football game in Carrizo Springs, the coach would tell us to wear our football helmets when we were leaving on the bus. The reason? Simple. Win or lose, the visiting team in Carrizo Springs always got "rocked" when leaving the game. Sure enough, rocks would fly, and the bus driver, who was qualified to run in a grand prix, always knew how to get us out of there without any but superficial injuries.

Carrizo was also a town of violence, and it took away from me a great and admirable friend, Sheriff "Doc" Murray. Doc, as everyone called him, was as honorable as any man I had ever met besides my father. I still remember being with my father at card games, and anytime Doc wasn't doing so well at cards, he would always say to me, "Lance, ole Sam (his pit bull at the jail) is going to get a kick in the butt when I get home." Doc and my father worked well together; their friendship and respect for each other was honorable. I will never forget having the opportunity to be with them and share those times of catching the "bad guys."

Unfortunately, Doc was taken too soon from this world, when the violence of that small town finally caught up with him. I was in college when my father received the bad news. Doc had been murdered in his own house. The motive, as in many horrible crimes, was money. I have always heard the saying "The love of money is the root of all evil"; I didn't take it to heart until Doc's tragic death. I remember my father asking me once again, and it would be our last time, if I wanted to accompany him to look for the murderers. I jumped at the chance because for me it was personal. We arrived in Carrizo Springs; my father, who was the Senior Ranger at the courthouse, had taken charge. I was afforded the opportunity to search for several hours in the area with the Rangers, but I always stayed close to my father. The tenacity and perseverance that I witnessed throughout the manhunt cannot be described, but it solidified my plans for what I was going to be when I graduated from college. The murderers were apprehended after a couple of days.

I went to Doc's funeral, the prettiest (if that word can be used to describe the occasion) memorial I have been to before or since. My father gave the eulogy, and a mariachi band played in the balcony. It was a great send-off to a fine man, who, like many good men, had left this world too soon.

*　　*　　*

I had a tryout with the Cincinnati Reds, in Stephenville. My fastball was clocked at 91 mph, but apparently I lived outside the scout's geographical area, and if he signed me, he wouldn't receive a commission. The next time he saw me pitch, which was in Odessa, I was humming fastballs at 89 mph and I broke the catcher's mitt. He admitted that if I had tried out for him in El Paso, he would have signed me, but he had already signed a left-hander and there weren't any positions open at the time. As it was, I went to Hays, Kansas, to play semipro ball for a summer. My parents drove all the way to Amarillo once to watch me play, and it was the worst day of my life. I struck out the first batter, then walked five in a row and was pulled.

There was some salvation, however, because a coach from Texas Tech was there, and he told my folks that he had a pitching coach who could help me. So I got a scholarship to Tech. In my year there, I'm not sure that pitching coach ever knew my name; I asked one of the players if he ever actually coached, and he said no, he just sits in the stands and watches. Eventually I was called in and told that I had made the team, but only as a reliever, and that I would not see much playing time. I was pretty angry, and told them I had come to Lubbock on their word that this pitching coach would spend time with me, and when you give your word, you keep it. So I walked, and not in the baseball sense. You don't lie to people.

It was also true that I had begun having trouble with my rotator cuff, which is a very bad sign at that age. I probably should not have thrown so much in Little League, since boys' bones and ligaments are still developing, and early overuse can contribute to injuries later on, as it did with me. So that makes it easier to look back on my lack of a pro career without a lot of regret. I loved playing ball, and I loved having that wicked sliding weapon, but it was time to move on.

I graduated from college with a major in political science–prelaw and a minor in criminal justice. I definitely was going to be working in the law some way, and my dad encouraged me to go to law school, pointing out all the roads you could take with it—the FBI, or a judgeship at some point. But as I got closer to graduation, I just wanted to be like Dad; I wanted to be the guy chasing down the bad guys. But I also knew, regrettably, that I could never fill his boots. If I had gone into the Rangers, people would have always compared me to him. Different time, different generation, and I knew it. I wanted to be my own man and make a name for myself in a different organization. I believed I had a great foundation, and I wanted to make a positive contribution to the profession. It just had to be a different one.

I tested for the Midland and Dallas police departments, and then purely on a lark I accompanied two buddies who wanted to take the test to get into the Border Patrol. I wasn't interested in the Border Patrol; I hated the uniforms—the agents looked like forest rangers. My buddies were both 4.0 students and had studied the manual—I didn't even know there was a manual—and we drove to El Paso in a two-seater Toyota with a camper shell in the back. It was freezing cold, and I was in the camper with a blanket. We all took the test—they didn't get in, I did. My dad has always given me grief that the test had a minimum passing score of 70, and I got a 70. He has never let me forget that he got a 71.

*   *   *

Lance Sterling pitching for Sul Ross State University,
Alpine, Texas, 1990.

It was just fate: Midland called with an offer to join the Midland PD, but I was off for four and a half months of Border Patrol training in Georgia. As did my father at Quantico, I had my adventures: I met a girl in a bar, we danced, we kissed, she drove me back to the base, I asked for a second date, and she said no, her husband was coming home from the navy. So I discovered that you can lie to people sometimes with what you don't say, and that's as bad as lying with what you do say. After Georgia, I spent seven years with the Border Patrol in Las Cruces, New Mexico. I was married for four years, had a son, Tyler Joaquin Jackson, who is the namesake of my dad, and later divorced. Thanks to a sympathetic supervisor during that ordeal, I made a lateral transfer to the Border Patrol office in Marfa, and moved back in with my parents until I resettled.

After rolling my truck three times on black ice, I found God on a frozen highway. I opened my eyes to life's blessings. I met my new wife and two darling stepdaughters. And unlike my dad, who was always happy in the

Lance Sterling, U.S. Border Patrol, Pinto Canyon
(about 25 miles south of Marfa), 2003.

field and never wanted managerial responsibilities, I am now the operations supervisor at my station. I choose to push a lot of paper now, but I miss my time in the trenches. I will always remember that invigorating sense of esprit de corps that I first felt around my dad when he was with other Rangers and that was so similar to what I felt during my time in the field. There was a special bond that was almost like family, and there was no doubt they would have done anything for one another.

I never found that as much in the Border Patrol—not that our service is so different, but the times and the culture now are different. One of my goals as an administrator is to try to provide some of that sense of belonging for my agents. I believe that, as managers, we are in our position not only to serve our country, protect our borders, and secure the laws that we are entrusted with, but also to serve the agents under our command. This is one of the major reasons I aspire to move forward. If I can accomplish this, then I believe that I will have succeeded and that my career choice, though roundabout, was meant to be.

I have no desire to switch to the Texas Rangers. One riot, one Ranger? No. One *family*, one Ranger. We are different men, and I have my own way of doing things, but his example is always there and has never steered me wrong.

I would just like to say in closing: God bless all those men and women who serve in uniform (military or civilian) and who do their jobs without recognition, and God bless my parents for allowing me to be along for the ride.

CHAPTER 17

Silver Badges of Courage

I've never quite known how society defines a hero. The dictionary says it is a person of distinguished valor or fortitude, or one who takes an admirable part in some remarkable action or event. There have been many times in the history of the Texas Rangers when that definition fit well, but it is equally true that I have never known a Ranger who actually regarded himself as a hero. All the Rangers I have known, whether Medal of Valor recipients or others who got into a tight situation, all had only one thing to say afterward: "I was just doing my job." Rangers are simply men who dedicate themselves to protecting the law-abiding public from predatory elements that have no respect for the innocent. That is what is on their minds first. If society chooses to regard law-enforcement officers as heroes for placing themselves between the people and chaos, then that is a commendable decision.

When I think of the qualities needed to be a successful Ranger, good, plain common sense comes first to mind. There is no better asset to have when it comes to enforcing the law and protecting the lives and property of the people. This notion of common sense enfolds a strong sense of knowing right from wrong, a fair sense of justice for all, and a sense of compassion for the underdog, and the weak, and the helpless. A Ranger needs to have a strong sense of fairness, to be able to stand his ground in the face of death or bodily injury, and to do what he has to do to protect others and himself. He must have keen senses and alertness, always aware of his surroundings and ready to respond to any situation. Guiding all these must be a strong honesty and integrity, not just with the people he serves, but with himself.

There is an old saying—I don't know where it comes from, and I don't believe it—that every man has his price. I know there is not enough money in the world to tempt me to disgrace myself, my badge, or my family. Even if I could be bought, you sure couldn't buy my badge, and without my badge, I wouldn't have been worth a damn to anyone. Money might be able to buy power and influence, but it can't buy self-respect or the respect of people of strong character. And if the Rangers lose their reputation for being honest and impartial, they will be useless. That proved true in the past. There was a reason Frank Hamer was sent to break up moonshiners and gambling joints: everyone knew he was incorruptible, unlike a whole cellblock's worth of county sheriffs, JPs, and local politicians. That was why lawbreakers feared him so: they knew he was honest.

And Rangers require tenacity, the ability to keep to a job until it is done. The majority of men who became fine Rangers came from hardworking families that instilled respect for parents, elders, and one's fellow man. Many came from a life that was close to Mother Earth—farming or ranching or burnt-back labor of some sort. Nothing so readies one for a long, arduous case or chase. And most of the great Rangers were strong family men. In this job, you're gone so much that your family can be neglected sometimes, but most of us simply could not carry on without the support of a good wife. (I guess Bigfoot Wallace was the exception; he never married.)

Learning is a commodity that comes in different forms. Some of the great Ranger captains have been classical scholars, but it counts equally when the learning is of a rural kind, knowing the sights and sounds and smells of the country. Growing up with these things, and acquiring an appreciation of natural learning, can be indispensable for becoming a Ranger. Animals, birds, and even insects tell him things—from a change coming in the weather to the presence of a predator. This promotes a sense of survival, that sixth sense that keeps him alert to danger. Deer learn these things; so do Rangers, and these environmental teachings can save his life or that of another. These elements came more often into play during the day of the frontier Rangers, men like Leander MacNelly and Jim Gillette, but they are by no means irrelevant today. Frank Hamer tracked in the wild, and so have I. Anyone who thinks that Texas today is less dangerous than it was during the Wild West has never visited inside a high-security prison. If some of those bad boys ever get out again, God help us.

I could not have been a Ranger for nearly twenty-seven years without spending some moments looking over my shoulder at the great Rangers of past eras, the men who embodied these qualities: Leander MacNelly and John B. Jones and Jack Hays, Bill McDonald and Frank Hamer, even my old captain, A. Y. Allee, who hired me into the Ranger service. It let me know that I was not serving in a vacuum, that I came from a tradition that expected not just bravery but honesty. And I have no doubt that that tradition has steadied many Rangers in moments of danger when, left to their own devices, they might have acted differently. In effect, we serve the tradition as well as the public.

Training in those old days consisted of a seasoned Ranger taking a rookie under his wing; it was tutelage, or an apprenticeship, if you will. No written exams or CD-ROMs for them; it was listen and do—or die—from the get-go. Nowadays we have a thousand-page manual just on how to investigate dead bodies, but still the best way to learn it is to get out there and do it, and having an old hand show you the ropes still puts you ahead of the game.

*   *   *

When I think of Rangers of past generations who inspired me and helped shape my career, I don't think at all of the stereotype of the Ranger as a tool that society uses to keep the downtrodden in line. The Rangers who moved me were the ones who went against the social and political grain to do what was right. Leander MacNelly was a big contributor to the Texas Ranger legend, in good ways and bad. There is no doubt that in the 1870s he and his company threw their weight around in the Nueces Strip (the area between the Nueces and the Rio Grande), and on various occasions he crossed the Rio Grande to recover stock stolen from American ranches. Once while pursuing 130 head taken from the King Ranch, he entered Mexico and hit the wrong hacienda, then found himself pinned against the river by Mexican troops. He captured their lieutenant and told the others that when he got his 130 cattle back, they would get their lieutenant back and he would leave. When word came from the U.S. government that he was violating Mexican sovereignty and was to leave Mexico at once, he replied that he didn't work for the federal government, he worked for the State of Texas, and he would leave when his job was done. This is a continuing tradition of the Rangers today. They don't quit until the job is done. MacNelly was short and slender, sickly from tuberculosis, and his voice was described as that of a timid Methodist minister. But he was not afraid of anything. He once was shot and wounded for arresting four white men who had murdered a freed black slave. It is a simple thing: enforce the law without prejudice or favor.

*　*　*

William J. McDonald is also one of my favorites. He was a good friend of Governor Jim Hogg in the 1890s, and men under his command once stated that he would charge hell with a bucket of water. He was sometimes criticized for being a publicity hound, but he became a bona fide legend for his raids on train robbers and cattle thieves. He was the most quotable of the old Rangers, and the source of the line most often associated with them. McDonald was sent to quell a riot in East Texas, and when he stepped off the train, a mortified city official asked whether they had sent only one ranger. McDonald replied quizzically, "Well, you only got one riot, don't you?" His other most famous saying is carved on his tombstone, in the town of Quanah: "No man in the wrong can stand up to a man who is in the right and keeps on a-comin'." His great-grandson, also named Bill McDonald, who was the agent in charge of the DEA in Del Rio when he retired, is a good friend of mine, and he has some of his famous great-grandfather's guns.

*　*　*

Some of my heroes weren't necessarily the Indian fighters or frontiersmen. For instance, you may not have heard of Marvin "Red" Burton. He didn't start out as a Ranger, but as a deputy sheriff in McLennan County. He was born on a farm near Mart, Texas, twenty miles east of Waco, in 1885, and married when he was only eighteen. He excelled in various jobs before becoming a Waco police officer, in 1919. Prohibition had just become the law, and a lot of officers were on the take from bootleggers, most of whose activities were carried out at night. When the chief called Burton in and told him that for the good of the department he would be working the day shift, Burton replied, "Sir, if I thought it was for the good of the department, I wouldn't say a word." Then he quit the city force and went to work for the county as chief deputy sheriff.

His boss was McLennan County sheriff Robert "Bob" Buchanan. On October 1, 1921, in the town of Lorena, thirteen miles south of Waco, the two faced off against the Ku Klux Klan, and several thousand people gathered to watch hundreds of robed Klansmen march on the black section of Lorena with burning crosses. From there the mob was going to go to the Baptist church for dinner and ice cream. Sheriff Buchanan let it be known that he wanted the leaders to lift their hoods so that if any violations of the law occurred, he would know who to hold responsible. Of course, they declined. When the march began, Buchanan met them, with Red Burton close behind.

Buchanan grabbed the first burning cross, threw it to the ground, lifted the carrier's hood—and all hell broke loose. When the sheriff went for a second Klansman, he was knocked to the ground (the Klansman who struck him first was a Waco policeman), swarmed on, and beaten. Red Burton was getting the same treatment. Two shots rang out, and Buchanan exclaimed, "Red, they've shot me," even as he pulled out a pocketknife and slashed and stabbed several of his assailants. Burton managed to pull his .38, drop the man who shot the sheriff, and hit several others. Buchanan staggered to his feet, and as two other Klansmen shot at him, Burton unholstered his .41-caliber Colt and shot them. One of the men trying to hold Burton was a leading businessman of the town, and Burton pressed his pistol into his stomach as he said, "Mr. Westbrook, I love you like a daddy, but if I am not released, I am going to kill you."

As the crowd milled around, uncertain what to do next, Burton reached a drugstore where the wounded sheriff had been taken. He took a .45 from a deputy there, got Buchanan into a car, and took him to the hospital in Waco. Other wounded had been taken there, and a huge crowd gathered, threatening to lynch Buchanan and Burton, but he walked, armed, through the crowd untouched. The county commissioners offered him vacation time, saying he needed to leave town for his own safety, but he refused. The Klan published wanted posters offering $5,000 for him, dead or alive. Another lynch mob gathered ten days later outside the jail, but Burton, now acting sheriff, made his rounds, a two-row sawed-off shotgun beneath his coat. There were threats and catcalls, but no one touched him. He stopped for coffee at the Riddle Café, taking a table near the rear of the restaurant. As the mob pressed against the window, the owner offered to take him out the back door, but he said, "I didn't come in your back door. I am going out just as I came in." He assured her that those outside wouldn't kill him, because they knew some of them would die if they did.

Texas governor Pat Morris Neff, who was from the Waco area and knew its racist attitudes very well, extended Burton a Ranger commission in 1922 on the basis of courage already shown. He served in the Rangers with distinction for over a decade, then became chief of police in Waco; he retired in 1951. There have been many courageous Rangers, but Red Burton absolutely was one of the bravest of the brave.

★ ★ ★

Frank Hamer is remembered mostly for his part in the killing of the outlaws Bonnie and Clyde, although the movie version that came out in the sixties was so libelous of Hamer's conduct that his family sued and collected a large settlement. One of the things that endeared Hamer to me was his commitment to fairness for the underdog. In the late 1920s, the Texas Bankers Association began offering "$5,000 for each DEAD ROBBER—not one cent for a hundred live ones." This quickly led to a disgusting scam involving some local law-enforcement officers, who would lure down-on-their-luck bums into situations in which they could be ambushed and killed, and the rewards collected by the conspirators. Hamer discovered the scheme, but failed to convince the bankers association to withdraw or modify the reward. For the only time in his life, Hamer alerted the newspapers to what was going on, causing a major scandal, and that was the end of the reward program.

Hamer also believed in fair play. He was once caught in a bad deal: he was the expert witness in a land dispute, whose losing party thought their only hope was to kill him. They hired three assassins, one of whom was an ex-Ranger named McMeans. When the attempt was made, in Sweetwater, Hamer was in the company of his wife, Gladys, and his brother Harrison Hamer, who was also a Ranger. Gladys shot one of the assailants when she saw him stalking Frank, who nevertheless was severely wounded by two gunshots fired by another. As one of the assailants fled, Harrison Hamer raised his gun to drop him, but Frank deflected the gun as he fired, saying, "Leave him. I'll get him later." Despite being wounded, he didn't want the man shot in the back. That took class.

★ ★ ★

Such conduct is not relegated purely to the early history of the Rangers. Since the creation of the Department of Public Safety, in 1935, only five Medals of Valor have been awarded to Texas Rangers. Johnny Aycock was the only Ranger to win two, and I devoted a chapter to him in *One Ranger*. Stan Guffey, who was with Aycock on the assignment for which he received the first one, was awarded one posthumously; he was killed by the kidnapper of a four-year-old girl. I worked with him in Company D before he transferred to Company F in Alpine.

I was with the Rangers in Uvalde when I first met Bill Gerth; he was a trooper with the Highway Patrol, and he worked with me on several cases. He was a top hand, locating and helping apprehend a number of wanted people. He then transferred to Kerrville, became a Ranger, and was stationed in Wichita Falls. He has the distinction of having been born on Pearl Harbor Day, December 7, 1941. Reared in the San Antonio area, he went into the Marine Corps in 1960, served three years, and joined the DPS immediately on his discharge. His first station was in San Antonio, and he then moved to Uvalde for five years, where he helped me out on a bunch of different cases, including pulling over a trailer full of stolen goats. Then he spent five and a half years in Kerrville, serving a total of eleven and a half years in the Highway Patrol. He made Ranger in September 1975 and retired the same time I did, October 1, 1993.

On May 19, 1983, as he was leaving his residence on Sisk Road in Wichita Falls, he received a radio dispatch regarding a bank robbery that had taken place some days before; the message included a description of the vehicle, a new Dodge truck with a camper on the back and California license plates. Bill was driving a solid-black state car, and he happened to pass a truck that fit this description, which was at the side of the road. Soon he passed the subject himself, who was on foot and walking back toward his truck. Bill looked at him in his rearview mirror and saw him turn and look at the car, but the subject didn't act as though he had been spotted by an officer. If Bill had been wearing his white Western hat—he had set it on the seat next to him—he would have been made immediately.

So Bill made a circle and came back around the vehicle. At this point the subject got hinky; he reached his car and lit out, and Bill called for backup. Billy Gilbert was the state trooper who heard the call and came in to assist—he's still a state trooper—and between the two of them, they managed to herd him back onto Sisk Road. When the guy finally emerged, he was brandishing a fully automatic Ruger Mini-14. He shot the windshield out of the trooper's car and pinned that officer down in the front seat, wounded by flying shrapnel. The subject was approaching the trooper's car to finish him off, and also had a city officer pinned down, when Bill Gerth got out of his car hefting a Remington Model 11 twelve-gauge shotgun with an eighteen-inch barrel. (I was very familiar with that kind of gun, since it was the first one issued to me in the Rangers. It kicks you on both ends.)

Bill said he had been on the range with that gun a few weeks before this incident, and he knew it shot high at twenty-five to fifty yards. Remembering this, he was able to knock the guy flat with a spread of buckshot. He thought he'd done very well, then the guy jumped up again, and Bill thought, well hell, the bell's rung and now it's round two. It turned out the guy was wearing a bulletproof vest—he was some kind of survivalist and was prepared for the end of the world, let alone a Highway Patrolman. He got to his vehicle as Bill discarded the shotgun and pulled out what he called his "real" gun, his Colt .45 Model 11, and fired off more rounds through the windshield of the assailant's truck. Looking under the truck, Bill could see the guy's feet as he fumbled with a huge janitor-style key ring while trying to open the passenger-side door and get to the arsenal of further weapons he had in there. Bill had been trained (see again the advantage of personal tutoring) by an old-time Ranger named Leo Hickman, who had had one eye shot out in an altercation. Hickman had told Bill that if he were ever in this situation, to ricochet bullets under the vehicle into a subject's legs or feet.

The subject was on his knees trying to get into his truck. Bill fired once under the truck and struck him in one leg, which caused him to holler. Bill fired again and hit him in the other leg, which he said really made him holler, and then finished him as he came around the truck. They later found a .308 sniper rifle and the money from the bank job in the truck. Saving the trooper's life won Bill the Medal of Valor. In relating this story to me afresh, he still wanted it mentioned that he did no more than any other peace officer would have done in the same circumstances, that he was just doing his job. Of course, it was lucky for the other two officers present that not many people were better pistol shots than Bill.

★   ★   ★

I also want to tip my hat to Sergeant Danny Rhea. He was born in 1947, the son of a military family, and joined the navy in 1967. But unlike the other men in his clan, he left the military and went to college, majoring in fine arts at Stephen F. Austin State University. Perhaps he would have fit in with some of those earlier Rangers who were classical scholars. He became a Highway Patrolman in 1976 and served in a number of stations for ten years before being promoted to the Criminal Intelligence Division, based in San Angelo; that was where I met him. He became a Ranger in 1988. Danny was the protégé of senior Ranger captain Bill Wilson and learned much from him. He served in Ozona for several years (I was in the same company in Alpine, so we worked together a good deal) before transferring to Sulphur Springs, in East Texas, which is a fisherman's paradise, and Danny is an ardent angler.

On January 6, 1998, a lunatic barged into the DPS office in Sulphur Springs with what he claimed was a bomb. The building was evacuated, and for over an hour Danny and others tried to talk him out, but when the guy pulled a handgun and aimed at one of the officers, Danny took him out with a Mini-14 .223, saving the life of another and winning a Medal of Valor. It turned out that the "bomb" was harmless, but Rangers have to respond to the perceived situation, not to a hopeful scenario. His handgun was real enough. Danny is retired now and living in San Angelo, where he does some security work and taxidermy.

*   *   *

And then there was my old friend Lieutenant Bob Favor, who didn't win a Medal of Valor but should have; I think they were not yet being issued at the time of his incident. He became a Ranger in 1967, the year after I did, and was stationed first in Corpus Christi. Being from Abilene, he didn't care for the coast (having spent forty-something months on a navy minesweeper, he had seen all the damned water he cared to see). He had just gotten moved into Corpus and was making the hundred-mile trip to Captain Allee's town, Carrizo Springs, headquarters of Company D, to report for duty (Corpus was in this district) when he got the call that Captain Allee, Tol Dawson, and a variety of sheriffs and deputies were out in the brush in Catarina, Texas, about fifteen miles southeast of Carrizo Springs, pursuing some subjects who had pulled an armed robbery in a little store on the highway between Carrizo Springs and Laredo.

Bob showed up, announcing to Captain Allee that he was reporting for duty, and Allee said, "Well, get out there and find those sons of bitches."

Bob thought to himself that he would know what a son of a bitch looked like when he saw one, and sure enough, Bob flushed one of the suspects, who flashed up with a handgun, but Bob dropped him with a shot in the stomach. He then approached the suspect and got the gun out of his reach. As Captain Allee came up and saw the robber still moving around, he jokingly said, "What the hell, Favor, did you run out of ammo?"

Bob said, "No, sir."

The Captain said, "All right, let's get him to the hospital." And that was Bob Favor's first day in the Rangers.

*   *   *

I really don't want to leave out Robert Mitchell, one of the finest captains that I ever knew in my career; I rank him next to A. Y. Allee, which tells you a lot. Bob was captain of Company F, whose men thought so well of him that they referred to themselves as "Mitchell's Rangers," which is an almost unprecedented honor from the rank and file. Like Captain Allee, Mitchell constantly worried about his men and their families and their welfare; any single one of them would have stood up and taken a bullet for him.

Ronnie Brownlow, who is now retired from the Rangers and a county sheriff in East Texas, where he's from, once faced a prison riot when he was in Company F. He walked into the locked-in area with the warden, talked to the leader of the rioting prisoners, and was able to negotiate a settlement of the trouble. Captain Mitchell suspected that Brownlow had gone into the situation with his two-shot derringer concealed as a "hide-out," at a stage when nobody was supposed to be armed. Normally, you wouldn't take a weapon into a negotiating situation.

Mitchell went up to Brownlow and asked him, "Tell me the truth, Ronnie. Did you take a gun in there with you?"

"Well, Captain, I can't lie to you. I did. I had my little two-shot .38 derringer."

Mitchell said, "What the hell could you have done with a two-shot derringer if all hell had broken loose?"

Brownlow answered, "Well, Captain I was going to X-ring the leader and use the last one on myself." (The X ring is the central circle on a shooting target.)

Knowing Ronnie, he was joking; he would have used it on another badass if he'd had to, and then fought his way out of there.

*   *   *

This is just a sample of the rich legacy I was honored to be a part of. I haven't even come close to talking about all the Rangers who deserved a Medal of Valor. Or, for that matter, even the ones I knew who dedicated their lives to protecting the people of the great state of Texas. But I do know that today's Rangers continue to uphold the same level of integrity and service, which in my view is even more difficult in today's high-tech era. I am sure that at some point their stories will be told.

God bless all the keepers of the peace.

Index